GUIDE TO ANALYSING COMPANIES

OTHER ECONOMIST BOOKS

Guide to Business Modelling
Guide to Business Planning
Guide to Economic Indicators
Guide to the European Union
Guide to Financial Markets
Guide to Management Ideas
Numbers Guide
Style Guide

Dictionary of Business
Dictionary of Economics
International Dictionary of Finance

Brands and Branding
Business Consulting
Business Ethics
Business Strategy
China's Stockmarket
Dealing with Financial Risk
Globalisation
Headhunters and How to Use Them
Successful Mergers
The City
Wall Street

Essential Director
Essential Economics
Essential Finance
Essential Internet
Essential Investment
Essential Negotiation

Pocket World in Figures

GUIDE TO ANALYSING COMPANIES

Bob Vause

THE ECONOMIST IN ASSOCIATION WITH
PROFILE BOOKS LTD

Published by Profile Books Ltd
3A Exmouth House, Pine Street, London EC1R 0JH
www.profilebooks.com

Typeset in EcoType by MacGuru Ltd
info@macguru.org.uk

Printed and bound in Great Britain by
Clays, Bungay, Suffolk

A CIP catalogue record for this book is available
from the British Library

ISBN 978 1 86197 985 8

The paper this book is printed on is certified by the © 1996 Forest Stewardship
Council A.C. (FSC). It is ancient-forest friendly. The printer holds FSC chain of custody
SGS-COC-2061

FSC
Mixed Sources
Product group from well-managed
forests and other controlled sources
Cert no. SGS-COC-2061
www.fsc.org
© 1996 Forest Stewardship Council

Contents

Introduction

THE AIM OF THIS BOOK is to provide an understanding of how to analyse and assess the performance of a company from the information provided about it.

Financial analysis is as much an art as it is a science. Combine any two figures from an annual report and a ratio is produced; the real skill is in deciding which figures to use, where to find them and how to judge the result. Before a constructive attempt can be made to analyse a company, a sound grasp of financial terminology and presentation is required. Thus Part 1 of this book explains the content and intent of the main financial statements that appear in a company's annual report: the balance sheet; the income statement or profit and loss account; and the cash flow statement.

All countries and companies share the basic accounting framework used in the production of financial statements, but the presentation of them is not standard. Adjustments may have to be made, but the outline provided in Part 1 is applicable to any company and any country. Some explanation of differences between US, EU and UK reporting practices is offered; translations of some of the terms found in European financial reports are given in a glossary in Part 3.

As far as possible, the examples given have been kept simple in order to emphasise or reinforce the subject matter; once the fundamental theory and practice is grasped there should be no problem in moving to more detailed and sophisticated analysis. In general, the book's examples focus on retail, service and manufacturing companies rather than banks and other financial institutions, which are subject to different legal and reporting requirements.

Part 2 of the book deals with the various methods of analysing different aspects of corporate performance. However, three important ground rules apply to each of these methods:

1 Never judge a company on the basis of one year's figures. Always look at three or, ideally, five years' figures.
2 Never judge a company in isolation. Always compare its performance with others of the same size and/or the same business sector and/or country.
3 When comparing companies always make sure, as far as you can,

that you are comparing like with like – in other words, that the basis of the data being analysed is consistent.

Profit and finance are two broad strands interwoven in the overall management of successful business organisations today. They also provide the basis for the analysis of a company. Each strand is equally important and both must be followed. Analysing a company's profitability without any reference to its financial position is of little value. Similarly, there is little point in doing a detailed analysis of a company's financial structure without reference to its performance. Profit is not sufficient on its own; a company must have the resources to allow it to continue in business and flourish.

To achieve an acceptable level of profit necessary to satisfy shareholders' requirements – to add value – is a common corporate objective. Without profit there can be no dividend or share value improvement, or reinvestment for future growth and development. A substantial part of this book focuses on various ways of identifying and measuring profitability. Shareholder value is more than just annual profit, and not everything is capable of quantification. Future expectations of a company's performance outweigh its track record in determining its share price – a factor that probably offers as good an indicator as any of shareholder satisfaction. Chapter 6 offers some general guidelines for undertaking the practical analysis.

When the practical analysis of a company is completed, the tables in Part 3 offer some benchmarks against which the ratios explained in Part 2 can be tested or compared. This reinforces the last lesson of financial analysis: comparison. Producing a series of ratios for one company can be useful in indicating trends in its performance, but it cannot provide an indicator of whether this is good, bad or indifferent. That can only be determined by applying the three rules stated earlier.

An important lesson from the 1990s is to invest in a company only when you are absolutely certain you understand the business and sector within which it operates. If you cannot see where the profits are coming from, don't invest. In all probability it is not a failure of your analytic ability but someone practising corporate legerdemain.

The major change on the horizon is the adoption of international accounting standards (IAS) of corporate reporting. Already progress has been made. All European Union listed companies now apply IAS in their reports. Allied to this, the internet will continue to improve the private investor's ability to access and analyse detailed and up-to-date performance and position figures.

As far as possible the book is written with a light touch. Companies get their momentum from people, whereas financial analysis of their activities is an art. Art combined with people should be fun; if it is not then you should leave it to those who enjoy it.

1
UNDERSTANDING THE BASICS

1 The annual report – and what underlies it

ANNUAL REPORTS ARE COMPLEX and difficult to decipher. The increasing volume and detail of legislation, regulations, rules, accounting standards and codes of practice all contribute to this. Each time there is fraud or mismanagement resulting in a major company's problems becoming public there is pressure either for a change in the role, duties and responsibilities of auditors or directors, or for disclosure of additional or more detailed information.

To read or interpret an annual report effectively, you need some understanding of the broad theory and the framework of financial accounting. The mechanics of double entry book-keeping do not need to be mastered, however, as it is extremely unusual for a quoted company to run into problems with debit and credit. The book-keeping process required to arrive at a balance sheet that balances can be taken for granted.

Double entry book-keeping

Italy claims to have been the first country in Europe to adopt double entry book-keeping. Luca Pacioli is normally given the accolade of being the first to publish on the subject. In 1494 he wrote *De Computis et Scripturis*, which included details of the mechanics of double entry book-keeping (debits, or left-hand entries in the books of account, and credits, or right-hand entries).

Under this system every transaction has two entries in the books of account. Whatever amount is entered on the right-hand side (credit) of one account, the same amount is entered on the left-hand side (debit) of another account. This guarantees that at the end of the financial year it is possible to produce an income statement (called the profit and loss account in the UK) disclosing the profit or loss for the year and a balance sheet with assets (debit balances) equalling liabilities (credit balances).

Who publishes accounts?

Every commercial business must prepare a set of accounts in order to agree its tax liability. Even when the organisation is a charity or otherwise tax exempt, accounts must still be prepared to provide those interested in its activities with appropriate information and the ability to assess the adequacy of management of the organisation's operations and assets. All public or nationalised enterprises are expected to produce and publish accounts in order to report not only to the state but also to the people.

Any company in which the public have been invited to become involved must publish an annual report containing a set of accounts. All other companies with limited liability submit accounts to the tax authority each year and file them, thus making them available for public scrutiny.

Limited liability

Most trading companies have limited liability. Shareholders providing a company with capital, through the purchase of stocks and shares, cannot be forced to contribute any further money to the company. Having paid the £1 or $1 for a share or unit of stock, they need pay no more. Should the company fail they can lose no more than the £1 or $1 invested; their liability is limited to this amount.

Private and public companies

A quoted or listed company is one whose shares can be bought and sold on the stock exchange. A private company cannot offer its shares for sale to the public, so different safeguards and reporting requirements apply, compared with those for public or stock exchange quoted companies.

Ownership and management

Shareholders of a private company are often directly involved in its management, with members of the family acting as directors. Shareholders of a public company are less likely to be directly involved. The management of a public company, its directors and managers, is normally clearly separate from the owners of the company, its shareholders. Thus there must be clear reporting requirements for public companies. The directors are acting as stewards of their shareholders' investments and each year are called upon to report the results of their management. At the annual general meeting (AGM) directors present the annual report and accounts to shareholders.

In the UK, a public limited company (plc) must publish more information than other private limited liability companies. This distinction is reflected elsewhere in Europe. The term public in plc refers to the size of the share capital of the company, so a plc does not necessarily have its shares quoted on the stock exchange. Public companies usually give a preliminary outline statement on the year's financial performance within three months of the end of the company's financial year; formal publication of the annual report follows soon after. For private companies, there can often be a delay of more than 12 months after the year end before a set of accounts is made available. In the UK, private companies have up to 18 months after their financial year end in which to file their accounts. Quoted companies publish interim accounts half-yearly in the UK and quarterly in the United States. There is continued pressure on companies to provide quick access to their figures. The US Securities and Exchange Commission (SEC) now aims for the filing of quarterly figures within 35 days and annual reports within 60 days of the period end.

Consolidated accounts

Where one company, the parent company, has a controlling interest in other companies, its subsidiaries, it is necessary to prepare consolidated or group accounts. These incorporate all the activities of all the companies concerned to provide an income statement, balance sheet and cash flow statement.

Since the early 1900s, US and UK companies have been required to publish group accounts. The Seventh Directive on European harmonisation dealt with group accounts, and since 1990 they have been mandatory for all EU companies. The intention is to ensure that shareholders and others interested in a group of companies have adequate information upon which to assess its operations and financial position.

In addition to the consolidated balance sheet, UK companies must also provide one for the parent company. This is normally called the company balance sheet. The presentation of a parent company balance sheet is not required in the United States.

Minority interests

Where a subsidiary is not 100% owned, the outside or minority interest – the proportion of the subsidiary owned by those other than the parent company – is shown separately in the accounting statements. Inevitably, some problems arise in identifying ownership and control when there are pyramid structures of shareholdings.

All intra-group trading is eliminated to avoid double counting of profits, so only revenue from dealing with customers outside the group of companies is shown in the income statement. However, minority interests must be credited with their proportion of any profit flowing from intra-group trading.

Details of subsidiaries

In the case of a group of companies, the annual report should provide details of all subsidiaries. The name, business, geographic location and the proportion of voting and other shares owned by the parent company should be shown.

If a subsidiary has been sold or otherwise disposed of, details should be reported as part of the notes to the accounts on discontinued operations, with the revenue and profit shown separately and the profit or loss on disposal treated as an exceptional item in the income statement.

The objectives of the annual report

The annual report is designed primarily to satisfy the needs of existing and possible future shareholders for information about a company. To do this it should be understandable and comparable, reliable and relevant. Financial statements are provided to assist and support their decision-making and to form the basis of a statement of the directors' stewardship of the funds shareholders have invested in the company. Financial accounts are not only a historic review; they also aim to assist users to predict the timing, nature and risks of future cash flows.

The annual report is an important document, containing not only the statutory financial statements, tables, notes and management reports but also anything else that the company may wish to disclose. It is the formal report by directors to their shareholders of their performance during the year and the financial position of the company at the financial year end. It also has an important public relations role.

A quoted company may have many thousands of shareholders, and even though only a few hundred are likely to turn up for the AGM, where the accounts are formally presented, all will receive a copy of the annual report as will anyone interested in the company who has requested one. Producing an annual report is therefore a significant cost; a listed company typically spends between $500,000 and $1m on this publication.

Who uses the annual report?

Shareholders and their advisers

Shareholders range from individuals owning a few shares to institutions owning a large number, and it is a mistake to assume the requirements of these two groups for information about a company are the same. Meeting the requirements of the financial advisers and security analysts in a single annual publication is probably even more difficult.

Shareholders own the company and use the annual report to discover how their investment has been managed by the directors during the previous year. Investments are normally made and retained for future income or capital gain. The annual report provides a basis for assessing past trends, but shareholders will be most concerned with the level of dividends and capital growth they are likely to see in the future. In assessing this they will look at a range of the measuring sticks covered in Part 2, including dividend cover and rate of return and debt/equity ratios.

The people who advise shareholders, those who earn their living on the strength of their analyses and forecasts of company performance, will look at a wider range of measures and will focus closely on indicators of the potential risks of investing in the company.

Shareholders and power

The majority of shareholders in a typical quoted company may make up 60–70% of the total number of shareholders but own less than 10% of the total number of issued shares. The bulk of the shares – and therefore effective control of the company – is almost always in the hands of a group of institutional shareholders, usually a few hundred, including insurance companies, trust and pension funds, banks and other financial institutions. When a group of institutional shareholders get together to tackle a company they wield formidable power that cannot be ignored by even the most autocratic directors. These are the shareholders that the directors listen to and try to satisfy. Because of this, and because they are well informed and highly competent in financial analysis, they are generally in a better position to know what is going on than the small shareholders.

Lenders

Lenders – providers of long-term and short-term finance to a company – include not only banks, other institutions and individuals but also suppliers offering goods and services to it on credit terms. They have a strong incentive to assess its performance. They need to be confident that the company can meet the interest payments due on borrowed funds and that the loans they have advanced to the company will be repaid when due. They are therefore likely to focus on profit and cash-flow generating capability, and measures of liquidity, solvency and gearing (see Chapters 9 and 10). In assessing this they – suppliers in particular – often rely on professional credit-rating agencies which will vet and monitor their customers.

Management

Like other interested groups, management is concerned mainly with the future performance and financial viability of the company rather than its past record. Management's key roles are planning and decision-making. Budgets are prepared and actual performance is compared with these. To run the company, its managers need timely and accurate information. The annual report gives them no help here. However, managers can be expected to take a keen interest in it – especially if they are entitled to bonuses based on the revenue or profit for the year. Such bonus arrangements open the door to a conflict of interest between the directors and shareholders, as the company's accounting policies are set by the directors, who will not be disinterested in the size of the bonus they get. To counter this potential conflict, changes in regulation and practice are gradually closing this particular gap between common sense and commercial practice.

Employees and unions

Employees and their advisers or representatives turn to the annual report to help them assess a company's ability to continue to offer employment and the wages it can afford to pay.

Employees who do not immediately turn to the pages detailing what the directors have been paid usually show greatest interest in the particular part of the business – the division, factory, section or department – in which they work. Evidence suggests they have less direct interest in, or sympathy for, the company as a whole. Generally, employees are less able to read an annual report, which can create difficulties. Companies are therefore increasingly providing employees with a separate report or briefing that provides a clear summary of important matters.

Government and the taxman

Annual reports and the information filed with them may be used by the government for statistical analysis. Company and personal taxation are often based on the statement of accounting profit given in annual reports. However, in most countries a company's tax liability is not fixed on the basis of the published annual report but on a separate set of accounts and calculations produced for tax purposes and agreed with the tax authority. One exception to this is Germany, where a company's tax liability is fixed on the basis of the published accounts (*Massgeblichkeitsprinzip*). As a result, German companies often understate profits in the income statement and undervalue assets and overstate liabilities in their financial statements.

Other users

Customers of a company will use its annual report to look for reassurance that it will be in business long enough to fulfil its side of any contracts it has with them. This is particularly important in the cases of, say, a large construction project spanning several years, or the provision of a product or service where future continuity of delivery and quality is essential. The failure of the supplier could have heavy cost implications for the customer.

Fundamental accounting concepts

Before reading a set of accounts, it is sensible to have some appreciation of the basis upon which they have been prepared. Financial accounting and reporting are governed by a number of what are referred to as concepts, principles, conventions, elements, assumptions and rules. These have evolved over many years. They have been moulded by experience and linked together to provide the framework for the construction of a set of financial accounts. They are applicable to every company.

Financial accountants, particularly auditors, are trained to be:

- Careful
- Cautious
- Conservative
- Consistent
- Correct
- Conscientious

These six Cs are in evidence in the preparation and presentation of the annual report.

The corporate persona

A company is a legal entity separate from its managers and owners. It can make contracts, sue and be sued just like an individual. For the purposes of law and accounting, it owns assets and has liabilities. Its net worth is the amount it owes to its shareholders. The last act of a company in liquidation before it ceases to exist is to repay the shareholders the net worth, if there is any.

Money quantification

If it is impossible to place a monetary value on a transaction or an event it cannot be recorded in the books of account. A rule of thumb for accountants is "if you can't measure it ignore it". This is one reason accountants have such difficulties with the intangible or qualitative aspects of a business. For example, the cost of the board of directors can be quantified to two decimal places and appear in the income statement each year. However, the question of what the directors are worth to the company is, at least for the accountant, impossible to answer and so they never appear in the balance sheet, as either an asset or a liability.

Accountants can be cautious in the treatment of intangibles or when quantifying "difficult" aspects of business costs and expenditure. However, if it becomes essential for a measuring rod to be placed against anything, accountants will prove to be well up to the task. For example, a company's employees can be quantified for inclusion in the balance sheet by using human asset accounting, and there are ways to quantify the environmental aspects of a business.

Enter the euro

In January 1999 the single European currency (the euro) began to be used by 11 member countries – the UK, Sweden and Denmark opting out for the present. It is not often that the monetary unit itself changes. This was the situation facing European companies when, in 2002, they were required to use the euro in their financial reports.

Impact of inflation

A major problem with monetary quantification is found when the measuring unit, say the pound or the dollar, changes in value over time. If, as occurs with inflation, the unit of measurement used in the accounts is worth more at the beginning of the period than at the end, the traditional accounting and reporting systems run into difficulties. Under conditions of continuous high inflation traditional accounting methods and reports are of little use.

For example, what value should appear in the balance sheet when a company purchases an asset at the beginning of the financial year for £500 and another identical asset at the end of the year that, owing to inflation, costs £1,000? Ignoring depreciation, is it practical or useful to add the two figures together and show assets "valued" at £1,500? The answer must be no, and some adjustment is required to provide a more meaningful guide to the value to the business of the assets employed at the end of the year.

Accountants have devised several possible solutions to overcome the problems of inflation in company reports. Current purchasing power accounting (CPP) restates all items appearing the financial statements by an appropriate inflation or price index. Current cost accounting (CCA) values assets at their current value to the business, either at the balance sheet date or at the time of the transaction, using a selection of price indices. Depreciation is then charged on the inflation-adjusted asset values, resulting in a more realistic charge being made in the income statement for the use of the assets during the year.

Cost valuation

Assets are normally shown in the balance sheet at a value based on their original or historic cost. The principal reason for this is that the original cost of an asset is in most cases indisputable and easy to discover and check. There is an invoice from the supplier or an entry in the bank account. To try to place any other value on an asset is inevitably more subjective, and a view or an estimate is required. What an asset cost is is undeniable. What an asset is worth is open to debate. Any valuation not based on historic cost will also change over time as it is subject to market forces.

Fixed assets are generally shown at their historic cost less depreciation, referred to as their net book or balance sheet value on the assumption that they will continue to be used in the future to support the business of the company. They are not shown at their scrap or resale value.

Going concern

Accounts are prepared at the end of the year on the assumption that

11

they will form part of a continuing flow of such accounts into the future. It is assumed that the company will continue in business for the foreseeable future. In other words, it is a going concern. UK listed companies must provide a statement from the directors that they consider their company to be a going concern.

There is no attempt in the balance sheet to set out the current market value or disposal value of assets. Assets are valued on the basis of the going concern assumption. The balance sheet simply shows the assets for this year, which can be compared with last year's and, in 12 months' time, with next year's.

Normally, the value of assets on the going concern basis is greater than if the company were to be wound up and the scrap or break-up values were used. As long as it is reasonable to make the going concern assumption, net book values can correctly be used in the balance sheet.

Going broke?

Where auditors have reason to doubt that a company is a going concern, they must draw shareholders' attention to this in their report. Directors of UK listed companies must, to meet the requirements of the Combined Code (see below) and Listing Rules, state in the annual report that they consider their company to be a going concern. A typical statement would be "the directors have a reasonable expectation that the company has adequate resources to continue in operational existence for the foreseeable future". This can be interpreted as saying "we do not expect to fail within the next 12 months".

Corporate governance

In the 1990s, after a series of examples of blatant mismanagement (if not fraud) in public companies, corporate governance became a major issue in both the UK and the United States. So that shareholders and others interested in a company might gain some confidence in its management and likely future viability, additional disclosure was demanded.

In 1998 the Hampel Committee concluded that a board of directors should always act in the best interests of their shareholders and in doing so adopt the highest standards of corporate governance – "the system by which companies are directed and controlled". Hampel reinforced and expanded on the recommendations of the Committee on the Financial Aspects of Corporate Governance ("Cadbury Code", 1992) and a group chaired by Sir Richard Greenbury ("Greenbury Code", 1996). The role of non-executive directors was given particular attention, with the recommendation that they should make up at least one-third of the board, and that all directors should be subject to re-election at least every three years.

In 1998 the Combined Code, encompassing Cadbury, Greenbury and Hampel, was issued and included in the Listing Rules to which all quoted companies are expected to comply. There were two sections, the first dealing with the principles of good governance and the second with best practice (see also Chapter 11). In 2003 the Higgs Report, on the role and effectiveness of non-executive directors, contributed to the development of the new Combined Code on Corporate Governance. Some of its requirements are:

- a report on the business as a going concern;
- an independent remuneration committee and disclosure of directors' total remuneration, share options and pension entitlements;
- a statement of directors' responsibilities for preparing the accounts;
- an audit committee and a statement by the auditors of their reporting responsibilities, and a review of Code of Best Practice compliance;
- a balanced and understandable assessment of the company's position.

There should be a competent board with collective responsibility for the successful implementation of corporate strategy to maintain and improve shareholders' investment. The directors' joint and individual performance in this respect should be evaluated and they are required to maintain a sound system of internal control and to review this regularly. There must be confidence in the company's ability to comply with law and regulation while maintaining efficient operations and financial control. Non-executive directors should make up at least half the board, and there should be a clear division between the role of chairman and chief executive officer (CEO). Where a company does not comply with any requirement of the Combined Code a detailed explanation should be given.

Prudence and separate valuation

The annual report will have a wide range of users with differing interests. It may be used as a basis for buying or selling the company's shares or even the company itself, or granting credit to, buying a product from, taking a job with, or lending money to the company. Because it is impossible in a single set of accounts to meet all the requirements of all users, it is best for the accountant preparing the financial statements to be cautious with the figures. It is better to undervalue than overvalue an asset. An investor in a company who later discovers that the asset backing is substantially below that shown in the balance sheet will be much more annoyed than if the reverse proves to be the case.

To help avoid overoptimistic definitions of profit in the income statement or valuations of assets in the balance sheet, accountants have developed the rule of prudence or conservatism, under which profit or asset values should never knowingly be overstated. For financial accounting and reporting this can be condensed into:

- when in doubt take the lower of two values;
- when in doubt write it off.

This simple rule has significant influence in the preparation and presentation of financial accounts. For example:

- Value inventory at the lower of cost or market value.
- Write off potential bad debts immediately, not when all hope of collecting the money has evaporated.
- If there are any doubts about revenue, recognise it only when it is collected in cash.
- In the income statement include only profits that have been realised during the year; it is not prudent to anticipate events.
- Take care to provide for all known or anticipated liabilities and losses to date, although not to the extent of creating hidden reserves.
- Recognise future losses as soon as they are known, not when they happen.

An important accounting principle is that of separate valuation. As a general rule, all assets and liabilities should be valued separately. It is not acceptable to present the total net value of a group of assets in the balance sheet – setting off the loss in value of one against the increase in value of another.

Realisation

Until an event or transaction has actually taken place it should not be taken into account in arriving at the profit or loss for the year. A major customer may, at the end of a company's financial year, promise a large order next month. This is good news for the company. It will be recorded in the management information and control systems, and plans will be made to adjust the order book and production schedules. However, until a formal and legally binding agreement is made and executed, nothing has occurred as far as the financial accounting system is concerned. No revenue can be brought into this year's accounts. The transaction has not yet taken place and so is quite correctly ignored in the financial statements. Profit is made or realised only when the transaction is completed, with ownership of the goods passing to the customer. Only when profit is realised can it become available for distribution to shareholders by way of dividend.

Asset values may increase as a result of inflation or market changes. This is beneficial for the company but it cannot claim that it has made a profit. Until the asset is sold any increase in value must be retained in the balance sheet. It can only be taken through the income statement as a profit when it is realised – that is, when the asset is sold.

Accrual and matching

The income statement shows the revenue generated during the year and matches it with the costs and expenses incurred in producing it. Income and expenditure should be included in the income statement at the time the transaction or event took place. This is usually when it is invoiced, not when the cash relating to the transaction is received or paid. All income and expenditure for the financial year is brought into the accounts without reference to when the transaction or event will have a cash impact. The difference between the timing of the transaction and its translation into cash is shown as either an accrual (money to be paid in the future) or a prepayment (money paid in advance).

Consistency and comparability

Accounting problems rarely have a single solution; usually there are several perfectly acceptable alternatives. This is a major dilemma for accountants. It has also given rise to the apocryphal story of a chief executive who is said to have advertised for an accountant with only one arm as he was tired of being told "on the one hand … but then on the other hand …".

A company can massage its profit for the year simply by changing its accounting policy: for example, by adjusting the inventory valuation or depreciation method. What may appear to be in the best interests of the company in one year may not be in the next. If companies were allowed to change each year their methods of asset valuation and depreciation charging or the treatment of costs and expenses, it would be impossible to compare previous years' accounts with the current ones. It should also be possible to use accounts to compare the performance and financial position of a company over a number of years and with that of other companies.

Unless there is a statement to the contrary, it can be assumed that the underlying accounting policies for the preparation of this year's accounts are the same as the previous year. As far as possible, from one year to the next, there should be consistency of terminology and presentation of all items included in the financial statements.

Companies can of course quite correctly decide to change an accounting policy. When this occurs the notes in the accounts should clearly state the nature of the change and the reasons for it. A company that habitually changes its accounting policies should be studied more carefully than one that does not.

Materiality and relevance

The annual report should provide its users with all useful and relevant information. Anything that is important or material should be disclosed. The test is whether failure to provide details will affect the decision-making of users. If it will, the details are material.

It is impossible to have precise rules on when an event or transaction becomes material. In general, if it is big enough to have an impact on the figures or important enough to influence any decisions likely to be made by those using the annual report, it is material and should be disclosed separately and clearly. In the United States the SEC requires the CEO to testify that the accounts are "materially truthful and complete".

As a rule of thumb, something is material to an accountant if it represents 5–10% or more of the total of whatever is being considered. For example, for a company with a $5m turnover any transaction of around $250,000–500,000 will be material. For one with a $50m turnover, a material event is in the $2.5m–5m range.

Reliability and understandability

To be of practical use financial statements must be reliable. The information they contain should be timely, free from error, unbiased, complete and clearly reflect the substance rather than the form of events. Directors have a duty to make their financial statements understandable. However, it would be unreasonable to require an annual report to be completely comprehensible to anyone picking it up. Some basic skill and expertise on behalf of the user is assumed.

Substance over form
To obtain a true and fair view it is necessary to separate substance from form for any transaction or event – "it's not what I say but what I mean". Merely to follow the legal form may not fully explain the commercial or business implications of what has occurred. It is more important for the basics of a transaction or event to be understood. A company's financial statements should clearly reflect the economic reality of any material transaction or event that has taken place during the year.

Accounting standards

The accounting profession developed rules and guidelines for best practice, but it was not until the 1930s that these began to be written down and codified. As companies grew in size and power and international business became more complex, there was pressure to formalise the process further so that best practice could be enforced. In other words, accounting standards were required.

In the UK, the Financial Reporting Council (FRC) was set up in 1990 with funding from the government, the City and the accounting profession, to promote good financial reporting. It has two branches. In 2001 the Accounting Standards Board (ASB) replaced the Accounting Standards Committee (ASC), which had overseen the introduction of 22 Statements of Standard Accounting Practice (SSAP). The Financial Reporting Review Panel (FRRP) is concerned with the policing of reporting and presentation of company financial statements.

The Accounting Standards Board
Company compliance with the accounting standards of the country in which it is listed is mandatory. At present, this means there are differences in the reporting requirements of a company listed in New York compared with one listed in London, Milan or Paris. It is to be hoped

that, in the near future, the acceptance of international standards will overcome this difficulty.

The ASB is an independent body, not tied solely to the accounting profession. Initially, it focused on the profit and loss account (income statement) and introduced two new financial statements: the cash flow statement and a statement of total recognised gains and losses. Compliance with all accounting standards is mandatory for all companies.

The broad aims of the ASB are similar to those of accounting standards organisations in other countries. The US equivalent is the Financial Accounting Standards Board (FASB), formed in 1973. They are to:

- define accounting concepts;
- codify generally accepted best accounting practice;
- reduce differences in financial accounting and reporting;
- provide new accounting standards when necessary;
- continually assess whether existing standards should be improved.

The first step the ASB takes when tackling a new area is to issue a Financial Reporting Exposure Draft (FRED). Then, after consultation and discussion, it issues a Financial Reporting Standard (FRS).

Statements of Recommended Practice (SORP) are developed for business groups or sectors which have specific needs for guidance on accounting matters. For example, they may, within ASB guidelines, be issued by the Pensions Research Accounting Group, the Charity Commission, the Association of British Insurers, or the Oil Industry Accounting Committee. SORPs apply only to the organisations they are designed for.

The ASB has an Urgent Issues Task Force (UITF) to respond quickly to problems of financial reporting and disclosure. The UITF publishes abstracts on the issues it has considered and these, although not mandatory for companies, can be expected to be incorporated in future ASB statements.

Companies must adopt accounting standards

Since 1985 UK companies have had to state that their accounts have been prepared according to the appropriate accounting standards. If a company does not strictly apply a standard there should be a note explaining why it has not. Careful attention should be given to any such notes, particularly if they are found in the auditors' report, although often the detail is complex and probably has been written with clarity well down the list of objectives.

International accounting standards

The International Accounting Standards Committee (IASC), set up in 1973, works towards worldwide harmonisation of the content and presentation of financial statements through the publication of International Accounting Standards (IAS). Following the restructuring of the IASC in 2001, these are now called International Financial Reporting Standards (IFRS) and prepared by the International Accounting Standards Board (IASB), which is currently based in London. These are listed at the end of this chapter.

The IASC works closely with the International Organisation of Securities Commissions (IOSCO), which endorses IAS, to ensure the compatability of international and national accounting standards. The Financial Reporting Standards Board (FRSB), with members representing Australia, Canada, France, Germany, Japan, the UK and the United States is working towards the "international convergence and harmonisation" of corporate reporting. As part of the move towards the adoption of international accounting standards, all 8,000 EU listed companies must now apply IAS in their financial reports.

Statement of accounting policies

The annual report contains a statement of the accounting policies that a company has applied in preparing its financial statements. Accounting policies should be reviewed and updated regularly and be the most appropriate for the presentation of the company's performance and position. A typical statement of accounting policies following IAS 1 and FRS 18 (issued in 2000) includes:

- the accounting standards applied;
- the method of consolidating group companies and associates;
- the treatment of acquisitions and goodwill, leases and foreign currency;
- whether historic cost or another basis has been used to value assets;
- the treatment of R&D and of the pension fund and costs;
- the inventory valuation method.

It is always worth studying the reasons given for a change in accounting policy. In most cases the change will be to bring the company into line with generally accepted accounting principles (GAAP), but sometimes the objective may be less straightforward. A change in depreciation policy or inventory valuation methods, for example, will affect not only asset valuation in the balance sheet but also the reported profit for the year.

When a company has changed its accounting policies, you should read the auditors' report to see if it gives the company a clean bill of health. If the auditors believe that some aspect of the financial statements fails to comply with legislation, accounting standards or GAAP, they have a duty to make this clear in their report to shareholders.

Generally accepted accounting principles

Every country has some generally accepted accounting principles (GAAP). These consist of a mixture of legislation, stock exchange rules, accounting standards, conventions, concepts and practice. The aim of GAAP is to ensure that the preparation and presentation of a set of financial statements conform with the current best accounting practice. The important words are "generally accepted" and "principles". GAAP do not comprise an unchanging set of written rules; they provide the skeleton upon which the accounts must be fleshed out. As circumstances and theory and practice change so do GAAP. Currently, a key issue is whether International Accounting Standards or US GAAP will take the dominant role in defining company reporting requirements.

European Directives

In the UK and the United States it is the accounting profession that oversees the development and implementation of accounting rules. In most of continental Europe this role is taken by government. The 1957 Treaty of Rome set out the objectives of what has become the European Union (EU). There is pressure for the harmonisation (convergence) of accounting and corporate reporting. To achieve this goal, directives are issued which member countries are expected to incorporate into their own legislation.

The Fourth Directive, adopted in 1978, dealt with accounting principles, accounts and allied information with standard formats enforced for the income statement and balance sheet. It also contained the true and fair view requirement in the preparation of financial statements. The Seventh Directive, adopted in 1983, concerned public quoted companies and the presentation of consolidated or group accounts, including the treatment of goodwill. This was adopted in the 1989 Companies Act in the UK.

All listed European companies are now expected to comply fully with IAS (IFRS). This still leaves some 4m companies exempt. The Fair Value Directive (2001) and the Modernisation Directive (2003) move towards the goal of a single financial reporting framework for all companies.

Stock exchange listing requirements

In the United States the Securities and Exchange Commission (SEC) imposes reporting and disclosure requirements on all quoted (listed) companies. In the UK the Financial Services Authority (FSA) took over this responsibility from the London Stock Exchange in 2000. The publication of interim reports and preliminary announcements and the division of company borrowing into bands of repayment time are all listing requirements (Listing Rules).

The stock exchange in the UK and the SEC in the United States impose reporting and disclosure requirements on all quoted or listed companies. The publication of interim reports in the UK and the division of company borrowing into bands of repayment time are stock exchange requirements.

The stock exchange also reinforces the application of accounting standards by requiring companies to provide a compliance statement and an explanation of any material deviations. The overall objective is to ensure that investors have appropriate information for their buy-hold-sell decisions.

Every company quoted on the stock exchange must comply with its listing requirements. This may call for revision of the presentation and content of the financial statements. Foreign companies listed on the SEC are often asked to disclose additional information to that required in their home country. In 1993 Daimler-Benz complied with US GAAP when it became the first German company to be listed on the New York Stock Exchange (NYSE). More recently, Siemens fully adopted US GAAP in order to gain NYSE listing in 2001.

Auditors

Every public company must employ an auditor. The auditing profession developed in the 19th century to protect shareholders' interests. Auditors are professional accountants who check the accounting records and all other relevant sources of data and information, and report that the financial statements give a true and fair view.

Auditors are independent of the management of the company. They are employed by the shareholders, not the directors. They report directly to shareholders in their report and attend the AGM.

Professional bodies

In the UK, the main professional body for auditors and accountants is the Institute of Chartered Accountants in England and Wales (ICAEW). The US equivalent is the American Institute of Certified Public Accountants (AICPA). In France, auditors are governed by the Compagnie Nationale des Commissaires aux Comptes (CNCC) and accountants by L'Ordre des Experts Compatables (OEC). Since 1947 French accounts have been based on a standardised format – Le Plan Compatable General (PCG). This was updated in 1999 to make listed companies IAS compliant. Since the mid-1990s there has been progress to update the PCG and make listed companies IAS compliant. Germany was later than most countries in founding professional accounting organisations. The Wirtschaftspruferkammer is for both auditors and accountants. In 1998 the German Accounting Standards Board (GASB) was recognised and began to issue standards forming the basis of German GAAP. In Italy, there are the Consiglio Nazionale dei Ragionieri e Periti Commerciali for accountants and commercial appraisers and the Consiglio Nazionale dei Dottori Commercialisti for doctors of economics and commerce.

All countries have many firms of auditors dealing with small and medium-sized companies, but for listed companies, particularly if they are multinational, there are only a few suitable auditing firms. These firms are capable of offering full professional auditing services anywhere in the world. They are as multinational as any company they may deal with and their names are well known. They can be expected to operate with the most exacting professional standards.

Size is important

It is unusual for major listed companies to be audited by small firms. Having the signature of one of the top firms on the auditors' report is considered a comforting sign for shareholders and other interested parties. An advantage of using their services is that they can be presumed to be completely objective and independent. If there is a difference of view or opinion they will, if necessary, be able to stand up to a company's management. For example, in 2000 PricewaterhouseCoopers (PWC) had some 10,000 partners and a fee income of $21.5 billion. A small firm of auditors, threatened with losing the business of a major company, might find the prospect made it more amenable to management's wishes. A large firm might not like losing the account any more than the small one, but it would not miss the income to the same degree. The Big Four accounting firms are Deloitte Touche-Tohmatsu, Ernst & Young, KMPG International and PCW. It is unlikely that you will see any other firm's name as auditor for a major international company.

However, experience of corporate misadventure through the 1990s cast some doubt on the effectiveness of large firms of auditors as a safeguard for shareholders. One particular problem was that, as a general rule, for every $1 charged for audit fees, professional firms seemed to generate more than $1 of non-audit income. Can complete independence be guaranteed if the auditing firm is reliant on consultancy or other professional fees from the same company? In one year, Arthur Andersen, as auditor of Enron, received $25m; in the same year it received $27m for consultancy work.

Auditing standards

Most countries have a set of auditing standards. These are the basis of the work of auditors and are mandatory for members of the profession. They are incorporated into generally accepted auditing standards (GAAS) and International Auditing Standards (IAS) produced by the International Auditing Practices Committee (IAPC).

Auditors' report

The audit report must state that:

- the accounts were prepared in accordance with the law and GAAP;
- the audit was conducted in accordance with GAAS;
- the financial statements show a true and fair view;
- proper accounting records have been maintained;
- all required information and records were made available;
- all explanations requested proved satisfactory.

Stock exchange requirements in the UK call for a statement of compliance with the code of practice relating to corporate governance. Thus there will be one auditors' report for the financial statements and one concerning corporate governance.

Auditors are expected to have looked at everything appearing in the annual report. They do not have a formal duty to audit the chairman's or chief executive's statement or the operating and financial review (OFR), but they should have ensured that these contain nothing that is misleading or inconsistent with the information in the financial statements.

True and fair view

The annual report should provide a true and fair view of a company's financial performance and position. The requirement for a true and fair view appeared in the 1947 UK Companies Act and was adopted in the EU's Fourth Directive, where it is seen to be the prime objective of annual reporting. In the United States, the objective of company financial statements is to "... present fairly ... and ... in conformity with GAAP".

In the UK and the United States the legal system is based on common law, whereas in most of the rest of Europe it is based on Roman law, which requires more precise detail and formal written rules. There is no definition of true and fair in UK legislation or in the Fourth Directive. It is a term that is difficult to define, but most people know what it means. Just as GAAP may evolve and change over time, so may what represents a true and fair view. It is a dynamic not a static concept.

In 1999 the ASB stated:

> Financial statements will not be true and fair unless the information they contain is sufficient in quantity and quality to satisfy the reasonable expectations of the readers to whom they are addressed.

Qualified report

The auditors' report is extremely important. When the auditors feel it necessary to make their concerns public this should influence any view taken of the company and its management.

Auditors must satisfy themselves that proper records have been kept and that the financial statements agree with these. If the auditors have not visited operating units of the company, their report must state that all necessary details have been provided. If the auditors are not satisfied with any aspect of the preparation and presentation of the financial statements, they are expected to draw this to shareholders' attention by qualifying their report.

For any major company a qualified audit report is damaging. However, qualification concerning the application of an accounting standard that reflects a basic disagreement on principle between the auditor and management is less likely to cause problems for a company than one where the auditors are of the opinion that the financial statements may be misleading.

Auditors and fraud

It is a common misapprehension that it is the auditors' role to search for fraud. An 1896 legal case in the UK provided a useful definition of the auditor as "a watchdog not a bloodhound". That a company has a clean audit report does not guarantee that there has been no fraud or, indeed, that the company will not fail the day after the accounts are published.

Auditors should satisfy themselves that the company's internal control systems are adequate. Directors are expected to make a statement to this effect as part of their report on corporate governance. It was a combination of less than effective auditing and sloppy internal management control that led to the dramatic demise of Barings Bank.

Directors

The annual report contains a list of all the members of the board of directors. New appointments and retirements are noted. At the AGM directors will be put forward in rotation for re-election to the board with a formal vote by shareholders on their appointment at the meeting.

It is worth reading any personal information on directors that is provided. Most companies now at least disclose their ages. Some also provide pen portraits of their experience and careers. Given the importance of the directors to a company, it is remarkable how little information is given about them in the annual report.

The relationship with shareholders

Directors are accountable to the shareholders. They have overall responsibility for the management of all a company's assets and capital. Part of the directors' responsibility involves providing shareholders with adequate information on the principal aspects of the company. At a minimum, directors provide details of the operations of the company during the year (income statement), its financial position at the end of the year (balance sheet), and its sources and uses of financial resources (cash flow statement).

At the AGM the directors present the annual report to shareholders, who then have the opportunity to raise any questions they wish. Such questions are not limited to the content of the annual report but may be on any topic. One of the important tasks of a company's chairman is to manage the AGM.

The directors' report

Each year directors must provide shareholders with a written report. This identifies the main business activity of the company, and should give shareholders a clear picture of the performance of their company and its financial position at the end of the year. If the directors consider that likely future developments may affect the company, they should draw this to shareholders' attention.

Directors' shareholdings

The annual report gives details of the number of shares each director of the company owns or has an interest in. Any share options or other schemes providing directors with opportunities to acquire shares should also be disclosed as should shadow share schemes, under which directors may receive benefits calculated in relation to share price movements.

Operating and financial review

In the UK, the Accounting Standards Board (ASB) has continued the process of improving accounting standards and the quality of information given in the annual report on the performance and business activities of a company. In 1993 it recommended that all listed companies include in their annual report an operating and financial review (OFR) statement, similar to the management discussion and analysis (MD&A) statement required of listed companies in the United States.

The OFR was updated in 2003, requiring additional information on the company's operations to support and enhance the accounts. This is not to be just another set of numbers; there should be discussion and comment on operational activities. It is intended not only to offer an historic perspective but to "assist the user's assessment of the future performance of the reporting entity by setting out the directors' analysis of the business". The intention is to provide a view of the company's current and likely short-term future performance. Ideally, there should be three sections offering a description of the business, its objectives and overall strategy, and its actual performance and financial position. It should also:

- be clear, succinct and readily understood by the general reader;
- contain only matters that are likely to be significant to investors;
- be balanced and objective, dealing even-handedly with both good and bad aspects;
- refer to comments made in previous statements;
- discuss trends and factors underlying the business;
- identify events, trends and uncertainties that are expected to have an impact on the business in the future;
- provide details of any significant events affecting the business that occurred after the financial year end.

Typically, an OFR contains many figures, graphs and ratios in support of the overview provided. A company should make clear how these relate to the financial statements in the annual report and ensure that any ratios used are adequately explained. An important principle is that all the information presented should be capable of comparison with that provided in previous years and with that of other similar businesses. The impact of any changes in accounting policies on reported performance or financial position should be clearly explained. A crucial rule of financial analysis is "when in doubt do it yourself". Never use pre-prepared tables or ratios as the basis for analysis unless you are confident of their source and accuracy.

Pro forma figures

When faced with uncertainty, poor performance, or the need to hide incompetence or fraud, directors may be attracted to presenting "pro forma" figures in their reports to investors. They develop their own measures of performance that do not necessarily correlate with the published accounts or support objective analysis. If you see the terms "adjusted", "normalised" or "underyling" being used in the review of a company's performance, be on your guard. An example of such a measure is to be found in the use of earnings before interest, taxation, depreciation and amortisation (EBITDA – see Chapter 7). A company showing a loss in the published income statement could produce a positive EBITDA figure for presentation by directors. If directors, in their discussion of performance, choose to use a measure other than one firmly based on the reported financial figures and GAAP, a clear explanation must be provided.

Corporate strategy for the lay person

The OFR (or the MD&A) is a good starting point for studying a company. It is intended to be read and understood by anybody and therefore free of specialist terminology and jargon. If figures or ratios are included, such as those concerned with gearing or earnings per share, they should be clearly linked to those contained in the published financial statements.

Each year the OFR sets out the historic performance and activity of the company together with some indication of future developments. Any major deviations from these should be explained the following year. It should not focus only on the good news and victories, as the statements in the annual report by the chairman chief executive often do.

The OFR should also link up with the statement of accounting policies by discussing any changes in the way in which the financial statements have been prepared or presented.

A company should not be expected to publish its corporate plan in the OFR, but it should discuss business trends and future events that will have an impact on the performance of the company.

The hindsight factor

There is only one attribute needed to ensure perfect financial analysis and investment: hindsight. A few days or weeks after a major event anyone can articulate precisely what occurred and the impact it had on a company and its share price.

It is easy to criticise the annual report as an ineffectual document. There are numerous examples of companies failing within a few months of publishing apparently healthy year-end results. With hindsight there may be clear evidence of the directors' incompetence, if not misrepresentation and fraud, although it is often the auditors who bear the brunt of criticism over their apparent inability to discover and draw attention to the true situation before the shareholders lost their investment.

International Accounting Standards

IAS
1   Presentation of financial statements
2   Valuation and presentation of inventories
7   Cash flow statements
8   Accounting policies
10   Post balance sheet events
11   Construction contracts
12   Income taxes
14   Segmental reporting
15   Operating leases
16   Property, plant and equipment
17   Leases
18   Revenue
19   Employee benefits
20   Accounting for government grants
21   The effects of changes in foreign exchange rates
22   Business combinations
23   Borrowing costs
24   Related party disclosure
27   Consolidated and separate statements
28   Financial reporting of interests in joint ventures
29   Financial reporting in hyperinflationary economies
32   Financial instruments
33   Earnings per share
35   Discontinued operations
36   Impairment of assets
37   Provisions and contingent liabilities
38   Intangible assets
39   Financial instruments
40   Investment property
41   Agriculture

2 The balance sheet

THE BASIS OF FINANCIAL ANALYSIS is the ability to read the accounts. This is a necessary skill for any manager and essential for those with ambitions for a seat on the board. The balance sheet is one of the key financial statements provided by a company in its annual report. For those with little or no financial knowledge it is often viewed as a puzzle, and one best left alone. To others it is seen as the pinnacle of the accountant's necromantic art, with some spectacular effects but no real substance.

The balance sheet provides much of the data and information necessary to support the analysis of a company's performance and position. It is the starting point for an assessment of a company's liquidity and solvency (Chapter 9), gearing (Chapter 10) and the calculation of rates of return on assets, capital or investment (Chapter 7).

Balance sheet presentation

Proof of the book-keeping

Originally, a balance sheet was prepared at the end of the financial year to provide proof of the accuracy of the double entry book-keeping system. It listed the balances in the books of account at the end of the year. If the two sides of the account balanced with debit (balances on the left-hand side) equalling credit (balances on the right-hand side), it could be assumed that proper records had been maintained throughout the year.

The balance sheet can be viewed as a set of old-fashioned kitchen scales. On one side is a bowl containing the assets (items of value the company owns or has the right to receive in the future), and on the other side is a bowl containing the liabilities (amounts the company owes to its shareholders or others providing finance and credit). For any business, one side of the scales represents what it has got and the other where it got the money from. The two sides must balance. It is not possible for a business to have more assets than sources of finance, to use more money than is available, or to have more finance available than is used.

It represents the final statement of the book-keeping process and was never intended to show the real value of a business. It is one of a continuing chain of year-end accounts. Today the balance sheet continues to fulfil its role as the final proof of the books of account.

The year-end position

The balance sheet provides a snapshot of the financial state of a company at the year end, setting out its financial position on the last day of the financial year. The basic equation of the balance sheet is:

$$\text{Assets} = \text{liabilities}$$

Under the rules of double entry book-keeping, assets appear on the left side of the balance sheet and liabilities on the right. The UK was an exception to this rule, with companies displaying assets on the right side of the balance sheet. This idiosyncratic behaviour dates back to the 1860s, when an error was made in the example of balance sheet presentation incorporated in a Companies Act. Assets were shown on the right side of the balance sheet instead of the left, and UK accountants followed the letter of the law for more than 100 years.

What to show?

It is not necessary to prepare an income statement to discover the change in shareholders' interest (profit or loss) for the year. If, at the end of the year, all the assets of the company are set down on one side of the page and all the liabilities on the other, the two sides will not balance. The difference represents the profit or loss for the year. If net assets have increased, a profit has been achieved; if they decrease, there has been a loss. When the income statement is prepared the final figure (retained profit) will provide the necessary 'proving' balancing figure for the balance sheet.

An important issue is what value to place on the assets and liabilities in the balance sheet: their 'cost', 'fair', or 'market' value. The cost of an asset can be defined with some accuracy; its true value is uncertain until it is actually sold. Whatever method of valuation is adopted, any changes in the value of assets and liabilities occurring during the year will have an impact on the shareholders' stake in the company. At present, the figures appearing in any balance sheet are a mixture of cost and some estimate of market value. Over the next few years accountants face the task of bringing some order and coherence to this aspect of the balance sheet.

Alternative formats for the horizontal balance sheet 2.1

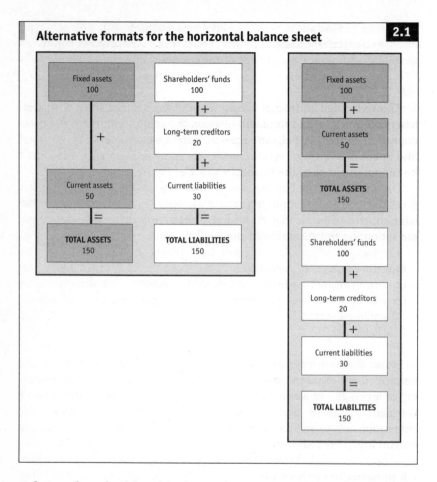

Balance sheet building blocks

A balance sheet normally consists of five basic building blocks. These appear in the balance sheet of any company, irrespective of the nature of the business or the country or countries within which it operates. The way in which the five building blocks are set out may depend partly on what is common practice or legally required within the particular business sector or country. For most companies and countries the balance sheet format is as follows.

Fixed assets	Shareholders' funds
Current assets	Long-term loans and creditors
	Current liabilities
Total assets	**Total liabilities**

This two-sided horizontal presentation of the balance sheet with total assets on one side and total liabilities on the other is standard for most countries. Indeed, in Belgium, France, Germany, Greece, Italy, Portugal and Spain this is a legal requirement. The horizontal balance sheet may be set out in either of the formats shown in Figure 2.1.

On one side of the balance sheet, fixed assets added to current assets gives the total assets employed at the year end. There are only three possible sources of funds that may be applied to finance total assets. These are set out on the other side of the balance sheet.

Capital and reserves or shareholders' funds (funds provided by shareholders)	100
Long-term creditors (long-term creditors and borrowing)	20
Current liabilities (short-term creditors and borrowing repayable	
within one year)	<u>30</u>
Total liabilities	<u>150</u>

How these three sources are combined to finance total assets employed is central to understanding the financial structure – the gearing or leverage – of a company. In assessing the adequacy or safety of a company's balance sheet, the proportion of finance provided by the shareholders is compared with that derived from other sources, outside borrowings, loans or debt.

UK presentation 1970s-style

Having proved their obstinacy on the question of which side of the balance sheet to place assets, UK accountants remained out of step with those in other countries. The traditional horizontal presentation of the balance sheet was replaced by a vertical one that linked current assets and current liabilities to highlight net current assets and net assets employed (see Figure 2.2 on the next page). Net current assets are defined as current assets less current liabilities. This balance sheet format shows net assets as follows.

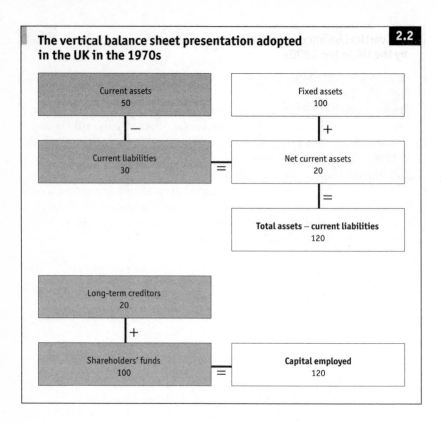

2.2

The vertical balance sheet presentation adopted in the UK in the 1970s

Net assets = fixed assets + net current assets, *or*
= total assets − current liabilities, *or*
= shareholders' funds + long-term creditors

The argument supporting this move was that it is useful to know to what extent a company could, if necessary, quickly pay its short-term creditors by using its short-term assets. Current assets, if not already in the form of cash balances, are assumed to be capable of being turned into cash within 12 months. Current liabilities are creditors due for payment within 12 months.

Net current assets

If a company is to pay its creditors within the next few months, where might it find the necessary cash? It would not be expected either to sell a fixed asset or to borrow long-term funds to provide cash to pay short-

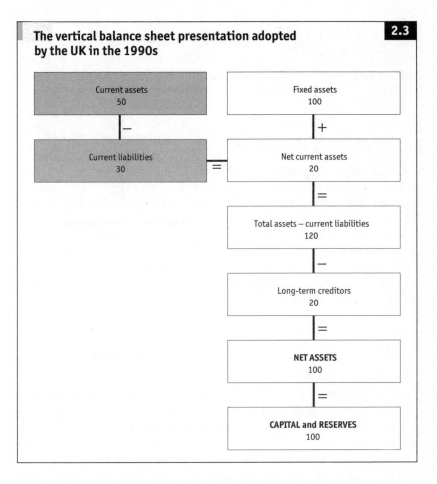

2.3

The vertical balance sheet presentation adopted by the UK in the 1990s

term creditors. For most companies it would be reasonable to expect this cash to be generated from within the current asset building block.

In paying creditors, a company would first use available cash balances, then collect cash owed to it by customers, and lastly turn its inventory into cash. A surplus of current assets over current liabilities – net current assets – in the balance sheet indicates that a company has more short-term assets that can be turned into cash reasonably quickly than short-term liabilities that require cash for payment in the near future.

UK presentation 1990s-style

The last move in UK balance sheet presentation was purely aesthetic. The horizontal format looked somewhat lopsided. The solution was to display the balance sheet in a column or table rather than as two sides: the vertical presentation. Net assets are defined in most UK balance sheets as follows.

Net assets = capital and reserves, or
           = (total assets − current liabilities) − long-term creditors

Today most companies in the UK use the vertical form of balance sheet presentation, retaining the emphasis on net current assets but focusing attention on shareholders' funds (capital and reserves) – see Figure 2.3 on the previous page. Other European countries maintain the more traditional horizontal format, with assets on the left and liabilities on the right. US companies generally present a balance sheet with total assets and liabilities but with one set above the other, providing a vertical format.

The UK form of presentation, using the five building blocks, produces a balance sheet as in Figure 2.3.

Liabilities

Shareholders' funds

One building block in the balance sheet indicates the amount of finance shareholders (stockholders) have provided for the company. This can have a variety of titles: capital and reserves, equity, shareholders' funds or interest, net worth.

The term net worth is a good basis for understanding what this building block represents. If the company with the example balance sheet shown in Figure 2.3 were to close down and turn its assets into cash (a process known as liquidation), there would be $150 in the bank, the value of total assets. Then it would pay amounts owed to the long-term and short-term creditors, $50, leaving $100 in the bank. This $100 represents the net worth of the company. After all borrowings and creditors have been paid, what is left, the net worth of the company, belongs to the shareholders. The last step, before the company ceases to exist, would be to repay to the shareholders $100, representing their investment or stake.

The section of a company's balance sheet giving details of the shareholders' funds normally contains three main headings:

- ◪ Called-up share capital or common stock
- ◪ Share premium account
- ◪ Profit and loss account or retained earnings

Shareholders have acquired the issued shares or stock of the company and are its owners. The shareholders' stake represents a long-term source of finance (capital) to the company. In most balance sheets the shareholders' stake is called capital and reserves. The two key items are share capital, the shares issued to shareholders, and the retained income or earnings, representing the profit retained (ploughed back) over the life of the company.

Retained profit is a liability

Under normal trading conditions a company retains some of the profit each year to assist growth and investment for its future development and success. In allowing the company to retain part of the profits made in a year rather than taking all the profit as dividends, shareholders are lending this money to their company. Thus retained profit is a liability to a company and is shown as such in the balance sheet. (See also Retained earnings, page 40.)

Share capital

Only shares or stock that have been issued and paid for by shareholders are shown in the balance sheet. These are referred to as the called-up or issued capital of the company. A company may have the ability to issue more shares from its authorised share capital. Most US companies disclose this information on the face of the balance sheet. In other countries, the details regarding the authorised and issued share capital are usually set out in the notes to the accounts.

It is possible for a company to purchase ("buy back") and hold its own shares – up to a maximum of 10% of share capital in the UK. These will be shown separately as Treasury shares or stock and as a deduction from shareholders' funds in the balance sheet.

Share price and the balance sheet

Shares are always shown in the balance sheet at their nominal value, for example, 25p, 10¢, €50. The market price at which these shares change hands is irrelevant; there is no attempt in the balance sheet to reflect the stock exchange value of shares.

If a company is wound up or liquidated, it sells its assets, turning them into cash. This is used to repay the short-term and long-term creditors, and what is left is returned to the shareholders, who may receive more or less than the nominal value of their shares.

Ordinary shares

Ordinary shareholders are a company's risk-takers. They may lose their investment completely if the company fails and there is insufficient money available to pay the creditors. They are the last to receive any money from the company. However, ordinary shareholders can lose only the nominal value of the shares they own, although they will normally have paid more than the nominal value for the shares on the stock exchange. They cannot be called upon to contribute any more funds to a company. Ordinary shareholders thus have limited liability.

The bulk of most companies' share capital is provided by ordinary shares (called common stock in the United States). In acquiring shares a shareholder obtains a stake or a share of the equity of the company. Legally, the owner of ordinary shares has a right to share in the profits and assets of the company as well as certain rights and obligations connected with its management.

A company may have several different types or classes of ordinary shares. Shares may carry different voting rights, with some shares having more or less than one vote per share. There may be differences in their right to participate in profits being preferred or deferred.

Preference shares

Preference shares were introduced in the 19th century to allow investors to participate with less risk in companies. Preference shareholders normally receive their dividends before the ordinary shareholders receive anything, and if the company is wound up they get their capital back before the ordinary shareholders. In other words, they rank preferentially for dividend and capital repayment. In return for these benefits, preference shares usually have a fixed rate of dividend and few, if any, rights regarding the management of the company. Issuing preference shares allows a company to raise long-term capital with a known cost: the dividend paid. However, the dividend paid on preference shares is not tax allowable as would be the interest paid on a long-term loan.

A company may issue cumulative preference shares. If in one year there is insufficient profit to pay the preference shareholders their dividends, the obligation will be carried forward to the following year when the arrears in dividends will be paid – again before the ordinary shareholders receive anything. Preference shares may be offered with the right to a share (to participate) in the profits beyond their fixed dividend. These are called participating preference shares.

Normally, preference shares are irredeemable. They form part of the permanent capital of the company and are not expected to be repaid. Sometimes companies issue redeemable preference shares. These can have a fixed date upon which they will be repurchased (redeemed), or the company may have the right to redeem them at any time.

In rare circumstances, a company may issue some participating redeemable preference shares.

Convertible shares

The term convertible can be attached to either shares or loans. Convertible shares may be issued providing the owner with the right, at some time in the future, to convert them into ordinary shares.

A bank may be approached by a company for a loan. The company wants to pay as little interest as possible, and the bank wants security for both interest and capital. The bank may be persuaded to charge a lower than normal rate of interest on the loan in return for the right to convert the loan into ordinary shares at an agreed price formula at some future date. The bank has security, as the money provided is not part of the company's share capital but a loan. Also, if the company flourishes and its share price improves, the bank can make a profit by converting the loan into shares.

Convertible redeemable preference shares may also be issued, although they rarely are.

Share premium account

If a company issues shares to new or existing shareholders, it offers them shares of the normal nominal value. It will take full advantage of the fact that its shares are being traded on the stock exchange at a price higher than their nominal value. So a company with $1 nominal value shares, taking account of the current quoted share price, decides to offer new shares at a price of $4 and the issue is taken up. As each share is issued and paid for the company's balance sheet is adjusted:

$$\text{Cash} + \$4 = \text{shareholders' funds} + \$4$$

For each share issued the company increases its share capital by $1. The remaining $3 is the extra amount above the nominal value, or the premium, that shareholders are willing to pay for the share. Share premium must be shown in a separate account as part of shareholders' funds and is deemed to be a capital reserve. A capital reserve can be used only for legally permitted purposes; for example, it cannot be used to pay a dividend to shareholders, but it can be used to cover the expenses of share issues. The company's balance sheet will show the following:

$$\text{Cash} + \$4 = \text{share capital} + \$1 \text{ and share premium} + \$3$$

Retained earnings

As a company generates and retains profit, the shareholders' stake increases proportionately. The balance sheet figure for retained income or earnings, or the profit and loss account in the UK, shows the total amount retained by the company over its life.

Retained profit is a revenue reserve. It can be used to pay dividends to shareholders and for almost any other purpose a company wishes.

Revaluation reserve

A company is allowed to revalue fixed assets appearing in the balance sheet in the UK, but not in the United States and Germany, or in recent years in France and Italy. In the UK, the revaluation has most commonly been based on the replacement cost of the assets concerned.

If a major fixed asset increases in value, perhaps as a result of inflation, this change may be reflected in the balance sheet. However, the increase in value of a fixed asset does not necessarily represent an immediate profit for the company. A profit is made or realised only when the asset is sold and the resulting profit is taken through the income statement. Until this event occurs the prudence rule requires that the increase in asset value is retained in the balance sheet. Shareholders have the right to any profit on the sale of company assets, so the shareholders' stake in the company is increased by the same amount as the increase in asset valuation. Thus the balance sheet still balances:

$$\text{Fixed assets} + \$x = \text{shareholders' funds (revaluation reserve)} + \$x$$

Current liabilities

To an accountant, the term current means short-term, with short-term being taken as less than one year. A current liability – a creditor due for payment – is therefore an obligation that the company can be expected to fulfil within the 12 months following the date of the balance sheet.

The current liabilities building block in the balance sheet normally has two main headings:

- Trade creditors or accounts payable
- Short-term loans, overdraft or commercial paper

The figure for trade creditors comprises money the company owes to its suppliers for goods or services delivered during the year. In most types of businesses suppliers are paid within 30–60 days, with the company taking 1–2 months' credit from them. Any creditors not due for payment within the 12 months necessary for them to be included as a current liability are shown elsewhere in the balance sheet.

Until a company pays its creditors it has the use of the cash owed to them. Thus creditors act as a source of finance. Companies exceeding acceptable levels of using short-term creditors to finance their business may be viewed as employing an aggressive financing strategy or they may be overtrading (see page 63).

All borrowing due for repayment within 12 months of the balance sheet date appears within current liabilities. In the UK, an overdraft, a form of short-term flexible borrowing, is technically repayable on demand so it is shown as a current liability, even if there is agreement with the bank to have the overdraft as a permanent source of finance.

Dividends also appear in this section of a balance sheet. At the end of the year the directors decide what dividend payment to recommend to their shareholders at the annual general meeting (AGM). The proposed dividend is charged as an expense in the income statement, but, because it cannot be paid until it is accepted by shareholders at the AGM, it is held in the balance sheet as a current liability.

The figure for tax shown in current liabilities can be taken as the amount owed by the company due for payment within the next financial year.

Long-term borrowing and creditors

Shareholders' funds represent a permanent source of finance and current liabilities (creditors due for repayment within one year) a short-term source of finance to a company. Between these two extremes is the third building block on the liabilities side of the balance sheet: debt or long-term creditors and provisions. These are sources of finance that do not have to be repaid within the coming year. In most companies, debt consists of a mixture of long-term creditors and medium-term to long-term loans.

The notes supporting the balance sheet should provide details of repayment dates of loans and the rate of interest charged on those loans. Often a debenture appears as part of the long-term financing of a company. A debenture is a loan secured on the company's assets, normally with an agreed rate of interest and a fixed repayment date. It is possible for a company to issue a convertible debenture offering similar rights to those outlined for preference shares.

The time when major loans fall due for repayment is an important factor in assessing the future viability of a company, as on the date of repayment the necessary cash must be available.

Another type of borrowing is through loan stock. Loan stock does not form part of the ordinary shareholders' stake and may or may not have the right of conversion into equity. It is often issued with warrants. The loan stock is not convertible, but the warrants allow the holder to purchase a fixed number of ordinary shares at an agreed future price and date. The advantage for the company is that the loan stock is repayable only on the set redemption date but new capital can be raised through the warrants.

Provisions

A provision is the setting aside of funds to provide for a future event that is likely to occur, but the precise amount of money involved or the time the event will take place are uncertain.

FRS 12 defined a provision as:

> Any amount retained as reasonably necessary for the
> purposes of providing for any liability or loss which is either
> likely to be incurred, or certain to be incurred but uncertain as
> to amount or as to the date on which it will arise.

The amount of any provisions, usually covering taxation and pensions costs, appears in the long-term creditors' section of the balance sheet with a note providing details.

Big bath provisions

The notes relating to provisions should be carefully studied and particular attention given to any changes observed from the previous year. There have been examples of companies making a provision for anticipated losses on closing down a business or the costs of major restructuring following an acquisition, and so setting aside significant amounts of profit in one year and then discovering that they had overprovided for the event and bringing the provision back to boost a future year's profit. This has occasionally proved a simple but effective tactic for an executive brought in to turn round a company. Investors expect to suffer in the first year and are delighted when "profit" returns in the second.

These were referred to as "big bath provisions" and effectively outlawed by FRS 12 and IAS 37, which allow provisions to be made only where the clear transfer of "economic benefits" is involved following a past event. A simple rule is to apply the "year-end test": if a company ceases to trade at the balance sheet date would it still have to pay the amount involved? If not, there can be no provision made as it relates to future, not past, business activity.

Assets

Tangible fixed assets

Two building blocks appear on the assets side of the balance sheet: fixed or long-term assets and current or short-term assets. Fixed assets are mainly tangible, such as the physical assets used to undertake the business of the company. They include land and buildings, plant and machinery, vehicles, and fixtures and equipment.

FRS 15 defines tangible fixed assets as:

> Assets that have physical substance and are held for use in the production or supply of goods and services ... on a continuing basis in the reporting entity's activities.

Tangible fixed assets have a finite useful working life. Investment in them ties up the company's available financial resources for a number of years. Fixed assets are normally depreciated, amortised, or written off over their useful life.

There is usually a single figure in the balance sheet for tangible fixed assets. This is their balance sheet value, net book value (NBV) or written down value (WDV), which represents their cost less accumulated depreciation charged over their life to the balance sheet date. As with almost every figure appearing in the balance sheet, it is to the notes in the accounts that you must turn to find any useful details. At a minimum there should, for each class of fixed asset, be details of the:

- cost or valuation of assets at the beginning of the year;
- accumulated depreciation charged to the beginning of the year;
- amount of depreciation charged during the year;
- amounts of additions and disposals made during the year;
- balance sheet value at the end of the year;
- company's freehold and leasehold property.

Depreciation

Depreciation can be viewed as representing the setting aside of income to provide for the future replacement of fixed assets. As assets are used their value reduces. They become worn out, run down or obsolete and need replacing in order to maintain or improve the productive efficiency of the business. Depreciation is charged in the income statement, thus reducing the reported profit for the year. It should also be deducted from the value of the fixed assets set out in the balance sheet, thus reducing the value of the company's assets.

FRS15 defines depreciation as:

> The measure of the cost or revalued amount of the economic benefits of the tangible fixed asset that have been consumed during the period.

Providing for depreciation

Depreciation is a provision, a setting aside of current income to meet future eventualities, so it could be shown as a part of the shareholders' funds in the balance sheet in the same way as retained profit.

Shareholders' funds	$		$
Depreciation provision	100	Fixed assets at cost	200

However, it has been traditional policy to deduct it from the fixed asset value.

	$	$
Fixed assets at cost	200	
Less depreciation	100	100

Inflation and fixed assets

Inflation can complicate the valuation of assets because $1 at the beginning of the year will buy more than $1 at the end of the year. When inflation is low, it is reasonable to use historic cost – what the asset cost when acquired – as a basis for the valuation of a company's assets and for depreciation.

A company that had not revalued property bought in 1960 would face two problems in relation to its balance sheet. First, the property would be undervalued because to replace it can be expected to cost significantly more than the 1960 figure. Undervaluing assets may improve the reported profit of the company, as a result of a lower than realistic depreciation charge being made against income, but it may prove dangerous by making the company an attractive target for takeover. If balance sheet values were used to set the acquisition price, it would be far below current market value. Second, if the property needs replacing or major investment to maintain it, the company may not have been setting aside sufficient profits, through the depreciation charge, for this to be possible.

The problem illustrated

For example, an entrepreneur starts a company in 2000 with an investment of $5,000, which is used to purchase an asset. The balance sheet at this point is as follows.

	$		$
Fixed assets	5,000	Capital	5,000
Cash	0		

The asset has a useful working life of five years and is depreciated or written off in income statement at the rate of $1,000 per year. The company makes $1,000 profit (after depreciation). In 2005 the company's balance sheet would appear as follows.

($)	Cost	Depreciation	Net		
Fixed assets	5,000	5,000	0	Capital	5,000
				Profit	5,000
Cash			10,000		10,000

The $10,000 cash balance is the result of five years' retained profit ($1,000 per year) and five years' depreciation charge ($1,000 per year). The business has doubled in size between 2000 and 2005.

The entrepreneur decides to replace the asset and continue the business. However, at the end of 2005 an identical asset to that purchased in 2000 costs $10,000; the price has doubled because of inflation. The investment is undertaken and the balance sheet shows:

	$		$
Fixed asset	10,000	Capital and reserves	10,000
Cash	0		

The company is now in exactly the same position as it was five years before: it has a new asset and no cash. Has the company really made the $5,000 profit shown in the balance sheet? Indeed, if it been paying tax at 50% it would have been necessary to borrow money to replace the asset at the end of 2005. This example illustrates the problems of financial reporting under conditions of inflation.

Let prudence rule
The overriding rule of prudence, supported by that of capital maintenance (see page 130), requires that a company takes account of the impact of inflation in the reporting process. There are many ways of countering or reflecting this in corporate reports. The simplest method is to use replacement cost as the basis for valuing assets and in charging appropriate depreciation rates. An alternative approach is to take an appropriate index of inflation, such as the retail price index, and apply this to the assets and liabilities of a company to bring them to current values – current purchasing power (CPP) accounting.

Foreign exchange
If a company trades with or makes investments in another country, it usually has to deal in a foreign currency. If exchange rates remained constant, accountants would have few problems. Unfortunately, for both accountants and companies, exchange rates fluctuate, not only from year to year but also from minute to minute.

The problem illustrated
At the beginning of the year a UK company invests £1m in building a factory in Zanado. The company intends to develop its business operations in Zanado as part of its long-term strategy. At the time of investment the exchange rate is £1=Z10. The company's balance sheet is adjusted to reflect this.

Cash	− £1m
Factory in Zanado	+ £1m (Z10m)

At the end of the year the exchange rate is £1=Z5. What should be shown in the company's balance sheet?

Factory in Zanado £2m (Z10m), or
Factory in Zanado £0.5m (Z5m)

It could be argued that the company had either a loss of £500,000 or a profit of £1m in connection with the investment. As the company intends to maintain its operational base in Zanado, to make such adjustments at the year end would not reflect reality. The company has not terminated its investment and has not incurred (realised) either a loss or a profit. It would be breaking the prudence rule to take the exchange rate related profit or loss to the income statement. Any changes in the value of the factory brought about by exchange rate fluctuations should be held in the balance sheet. The company has invested Z10m in a factory in Zanado and this asset is still retained at the balance sheet date.

Which rate to choose?
If the investment in Zanado represented a subsidiary company, consolidated accounts would be prepared at the end of the financial year. To consolidate the subsidiary, some basic rules of procedure are required. There are several options available in choosing the exchange rate that best reflects both the trading during the year (for the income statement) and the year-end position (for the balance sheet). The options are:

- the average exchange rate for the year;
- the exchange rate applicable at time the transaction occurred;
- the exchange rate applicable at the end of the financial year.

It is reasonable and practical to use the exchange rate applicable at the year end (the balance sheet date) for the consolidation of overseas assets and liabilities. It is most common for the net worth of a foreign subsidiary to be taken into the accounts at the exchange rate applicable at the balance sheet date. For profit and loss transactions, normally either the exchange rate at the date of the transaction or the average rate for the year is used.

In the UK and the United States, companies usually take the transaction gains or losses of trading into the income statement and the gains or losses on assets or liabilities to the reserves in the balance sheet.

It is normally accepted that a prudent company would endeavour to reduce or minimise its exposure to risk through exchange rate fluctuations by covering the potential risks. For example, a company might borrow in the foreign currency a sum equivalent to the amount of the investment it is going to make in the foreign subsidiary. This approach, which is called hedging, means that any change in exchange rates is automatically adjusted on both the asset and the liability side of the balance sheet.

Intangible assets

The majority of assets shown as fixed assets in the balance sheet are tangible, but there may be other long-term assets that are described as intangible. As a general rule, accountants and auditors do not like intangible assets, which are fraught with potential danger. As their name implies, they are not physical items capable of normal identification and verification as are land and buildings or a piece of machinery.

There are at least four ways for intangibles to appear in a balance sheet:

- expenses are capitalised in the balance sheet and not charged against profits in the income statement;
- a value is placed on "new" assets of the company;
- another company is acquired (see page 53);
- an intangible asset is purchased (for example, a brand).

Capitalising expenses

A company may decide that rather than charging an expense in the income statement it will be taken to the balance sheet as an asset. This is referred to as capitalising an expense. It increases reported profit by reducing the amount of expenses being charged in the income statement.

Brand names

Until recently, it was not considered prudent for companies to include intangibles such as brand names as an asset in the balance sheet. Yet it is reasonable to consider brands as important assets for many companies. Names such as Coca-Cola, Rolls-Royce, BMW and Perrier are worth something in their own right.

In the late 1980s in the UK, some companies, mainly in the food and drink sector, began to include brand names as an asset in their balance sheets. Their argument was that brands were a valuable commercial asset and that excluding their value from the balance sheet resulted in a potentially dangerous undervaluation of the company.

There is no generally accepted practice in this area. Marks & Spencer does not put its St Michael brand in its balance sheet, but in 2000 Diageo valued its brands – including Johnnie Walker, Smirnoff, Pillsbury, Al Paso and Burger King – at £4,875m in its balance sheet, representing almost one-third of the total assets of the company. The CEO of Diageo's United Distillers & Vintners division was reported as stating that nine of its "global power brands" produced 70% of operating profit for the company. Clearly, in attempting to place a value on some companies it is unwise to ignore brands. Where a company has created an intangible asset such as a brand name, this can be taken to the balance sheet only if it has a quantifiable market value ("fair value"). This normally prohibits the capitalisation of internally developed brands, patents, client lists and media titles.

Placing a value on a brand

Brands can be divided into two classes: those that are internally developed by the company itself; and those acquired by purchase as an asset from another company. The only time an indisputable value can be placed on a brand name is when it has just been sold. At any other time brand valuation is more of an art than a science. A "value" could be produced by taking the annual "cost" to the company of supporting and developing the brand name and multiplying it by the anticipated life of the brand. Alternatively, the annual "profit" generated by the brand could be used as a basis for valuation.

UK companies can decide at any time to include the value of a brand in the balance sheet. They are not limited to when they acquired the brand or when it became a clearly identified asset through internal investment and development. As large sums are often involved the decision to capitalise a brand, this can have a dramatic impact on the balance sheet. The assets increase in value, and with the balancing move in shareholders' funds the apparent balance sheet gearing also changes.

Treatment of intangibles

In 1998 (FRS 10 "Goodwill and intangible assets") the ASB defined intangible assets as:

> *Non-financial fixed assets that do not have physical substance*
> *but are identifiable and are controlled by the entity through*
> *custody or legal rights.*

It is important to study the notes in a company's annual report on intangible assets, particularly if they are appearing for the first time. The balance sheet notes should provide details of the basis of their valuation.

In valuing a company or assessing its financial position, the treatment of intangibles can be crucial. It can be argued that intangibles are by their nature of debatable value and should be ignored in placing a value on the assets employed in a company. Their inclusion, the argument goes, makes it difficult to get an appreciation of the assets that might act as security for creditors and providers of funds to the company. Alternatively, if a company is being valued as a going concern on a continuing business basis, more often than not intangibles form an integral part and should not be ignored. Intellectual property rights (IPRS) offer an example of 21st-century intangibles. These include patents, copyrights, database rights, trademarks, know-how and confidential customer lists. Although difficult to value, they are often essential to placing a realistic valuation on a company. Prudence and caution may say remove intangibles, but commercial reality may say the opposite.

Goodwill

One intangible that has presented many problems for accountants is goodwill, which is defined as the amount paid by one company for another over and above the value of its assets, referred to as "purchased goodwill". Brands therefore often form part of goodwill, and in the UK under FRS 10 and IAS 38 they receive the same accounting treatment.

Goodwill is an important and controversial intangible asset and can only arise when dealing with a group of companies. It is produced when one company acquires another. The calculation of goodwill is straightforward. It is its treatment in the balance sheet that is complex and is the subject of considerable difference of opinion.

For example, company A offers to purchase company B for $2,000 cash. Their balance sheets are as follows.

($)	A	B		A	B
Assets	5,000	2,000	Share capital	2,000	1,000
			Reserves	2,000	500
	_____	_____	Creditors	1,000	500
	5,000	2,000		5,000	2,000

Company B has share capital and reserves or net assets of $1,500. Why might company A be prepared to pay $500 more than the balance sheet value for company B? There could be many reasons. Company B may have intangible assets such as brands, patents and research and development, which, though of value, do not appear in its balance sheet. Company A may wish to gain the benefit of B's management team with its flair, experience and expertise. (Management does not appear in either company's balance sheet.) Or A may be attracted by the potential profit streams that could be generated from B.

Goodwill can arise only at the time of an acquisition; it is not recalculated each year. It may prove particularly significant where service or people-oriented businesses are concerned. If an advertising agency or an insurance broker is acquired, it is reasonable to assume that the principal asset being sought is the employees of the company, rather than the fixed assets. The net assets, or balance sheet value, of such a company might be minimal and the resultant goodwill high.

For whatever reason, company A decides that $2,000 is an acceptable price to pay for B. Company B's shareholders agree and it becomes a subsidiary of A, and consolidated accounts are prepared. Everyone is happy, except the accountant of company A. There is a basic mismatch in the transaction. Company A is paying $2,000 for assets in B which are valued at $1,500, so the accounts do not balance.

Cash paid out $2,000   Assets acquired $1,500

There is $2,000 cash going out and only $1,500 of assets coming in. To solve this dilemma the accountant simply adds goodwill valued at $500 to the assets acquired in company B. The books now balance.

Cash paid out $2,000   Assets acquired $1,500 + goodwill $500

However large or complex the balance sheet of the company being acquired, and however fierce and acrimonious the takeover battle, the calculation of goodwill is the same:

price paid − value of assets acquired = goodwill.

Accounting for goodwill

The considerable conflict and debate generated by goodwill arises not so much from its calculation but from its treatment in the accounts of the acquiring company.

Goodwill could be treated as an asset in company A's balance sheet ($500) and be written off (amortised) over a reasonable number of years in the income statement or deducted from shareholders' funds.

Until 1998 UK companies did not write off goodwill in the income statement but charged it directly against the reserves in the balance sheet. Thus it was possible for the elimination of goodwill to have no impact on the reported profit appearing in the income statement. With the publication of FRS 10 the UK fell into line with the practice adopted by most other countries. Goodwill is shown as an asset in the balance sheet and written off over its estimated useful economic life – normally not more than 20 years – using the straight-line method of depreciation. In the United States, goodwill is tested each year for impairment but not necessarily charged as an expense in the income statement (FAS 142). The treatment of goodwill can contribute to a difference in the reported profit of a UK and a US company.

Negative goodwill

It is possible for an acquisition to be made for less than the balance sheet value of net assets. The acquirer has made a very good purchase or the acquisition is loss-making and seen as having poor future prospects. The accounting result, "negative goodwill", is not allowed in the United States, but elsewhere it is normally shown as a deduction from any existing goodwill.

Impairment of asset values

To assess a company's performance or financial position, it is essential to have a realistic figure for the value of assets employed. If the value of a company's assets falls and is unlikely to recover – a permanent diminution – the balance sheet should reflect this event and the income statement take the loss. Assets should never knowingly be overvalued: an asset should not be shown in a balance sheet at an amount greater than can be realised from it. In 1998 the ASB published FRS 11 "Impairment of fixed assets and goodwill" (similar in scope to FAS 142 and IAS 36 "Impairment of assets") to provide guidance on this issue.

Companies must regularly review all principal fixed assets – tangible and intangible – to ensure that the balance sheet offers a reasonable valuation. The value of an asset may fall because of many adverse events or conditions, such as obsolescence or damage, initiatives by competitors, or significant and permanent changes in the marketplace. These are referred to as "impairment factors". In the UK, when goodwill or any other fixed asset is being written off over more than 20 years, it must be reviewed for impairment each year. At the end of the first year following an acquisition, companies must review the associated goodwill for impairment.

When assets are being written off in under 20 years and a company becomes aware of any significant impairment factors, it must undertake an objective review of the value of all of its tangible and intangible assets. This is called an impairment review, and it consists of comparing balance sheet values ("carrying values") of assets with their recoverable amount. An asset's recoverable amount is either the net realisable value for which an asset could be disposed of or the net present value of the future cash flows it is expected to generate over its expected useful life ("value in use"). Where assets are seen as being impaired, they are written down in value in the balance sheet and the loss of value is shown separately in the income statement.

Although this may appear to overcome many of the problems previously met in company valuation, it must be remembered that the only "facts" being offered are based on estimates and forecasts made by the reporting company. At least goodwill can never be revalued upwards above its original cost.

Acquisitions and mergers

When one company acquires another, the acquiring company may have a choice of how it treats the acquisition in its accounts. The choice is between acquisition accounting and merger accounting.

Under acquisition accounting, the assets and liabilities are taken into the acquiring company's balance sheet at their fair value at the date of acquisition, and the profits of the acquired company are brought into the consolidated accounts only from the date of acquisition. Where shares form part of the acquisition price, they are taken at their market value when calculating the figure for goodwill.

Merger accounting treats the companies involved as if they had always been a single entity. The acquisition, rather than being seen as a takeover, is viewed as a combination or merger of interests where one company does not dominate the other.

In merger accounting, shares used for the acquisition are valued at par (their nominal or face value) and the balance sheet value of assets is used. The two balance sheets are added together to form the new company. There is no difference between the price paid and the value acquired, so no goodwill is created. There is no requirement, as under acquisition accounting, to write off any amounts either in the income statement or against balance sheet reserves.

Continuing with the example used earlier, company A's balance sheet reflects the transaction with cash reducing by $2,000 and being replaced by an investment in company B's shares valued at $2,000.

($)	A	B		A	B
Assets	3,000	2,000	Capital	2,000	1,000
Share in B	2,000		Reserves	2,000	500
			Creditors	1,000	500
	5,000	2,000		5,000	2,000

Following the acquisition the group or consolidated balance sheet is prepared.

Group AB ($)

Assets	5,000	Share capital	2,000
Goodwill	500	Reserves	2,000
		Creditors	1,500
	5,500		5,500

Minority interests

As a rule, when more than 50% of the shares of one company are acquired by another it is necessary to consolidate the subsidiary into the parent company's group accounts.

In practice, often less than 100% of a company's shares are acquired. If company A purchases only 80% of company B's shares for $2,000, A still controls B. It owns the majority of its shares and so has gained a subsidiary company which it will consolidate in its accounts. But 20%, a minority, of B's shares are owned by outside, non-company A shareholders. Company B is not a wholly owned subsidiary of A. In this situation the consolidated balance sheet will appear as follows.

Group AB ($)

Assets	5,000	Share capital	2,000
Goodwill	800	Reserves	2,000
		Creditors	1,500
		Minority	300
	5,800		5,800

The minority, sometimes called the outside interest or outside share-holders, represents company B's shareholders other than company A. The consolidated balance sheet reflects that 20% of the $1,500 net assets or capital and reserves of B ($300) are owned by shareholders outside the group. The goodwill figure is derived from the fact that $2,000 is paid for $1,200 net assets in B. In other words, $2,000 is paid for $1,200 (80%) of B's capital and reserves or net assets.

The presentation of minority interests varies, but most companies show the outside shareholders' stake in the capital and reserves section of the balance sheet.

Shares rather than cash

Company A might consider issuing shares to acquire company B rather than using cash. If A's $1 nominal value shares are quoted at $2 on the stock exchange, it could issue 1,000 shares ($2,000) in exchange for all the 1,000 shares in B. If B's shareholders agree, the acquisition can take place without any cash being involved. Company B is now a wholly owned subsidiary and the group balance sheet is as follows.

Group AB ($)

Assets	7,000	Share capital	3,000
Goodwill	500	Share premium	1,000
		Reserves	2,000
		Creditors	1,500
	7,500		7,500

The share premium arises from the issue of 1,000 $1 shares at $2 each. This method of accounting for acquisitions is called the acquisition basis. In presentation of the consolidated balance sheet in the UK, the goodwill would be written off against the shareholders' reserves.

Group AB ($)

Assets	7,000	Share capital	3,000
		Share premium	1,000
		Reserves	1,500
		Creditors	1,500
	7,000		7,000

Companies that have acquired another company may be in a position to opt for the use of merger accounting rather than acquisition accounting. Under merger accounting, a different approach from that outlined above is adopted.

◗ The retained profit of company B is included in the group accounts.
◗ No goodwill is produced.
◗ There is no share premium account. It is assumed that there was a simple share exchange between the two companies with the assets being taken across at their book values, thus no fair value is placed on them.

The key requirement for the adoption of merger accounting is that the majority of the acquisition is completed through the issue of shares; that is, at least 90% of the acquisition consideration is satisfied through shares. This is called pooling of interests in the United States. If merger accounting were applied, the group balance sheet would be as follows.

Group AB ($)

Assets	7,000	Share capital	3,000
		Reserves	2,500
		Creditors	1,500
	7,000		7,000

One attraction of the merger method is that even if the acquisition is completed towards the end the financial year, the full profits of company B are taken into company A's income statement, with the total retained profit appearing in the reserves, as shown above. This would not be the case under acquisition accounting, where only post-acquisition profits are taken into the group accounts. If A is performing badly, the addition of B's full-year profit could transform the apparent position and make a dividend payment possible. Merger accounting may offer a quick fix to a company's profitability. Furthermore, there is no potentially annoying goodwill to be written off. All B's assets would be taken into the consolidated accounts at their balance sheet values.

The DaimlerChrysler AG combination in 1998, adopting US GAAP, used the pooling of interest treatment – the accounts of the two companies were combined without showing one taking over the other – and no goodwill was shown. In 2001 the FASB banned the pooling of interest treatment of mergers and acquisitions. It is now only possible to write off goodwill due to impairment.

Fair value and provisions

The basis for the valuation of assets and liabilities of a company being acquired is their fair value at the acquisition date. This can be interpreted as what could be expected to be received in exchange for the assets concerned – an arm's length transaction or a reasonable open market price. If the fair value of the assets of company B was $2,200, the goodwill produced under the acquisition method of accounting would reduce to $300, and the value of assets in the consolidated balance sheet would increase to $7,200.

In the calculation of almost any figure in a set of accounts there is scope for initiative and discretion. It is often difficult to answer the question: "What is it worth?" There may be several reasonable alternative valuations that can be made. Often the acquiring company may prudently make provisions for the future reduction in value of the assets being acquired.

Company A may consider that the total assets of company B should be valued at $1,500 rather than $2,000 owing to the current business environment. The fair value of the net assets being acquired becomes $1,000 (assets $1,500 – creditors $500). A provision of $500 has been made against the original value of company B, perhaps relating to the stock of goods being held at the year end. The agreed purchase price has not changed and goodwill becomes $1,000 (purchase price $2,000 – net assets $1,000).

The treatment of the acquisition in the consolidated balance sheet is now as follows.

Group AB ($)

Assets	6,500	Capital		3,000
		Share premium		1,000
		Reserves	2,000	
		Less goodwill	1,000	1,000
		Creditors		1,500
Total	6,500			6,500

Company A has made prudent provision for the possible reduction in the value of the assets it has acquired. But what if next year those assets achieve a value of $2,500, the stock of goods being sold for $1,500? In the consolidated income statement there is an extra $1,000 profit, which, if not distributed, is taken to the reserves in the balance sheet. This is an unexpected but welcome boost to the group's profitability and an improvement in its reserves. In this way it may be possible to massage group profitability.

Associated companies and joint ventures

Normally, when one company owns or controls more than 50% of the shares in another that company is treated as a subsidiary of the other, and its accounts are consolidated into those of the parent company.

If company A owns less than 50% of the shares in company B and thus is a minority shareholder, A will show the investment in its balance sheet, normally as part of fixed assets, and the share of B's profits will be taken into A's income statement.

How the investment is defined depends on what proportion of company B's shares are owned. The simple guideline is that if a company owns less than 20% of the shares, the investment is treated as an investment. If more than 20% but less than 50% of the shares are owned, in the UK this is termed a "participating interest", and if there is also the ability to significantly influence the operating and financial activities of the company, it is shown as an "investment of an associate."

The 1990s saw an increasing number of strategic alliances, investment partnerships and joint ventures between companies. FRS 9 defined a joint venture as:

> *An entity in which the reporting entity hold an interest on a*
> *long-term basis and is jointly controlled by the reporting entity*
> *and one or more other ventures.*

Enron claimed profits and hid enormous debt from investors through the creative use of a complex web of joint-venture vehicles – some 3,000 at the time of its collapse. Remember the golden rule: beware if you cannot understand what the company is doing or where the profits are coming from.

Equity and gross equity method

FRS 9 requires more detailed information on associates and joint ventures to be provided in the income statement, cash flow statement and balance sheet. Associate and joint ventures are shown in the investor's accounts on the basis of the equity method of accounting. Under this method the balance sheet initially shows the investment at its cost and adjusts this each year for the investor's share of the results – which are taken into the income statement – and for changes in net assets.

The investing company's share of a joint venture's turnover, profit, interest and tax should be separately disclosed in the income statement, and the balance sheet should show its share of the gross assets and liabilities.

Current assets

Any item appearing as part of current assets can be taken as being either cash or capable of being turned into cash within 12 months of the balance sheet date. The three main headings found in this section of the balance sheet are inventory, debtors and cash.

Inventory

Year-end inventory shown in a company's balance sheet normally consists of a mixture of raw materials, work in progress and finished goods. In the UK, this is referred to as stock. For retail companies, the year-end inventory consists almost entirely of finished goods in the shops or in the warehouse.

The basic rule for the inventory valuation is that it should, according to the prudence rule, be shown in the balance sheet at the lower of cost or net realisable value; that is, what it cost to make or what someone might reasonably be expected to pay for it if it is no longer worth what it cost to make.

Debtors

Debtors or accounts receivable represent the amount owed to a company by customers for goods or services that have been provided but at the end of the year have not been paid for in cash. The amount due is shown as trade debtors at the year end.

If a company has experienced bad debts during the year, these should have been accounted for in the income statement. It is standard practice for companies to make a regular provision each year for bad or doubtful debts; a percentage of sales revenue is assumed to be non-recoverable. The figure for debtors appearing in the balance sheet can be taken as being good debts that the company realistically expects to collect in the next few weeks under the normal terms and conditions of trade.

Most sales are paid for by customers within two or three months. Be cautious when the terms "long-term receivables" or "deferred" debtors or revenue appear. This indicates that the company has made a sale but is shifting some or all of the income into future years, possibly as a means of smoothing volatile or uncertain earnings. Alternatively, the company may be suffering sales resistance and offering customers extremely generous and extended credit terms.

Debt factoring and securitisation

Companies sometimes enter factoring arrangements, whereby they "sell" their debts to another company and have cash immediately available for use in the business. Details of major factoring arrangements should be given in the notes to the accounts. The term "securitisation" may be linked to trade debtors or other assets. It refers to the packaging of assets for sale to generate immediate cash flow, and was first developed by American banks in the 1970s to raise finance from the sale of mortgage loans.

Cash and investments

Cash is defined as being the cash held by a company at the balance sheet date, including all deposits that are repayable on demand. These are sometimes referred to as cash equivalents or liquid resources. Investments held by a company at the end of the year are included in current assets only if they are short-term. Any investment shown in this section of the balance sheet can taken as being liquid, that is, capable of being turned into cash within a reasonably short time.

3 The income statement

T HE INCOME STATEMENT (called the profit and loss account in the UK) deals with the operating activities of a company and is intended to provide a report on its performance during the year. The statement gives details of a company's income and expenditure for the year. Where sales revenue is greater than costs a profit is produced; where the reverse occurs a loss results – hence profit and loss account.

Profit considerations

Different profits for different purposes

A considerable amount of time could be spent discussing various definitions of profit. A starting point for an accountant might be that "a profit is produced when income is greater than costs"; for an economist it might be "what you can spend during the week and still be as well off at the end of the week as at the beginning". The accountant's definition necessitates the practical application of the principles of realisation and accrual. The economist's definition would probably include capital maintenance as one of accounting's basic principles or rules.

Profit can be defined as the difference between a company's capital at the start and at the end of a period. Profit can arise only when net assets have increased. For example, a company starts business with capital of $1,000 and uses this to purchase an asset that is later sold for $1,500. Inflation is 10% per annum, and the replacement cost of the asset at the end of the period is $1,300. What profit has the company made?

The simple answer, of course, is $500. Traditional historic cost accounting shows opening capital of $1,000, closing capital of $1,500 and, ignoring inflation, a profit for the period of $500.

Sales revenue	–	cost of sales	= profit
$1,500	–	$1,000	= $500

If the purchasing power of the company is to be maintained, the impact of inflation must be taken into account. Financial capital maintenance calls for $100 (10% of the opening capital) to be set aside, resulting in a profit of $400.

Sales revenue	−	cost of sales	= profit
$1,500	−	$1,100	= $400

If the intention is to maintain the physical operating capability of the company, sufficient capital must be available to replace the asset and continue the business. Operating capital maintenance requires $300 to be earmarked for the replacement of the assets and profit becomes $200.

Sales revenue	−	cost of sales	= profit
$1,500	−	$1,300	= $200

One of the difficulties in reading income statements is to decide what should be taken as the profit for the year. This depends on what is being looked for and why. There are different profits for different purposes. It is impossible to have a single profit for a company, let alone a single profit for all companies.

Matching and accrual

The income statement covers a company's financial year, which normally, but not always, consists of 12 months or 52 weeks. If the income statement's main purpose is to show the profit for the year, it is important that income and expenditure be matched to relate to the year in question. There may be a difference between when a transaction occurs (cash is paid or received) and when it should appear, or be recognised, in the income statement. For example, what happens when materials are used to produce products that are sold this year but are not due to be paid for until the next financial year? Or when materials have been received and paid for this year but have not yet been used in production? In the income statement, the income produced during a financial period is set against the costs associated with that income: income and expenditure are matched.

Profit is not cash

It must not be assumed that the profit displayed in the income statement is represented by cash at the year end. A company may show a profit for the year, but this does not mean that it has cash available. Even if a company makes no capital investments in projects to sustain the business for the future, a profit in the income statement is no guarantee that adequate cash or liquid assets will appear in the balance sheet at the end of the year.

When preparing an income statement, an accountant includes the total sales revenue produced during the year. This figure includes both cash and credit sales. A company offering customers credit terms is, in effect, lending them its money until payment is made. A sale may have been made, and therefore included in the income statement for the year, but no cash has been received.

Money owed by customers is referred to as either debtors or receivables. Credit sales are included in the figure for sales revenue in the income statement and appear in the balance sheet as a heading within current assets. When customers pay the amount due, the figure for debtors or receivables is reduced and the cash balance increased by the same amount in the balance sheet.

A company taking advantage of credit terms offered by its suppliers receives materials and services for use during the year but does not necessarily pay for them before the year end. Until the suppliers are paid, the money they are owed is shown in the balance sheet as part of short-term current liabilities. When the suppliers are paid, current liabilities and the cash balance are reduced by the same amount.

The timing difference between the recognition of a transaction or event and the associated cash movement can have important implications for a company.

Overtrading

What happens when credit given exceeds credit taken? A company may be achieving a healthy profit margin on sales but, at the same time, offering its customers much better, longer, credit terms than it can obtain from its suppliers. The terms of credit given and taken have no impact on the profit disclosed in the income statement, but they can significantly affect the cash position or liquidity of the company.

For example, a company starts the year with $200 cash. With no credit given or taken, sales revenue is $1,000 and costs are $800. A profit of $200 is shown in the income statement for the year and a cash balance of $400 in the year-end balance sheet.

$200 cash + ($1,000 sales revenue − $800 costs) = $400 cash

If credit is given and taken, at the end of the year the company is owed $500 of the $1,000 sales revenue and, taking advantage of credit terms offered by suppliers, owes $100. The cash position then changes.

$200 cash + ($500 sales revenue − $700 costs) = $0 cash

In both examples, the net current assets have moved from $200 at the start of the year to $400 at the end. However, with the credit policy adopted in the second example, the cash position has deteriorated from $200 at the beginning of the year to zero at the end. Although the company may be trading profitably with $200 profit, it is running down its liquid resources to possibly dangerous levels. This is often referred to as overtrading; profit is being generated at the expense of liquidity.

If the company extended further credit or a major customer became a bad debt, it would be forced to borrow money to keep trading. Before such an event occurred, the company might be well advised to look for alternative forms of finance for its future operations and growth.

Since the dangers of overtrading are so clear, why do companies get into such positions? Overtrading is most commonly associated with growth. A traditional means of increasing sales revenue is to offer good credit terms to customers. If the financial implications of the sales policy are not taken into account, a company may show rapid growth in revenue and profit but run out of cash and be unable to continue trading. Another reason for adopting a credit policy may be because everyone else does. If a business has traditional terms of trade with customers or if all the companies in the sector decide to change their credit terms, it is difficult for one company, particularly a small one keen to gain market share, to act differently.

How long is a year?

The standard reporting period for all countries and all companies is 12 months and accounts are presented each year. Although this is logical and useful, the calendar year is not necessarily the best timescale for company reports. Annual reports may be suitable as a basis for assessing the performance and position of retail companies but not for companies involved in gold, oil or gas prospecting or planting oak trees.

In connection with a company's income statement, it is important to be aware that occasionally the year may consist of more or less than 52 weeks or 12 months. If this is the case, it must be taken into account before analysing the figures or drawing any conclusions from comparing one company with another.

It is quite common for companies to have a trading year end for the last Friday of one month of the year or to be operating on internal reports covering 13 periods of 4 weeks in the year. As a result, some years may have 53 rather than 52 weeks. In practice, this does not have much impact on the analysis of the company concerned.

More significant is where there is a major change in the annual report year end. A company may wish to move its year-end reporting in line with other similar companies, or it may have become part of a group of companies having a different year end. This can cause problems for financial analysis, particularly if seasonality is involved, such as a retail company moving from an end-December to an end-March year end.

Continuing and discontinued businesses

The income statement will normally show revenue and profit divided into that produced from continuing businesses, discontinued businesses and acquisitions made during the year. This makes it easier to analyse the company, with details of the continuing operations providing the best basis upon which to forecast likely future performance.

Any material events or items should be disclosed; material can be taken to be more than 5–10% of whatever is involved. If a company acquires another during the year and the resulting additional revenue or profit is more than 10% of the total for the group, it would be reasonable to assume that this information will be disclosed separately, either on the face of the income statement or in the notes.

If a company disposes of or otherwise divests itself of a business this is called a discontinued business. When this occurs, the comparative figures are restated to highlight the revenue and profit or loss of that business. In the UK, when a company has acquired or disposed of a business during the year, the details of these acquisitions and discontinued operations should appear in the profit and loss account. The division between continuing and discontinued businesses is shown in a similar way for operating profit. This makes it easier to assess revenue and profit trends and therefore what the company is likely to achieve in the forthcoming year from its continuing businesses.

Associates and joint ventures

FRS 9 added to the information shown on the face of a UK company's profit and loss account. The investing company must identify separately its share of the turnover, operating profit, major exceptional items, interest and taxation of any joint ventures. It is common practice for companies also to show the equivalent data for associates.

Turnover	£
Continuing operations	1,000
Acquisitions	<u>100</u>
	1,100
Discontinued operations	<u>50</u>
	1,150
Share of turnover of:	
Joint ventures	250
Associates	<u>100</u>
	1,500

Segmental reporting

It is interesting to know a company's total sales revenue for the year, but it is much more useful to be able to see in which businesses and where in the world the revenue was generated. One of the most useful notes in a company's accounts to help you understand what, where and how well it does is that provided by what is called segmental information or reporting, or disaggregated information. The segmental report analyses a company's turnover, profit and assets employed by major sector of activity and location, thus making it possible to study individual businesses within a group or conglomerate and to use the data to compare them with other, perhaps single business, companies.

A segment can be defined using the materiality rule of 10%. If a business represents more than 10% of the turnover, profit, or net assets of a company, it can be expected to be reported separately in the segmental analysis report.

Segmental reporting is covered by a combination of legislation, accounting standards (including SSAP 25, FAS 131, and IAS 14) and stock exchange listing requirements.

Generally, the three main areas of interest are revenue, profit and assets employed. For segmental reporting the most common definition of profit is operating profit and of assets is net operating assets. Companies may opt to provide more than the minimum requirement. Some provide segmental cash flow information and capital investment details. Increasingly, employee statistics are incorporated, showing not only number of employees but also where they are based.

There are often practical problems in allocating costs and expenses. For example, how can the total cost of the group main board directors be allocated, by product or by market? Such costs are defined as common costs, and when they are not spread among the segments they appear as a single line in the segmental report. Inter-segment trading may create some technical problems for accountants and directors, and may be shown separately in the report.

The division into segments or sectors is normally based on products or services and markets or distribution channels that the company operates, but the way a company is organised or structured can influence the presentation. The segmental details for turnover, profit and assets are shown by location, and additional details may be provided for sales revenue by destination.

The final decision on what classes of business and what geographic areas are provided in the segmental report is made by the directors of the company. The criteria should be for them to consider whether the segmental information they plan to provide will be useful to those reading the annual report.

Presentation format

Most countries require that the income statement includes comparative and consistent figures for the previous year. The US Securities and Exchange Commission (SEC) requires public companies to provide comparative figures for the current and previous two years. Figures for earlier years are included in the company's five-year or ten-year historic performance table to be found elsewhere in the annual report.

Although there is some evidence of progress towards standardisation in income statement content and presentation, there are still wide differences among both countries and companies. For example, in the UK companies can choose from four different formats.

Two of the most common forms of presentation of an income statement start with the sales income for the year. Costs and expenses are then either subdivided by function – cost of sales, distribution, administration (the function or cost of sales format) – or displayed according to their nature or type – materials, wages (the output format). Most countries allow companies to choose whichever format is most appropriate to their needs, but some enforce a single format. For example, in Belgium, France, Italy and Spain costs can only be presented by their nature; in the United States only the cost of sales or function format is allowed. As a result it can be impossible to get strictly comparable data for companies. This is a strong argument for international standards in financial accounting and reporting.

A typical income statement format and presentation is as follows:

Turnover
minus Cost of sales
Gross profit
minus Other operating expenses
Operating profit
plus Other income
Profit on ordinary activities before interest
minus Interest (net)
Profit on ordinary activities before tax
minus Tax
Profit on ordinary activities after tax
minus Minority interests
Profit attributable to shareholders
minus Dividends
Retained profit

For UK companies, details of the share of the turnover, profit, interest and tax of any joint ventures and associates will also be disclosed. This will be done either on the face of the profit and loss account or in the notes for each item.

Some companies provide more detailed information of the materials used, distribution, administration and other operating costs and expenses of the year.

Distribution costs	Administrative costs
Advertising	General management costs
Sales and marketing	Cost of administration building
Warehouse costs	Professional fees
Transport costs	R&D

Nuts and bolts

Sales revenue

The first figure appearing in an income statement is normally that of sales revenue, turnover or income for the year. In most cases it is shown net of any sales taxes. However, some companies show the gross revenue for the year. Watch out for this when comparing companies within a sector for size, growth, or profitability; many of the ratios discussed in this book will be distorted if gross rather than net revenues are used as their base.

The income statement should provide a single figure for sales revenue. However, it should not be assumed that there can be only one correct figure. A sale is not always easy to define. Is sales revenue to be recognised when the order is placed, when the customer's cash is received, or when the goods are shipped? How should revenue flowing from a five-year service or rental contract or a three-year construction project be treated?

Deciding which figure to use for sales revenue is not as simple as it might seem. In July 2001, the ASB published a discussion paper, *Revenue Recognition*, of over 150 pages. Businesses face a variety of problems in deciding at what point a sale should be brought into the income statement. It may be assumed that when the right to or ownership of the goods or services provided has passed to the customer that is the point at which a sale is recognised and taken into the income statement.

Internet and software companies have caused problems for accountants as they devise rules for defining sales revenue. For example, how are customers' rights of return to be treated? Issues of consistency, comparability, prudence, accrual, realisation and substance over form have to be faced. A simple test is whether, following the transaction, an asset has been created – and a debtor now exists. If this is the case, the revenue should be recognised in the income statement.

Creating sales

The 1990s provided numerous examples of creativity enabling companies to show substantial and consistent revenue growth, at that time mistakenly seen as a key indicator of performance and success. Examples included:

- goods on sale or return to customers treated as sales;
- secret "side agreements" with customers giving them the right to cancel the sale, but including it in sales income for the year;
- all potential income from a long-term contract taken immediately rather than spread over the life of the agreement;
- taking a sale into income before the customer signs a legal agreement;
- failing to make adequate provision for bad debts;
- taking 100% of a sale as income even though the customer has paid only a 10% deposit;

- shipping goods early before the customer expected and including them as sales revenue for the current year – an extreme example was, when customers would not take delivery, to hire a warehouse, ship goods to it and record the sales revenue as bona fide;
- grossing up sales, as when a travel agent sells a $1,000 ticket on which 10% commission is earned, but takes the full $1,000 as sales revenue;
- treating investment income as sales revenue;
- lending money to customers to finance their purchases – the loan goes to the balance sheet and the 'sale' to the income statement;
- showing income from the sale of assets as operating revenue.

Such creativity is not, at the time, easy to spot. However, some of the analysis discussed later may help to highlight inconsistencies or blips in the financial statements and at least trigger a caution signal. The application of accounting standards (FRS 5, IAS 18) and developments in US GAAP are working to improve investor confidence in the annual report as a source of reliable information.

Cost of sales

Cost of sales can be considered to be the cost of materials and employees and other direct and indirect costs involved in generating sales revenue including:

- direct materials;
- direct labour;
- all direct production overheads including depreciation;
- inventory change;
- hire of fixed assets;
- product development expenditure.

Companies do not normally provide any further analysis of the cost of sales, although additional information can be found in the notes following the income statement on, for example, employee numbers, fixed asset depreciation and leasing, and research and development.

Change in inventory

Cost of sales includes the change in inventory between the beginning and end of the year. This is part of the matching process. Sales revenue for the year should be charged only with the cost of goods used in producing that revenue. Items remaining in store at the end of the year should not be charged against the year's revenue.

The value placed on inventory at the beginning and end of the year can be an important factor influencing the reported profit of a company. The basic accounting routine applied to arrive at the cost of sales charge in the income statement is as follows.

$$\text{Opening inventory} + \text{purchases} = \text{goods available for sale}$$
$$- \text{closing inventory} = \text{cost of sales}$$

Inventory is often attractive not only to employees (shrinkage and wastage are euphemisms for theft) but also to those preparing a company's accounts for the opportunities it allows them to be creative. For example, if a company, for whatever reason, were to increase the value of inventory at the year end by $1,000, there would be an automatic improvement in the reported profit of $1,000 for the period brought about by a reduced cost of sales.

($)	Low inventory value		High inventory value	
Sales revenue		10,000		10,000
Opening stock	1,000		1,000	
Purchases	8,500		8,500	
	9,500		9,500	
Closing stock	3,500	6,000	4,500	5,000
Profit		4,000		5,000

The balance sheet asset value for inventory is increased and the profit for the year improves. Nothing physical has occurred to the inventory; only its value has changed. For every $1 added to the value of closing inventory there is an extra $1 at the bottom line of the income statement.

Although companies may be reluctant to admit that inventory is worth less than it cost to make, the prudence requirement in financial reporting should ensure that companies follow the simple rule of showing inventory at the lower of cost or net realisable value. The lower inventory figure shows caution both in balance sheet valuation and in defining the profit for the year.

Two of the most common methods of valuing inventory are called first in, first out (FIFO) and last in, first out (LIFO). FIFO assumes that the oldest items of stock are used first. As the inventory is used or sold, it is

71

charged to production or sales at the earliest cost price. In the UK, this is the most common method of inventory valuation. LIFO is the method often used by US companies. The newest items of inventory are assumed to be used first – the reverse of FIFO.

Purchases	$	FIFO	$	LIFO	$
1,000 × $5	5,000	1,000 × $5	5,000	1,000 × $7	7,000
1,000 × $7	7,000	500 × $7	3,500	500 × $5	2,500
2,000	12,000	1,500 cost of sales	8,500	1,500 cost of sales	9,500
		500 inventory × $7	3,500	500 inventory × $5	2,500

If prices are rising, FIFO may be assumed to value inventory close to its replacement cost in the balance sheet ($3,500), but the charge for cost of sales in the income statement ($8,500) will be comparatively low. Under inflationary conditions, LIFO will value inventory at lower than replacement cost in the balance sheet ($2,500), but the charge for cost of sales in the income statement ($9,500) may be more realistic.

A third, less popular, method of cost of sales calculation and inventory valuation is to use average cost. In the above example, the average cost is $12,000 ÷ 2,000 or $6 per unit. The average cost method would provide a closing inventory of $3,000 and a cost of sales charge of $9,000. The use of weighted average cost is common in Japan.

There are traditional ways of putting a value on year-end inventory. The balance sheet value of a retail company's inventory is often calculated by taking the selling price of the goods on shelves at the end of the year and deducting the normal profit margins applied.

An important influence on the method of inventory valuation adopted may be what is allowable for tax purposes. Continuing with the example, if company A applies FIFO it produces a taxable profit of $1,500; if company B adopts LIFO it produces a taxable profit of $500.

($)	A	B
Sales revenue	10,000	10,000
Cost of sales	8,500	9,500
Profit	1,500	500

In France, Germany and the United States, LIFO is accepted for tax purposes, so it is a commonly used inventory valuation method. In the

UK, only FIFO is accepted for tax purposes. Italy is more relaxed, allowing LIFO, FIFO and average cost valuation methods.

Gross profit

Some companies provide a figure for gross profit. This is produced by deducting the cost of sales from sales revenue for the year. Other operating costs and expenses are deducted from gross profit to provide the operating profit for the year.

Auditors' fees

Part of the administration cost included in the income statement is the fees paid to auditors. The figure shown should clearly distinguish between fees for audit and those paid to the same firm for other work such as consultancy assignments or special investigations.

Employee details

As part of the annual reporting process, companies disclose how many full-time and part-time staff were employed, either at the end of the financial year or, more commonly, the average during the year. The total payments made to employees is also shown. The employee or staff cost heading covers all wages and salaries, social security costs, pensions costs and other employment-related payments.

Anyone legally contracted to work for the company is an employee, including part-time workers and directors. Where a company has a contract with a self-employed person, who by definition is not an employee of the company, the money involved is normally shown under the other costs and charges heading. Directors who have a service contract with the company are classed as employees. Thus the total cost of directors is included in the figure for staff or employee costs, although there should be a note in the accounts detailing this amount separately.

Directors' remuneration

The actions and activities of a company's directors form an important part of corporate reporting. In most countries there has been a flow of legislation, regulation or stock exchange requirements covering disclosure of details of a company's financial dealings with directors.

The Cadbury Report stated:

> *The overriding principle in respect of board remuneration is that of openness. Shareholders are entitled to a full and clear*

statement of directors' present and future benefits, and of how they have been determined.

The Combined Code requires that three or more non-exective directors form a remuneration committee. This committee is to develop and oversee the company's remuneration policy and the individual rewards of each executive director and the chairman – including benefits in kind, bonuses, share options and any long-term incentive schemes. The company's website should provide full details of the remuneration committee.

Make a loss, take a profit

There have been many examples of directors receiving substantial sums in return for giving up their tenure of incompetence in managing lossmaking companies. Any payment in compensation for loss of office and any significant payments made to directors – including former directors – should be fully disclosed in the annual report.

Best practice requires directors' rewards to be firmly based on appropriate objective performance-related measures. Directors may be rewarded above their basic salary in relation to internal performance targets, such as sales revenue or profit, or with reference to the relative share price of their company. An increase in the company's market capitalisation might prove effective as the basis for executive reward schemes. Whatever approach the company adopts, it should be clearly set out for shareholders in the annual report.

Greenbury and Hampel recommended that directors be given service contracts of no more than one year's duration. The Combined Code ensures that shareholders are provided with sufficient information on each director to decide on their re-election at least every three years.

As a general rule, directors must disclose all their financial dealings with a company. Directors are employed by and are therefore servants of the shareholders.

The note in the accounts giving details of the directors' aggregate remuneration or emoluments should clearly indicate the total amount paid to directors for services in connection with the management of either the holding company or any subsidiary. Pensions paid to past and existing directors should also be shown. The extent of disclosure should make it possible to see all the payments made. For example, if a retired director is allowed to continue using a company car, the estimated value of this benefit should be shown separately as part of pensions.

Share options

Many companies operate share (stock) incentive plans (SIP). These give all employees the opportunity of owning shares in their company. Other companies offer selected employees, as a reward for past or an incentive for future performance, the right to purchase shares at a favourable price. Share options can be a more effective means of providing employees with net income than straightforward taxable remuneration. In the 1990s many e-companies offered share options. The cost to the company appeared negligible, and no cash was involved. The potential reward for the individual could be significant, and this was expected to ensure loyalty and top performance. In 2000, when many of these companies joined the "99% Club" – their share price dropped to 1% of its previous highpoint – the true value of the share options was revealed.

An important issue is timing: when does the benefit from the share option occur? Is it on the granting of the option or when the option is exercised? Whether it is appropriate to charge the income statement with the cost of share options is the subject of fierce debate between businessmen (anti) and accountants (pro). To date businessmen seem to be winning the battle. Share options act to reduce shareholders' investment: when the shares are issued their holding is worth less. There is a transfer from shareholders to management.

A strict legal interpretation is that the benefit arises at the time of granting the option, the benefit being the difference between the option and the market price at that time. However, both the company's share price and its future performance are uncertain, and it can be argued that it is impossible to value an option at this point. Companies must provide shareholders with full details of any share option schemes for directors, including the profits made from exercising any option. The basic information should include for each director:

- the number of shares under option at the beginning and end of the year;
- the number of options granted, exercised, or lapsed during year;
- the dates of options and the exercise price and market price of the shares when exercised.

These requirements result in some weighty notes in the annual report. Do not be put off as their study may well repay the effort of analysis.

Pensions

Typically, employees and the company make contributions to a pension fund. The money is invested in appropriate assets and pensions paid to employees on their retirement. This can result in significant sums of money being kept in a company pension fund. Such pools of money have been attractive places for unscrupulous directors to dip into, as the late Robert Maxwell demonstrated, resulting in a tightening up in the UK of pension fund safeguards. Currently, a company pension scheme's funds are under the control and stewardship of independent trustees.

The management and reporting of pension funds is complex and difficult. FRS 17 "Retirement Benefits", covering all post employment benefits to which a company is committed, became mandatory in 2005. The annual report should provide details of:

- the nature of the scheme;
- the cost for the period;
- any surplus of deficit at the year end;
- assets and liabilities valued as at the balance sheet date.

The service cost of pensions for the year is shown in the income statement and any actuarial gain or loss on the scheme is taken to the statement of recognised gains and losses (STRGL). The balance sheet shows an asset or a liability representing the net value of the assets and liabilities for the scheme – normally termed "post-employment net assets/liabilities".

Operating profit

An important measure and indicator of performance for any company is the profit made from running the business; that is, the profit generated from its operations. If gross profit is not shown, operating (trading) profit is the first profit disclosed on the income statement and is calculated by deducting the cost of sales plus other operating costs from turnover. Whichever form of presentation is adopted in the income statement the operating profit is shown as a separate heading. It is reasonable to assume that the operating profit of different companies can be compared on a common basis.

Profit or loss on sale of an asset

If a company sells an asset (such as a machine, a vehicle or a company) during the year, the balance sheet value is deducted from the income from the sale of the asset to give a profit or a loss, which is shown under a separate heading in the income statement. If the asset being sold is a subsidiary company, there may be a potential difficulty in the treatment of the goodwill. If, as previously was the case in the UK, the goodwill was written off against reserves at the time the subsidiary was acquired, it must be written back and added to net assets to provide a value against which the profit or loss on sale is assessed. On the sale of a subsidiary goodwill is written back, so it will not appear on the face of the income statement. However, it should be referred to in the accompanying notes. (Goodwill is discussed in more detail in Chapter 2.)

Other income

In addition to revenue from selling services or goods, a company may have investments that earn income in other companies. How such investments are treated depends on the degree of control the company has over the companies in which it has investments. As a simple guide, if more than 50% of the voting shares of a company are owned, it is treated as a subsidiary and its accounts are consolidated into those of the company owning the shares. If less than 50% of the shares are owned, consolidated accounts are not required.

As a general rule, applying in the UK, the United States, Belgium, France and Germany, it is assumed that a holding of 20% or more of a company's voting shares gives a significant degree of control and this investment is defined as an associated undertaking. The income flowing from the investment and any joint ventures is shown separately in the accounts.

Depreciation and profit

Capital maintenance is an important aspect of corporate reporting. In order to continue in business in the future, a company is expected at least to maintain the current level of investment in operating assets and to replace assets as they wear out or become obsolete. Capital employed is on one side of the balance sheet and assets are on the other. If assets are maintained, so must capital be maintained. One way of achieving this is through depreciation, the setting aside of current revenue for future reinvestment in the business.

It is possible to consider depreciation in at least three ways.

1 In the balance sheet a company is expected to provide a reasonable representation of the value of its assets. In normal circumstances a new car is worth more than an old car. As an asset gets older and its value decreases, it is reasonable to expect this change in value to the business to be reflected in the balance sheet.

2 As a company carries on its business, it uses resources. It incurs costs and expenses, uses labour and materials, and uses up some of the value of the fixed assets, machinery and vehicles employed in the business. To produce the profit shown in the income statement, all costs and expenses are deducted from revenue. The direct costs are charged and some allowance is made for the cost of using the fixed assets during the year. Part of the value of the plant and machinery has been used up during the year. To reflect this wear and tear of fixed assets, an amount is charged in the income statement. Thus depreciation may be considered to be the cost of the various fixed assets being used during the year.

3 If a company is to continue in business, at some stage it will have to replace its fixed assets as they wear out or become obsolete. To provide for this eventual asset replacement, the company prudently sets aside funds for this purpose. Depreciation is charged in the income statement, but it is not actually paid out to any third parties; it is retained in the company.

A company that fails to charge depreciation breaches not only the requirement for prudence in financial reporting but also the fundamental requirement of capital maintenance.

There are many ways of calculating the depreciation charge in an income statement. For example, a company purchases an asset with a working life of four years for $1,000. It produces a profit, before depreciation, of $300 per year, 50% of which is distributed as a dividend to shareholders. At the end of the fourth year the replacement cost of the asset is $1,000.

If no depreciation were charged, the company would retain $600 profit (50% of $300 for four years). At the end of the asset's life there would not be sufficient funds available in the balance sheet for replacement. Had the company charged $250 per year for depreciation (writing the asset off over the four years of working life), the distributable profit would have been only $50 per year. If 50% of this had been paid to shareholders as dividend, there would have been $1,100 of retained profit at the end of the fourth year.

Straight line depreciation

The simplest and most common approach to calculating depreciation is the straight line method. The cost or value of the asset is divided by its anticipated useful working life to produce the annual depreciation charge.

Cost of asset	$1,000
Estimated useful working life	4 years
Depreciation charged in the income statement per year	$250

Reducing balance depreciation

A second approach is the reducing balance method, which is applied commonly by US companies and also for tax purposes in the UK. A constant percentage of the reducing asset value is charged each year.

Cost of asset	$1,000
Depreciation rate per year	50%

In the first year $500 depreciation is charged in the income statement. This reduces the value of the asset to $500, and so in the second year the depreciation charge is $250.

Accelerated depreciation

A third approach is the sum of the digits method. The anticipated useful working life of the asset is ten years. All the digits – 1, 2, 3, 4, 5, 6, 7, 8, 9, 10 – are added together, producing a total of 55. In the first year the depreciation charge is 10/55ths of the asset value, in the second year 9/55ths, and so on, until in the final year 1/55ths is charged to fully depreciate the asset.

The sum of the digits and reducing balance methods are examples of accelerated depreciation, since the greatest charges for depreciation are made in the early years of the life of the asset. This, for example, is realistic for a car, as just driving it out of the showroom results in a big drop in its value.

If an asset costing $20,000 has an expected useful life of four years, the various methods of deprecation would show the following.

Year	Straight line $	Reducing balance $	Sum of digits $
1	5,000	10,000	8,000
2	5,000	5,000	6,000
3	5,000	2,500	4,000
4	5,000	1,250	2,000
Total	20,000	18,750	20,000

With the reducing balance method the asset is never fully depreciated. There will always be some, however insignificant, value remaining. In the example $1,250 remains as a balance sheet value at the end of four years.

The three methods of calculating depreciation will, each year, result in different charges for the asset being made in the income statement and in the balance sheet value. Depreciation policy is important when assessing the financial performance and position of a company.

Always read the notes on fixed assets and their depreciation carefully. A company's asset valuation and depreciation policies should be reasonable, prudent and consistent. If this is not the case, you need to satisfy yourself that profits are not being manipulated. It is possible to boost reported profit if all expenses relating to an asset, including interest charges for its finance, are capitalised rather than charged to the income statement. Compare the company's policy with that of others in the same sector to make sure there is conformity.

It is not difficult to imagine a situation in which a company would prefer not to operate a prudent depreciation policy. Low profitability might be bolstered by not charging depreciation in the first year of a new asset being brought into operation. The company might argue that as the new investment – particularly if it is land and buildings – was operational for only part of the year, it is reasonable that it should not be subject to depreciation. Thus the new investment would generate revenue but not be burdened with the "cost" of depreciation. Once such an approach is accepted the consistency rule will ensure its application in future years.

Taxing matters

The pre-tax profit reported in a company's accounts is unlikely to be the profit used to calculate the eventual tax liability. A simple means of assessing this is to find the tax rate being paid on the reported profit of a company. This can be roughly judged by dividing the pre-tax profit by the tax due shown in the income statement. The resulting figure can then be compared with the rate of company taxation for the country involved. As a general rule, the actual tax rate will be found to be well below the standard rate imposed on companies. The rate of tax being paid should be disclosed. The amount of tax due will be disclosed in the balance sheet as part of the year-end current liabilities.

Tax allowable depreciation

If companies were allowed to set their own rates of depreciation in arriving at their taxable profit without any external controls or guidance, no company would need to end up with a tax liability. The standard practice in most countries is to have two rates of depreciation, one that is allowed and accepted for tax purposes and a second that is applied by companies in the presentation of their annual reports to shareholders. Inevitably, there is a difference between the profit a company declares to its shareholders and the profit it declares to the tax authorities. Accounting profit is defined under generally accepted accounting principles (GAAP), but taxable profit is defined by government legislation.

Deferred taxation

Depreciation is often a cause of a significant difference between a company's reported and taxable profit. A company has little option but to accept the tax rules prescribed by the country or countries in which it operates. If tax incentives are offered to encourage investment, any company can be expected to take full advantage of them. However, this can lead to an apparent distortion in the reported after-tax profits of a company. This is the result of what are called timing differences.

The impacts of the investment and its associated tax implications may not occur in the same period. This can distort the reported after-tax profits of the company and is overcome through the use of a deferred taxation account, sometimes referred to as a tax equalisation account.

For example, a company purchases for $5,000 a machine with an expected working life of five years and no residual value. The tax rate is 50%. For tax purposes the machine can be fully depreciated in the first year. The company has a profit before depreciation of $10,000 per year.

($)	Year 1	Years 2–5
Profit before depreciation	10,000	10,000
Depreciation	1,000	1,000
Pre-tax profit	9,000	9,000
Tax	(2,500)	(5,000)
Deferred tax	(2,000)	500
After-tax profit	4,500	4,500

FRS 19, introduced in 2002, requires deferred tax to appear in the balance sheet.

Year 1	Year 2	Year 3	Year 4	Year 5
$2,000[a]	$1,500	$1,000	$500	$0

a 50% of $4,000 is the year-end value of the machine.

Reconciling the books

Companies keep at least three sets of books. One is for management to enable them to run the company; the second is for the tax authorities to calculate the annual tax liability; and the third is presented to the shareholders in the annual report. The three sets should, under normal sound accounting practices, be capable of reconciliation.

Capital or revenue

The decision on whether something should be treated as capital (balance sheet) or revenue (income statement) in the year reinforces the links between the balance sheet and the income statement in connection with the treatment of fixed assets. Revenue expenditure is related to the normal business activities of the company or is concerned with maintaining the fixed assets. Capital transactions are normally intended to provide a long-lasting asset to the company.

The treatment of research and development (R&D) costs is a good example of the potential importance of the capitalise or expense decision, the result of which can have a significant impact on both the income statement and the balance sheet.

For example, a company invests $1,000 in R&D each year. It is considered that the life of the R&D investment is ten years. It is expected that the new products and services delivered by the R&D investment will come on stream over the next ten years. The company's policy is to provide shareholders with a regular annual $250 dividend as shown in year 1.

($)	Year 1	Year 2a	Year 2b
Profit for the year	1,500	750	750
R&D expense	1,000	1,000	100[a]
Profit	500	(250)	650
Dividend	250	0	250
Retained profit	250	(250)	400

a Balance sheet asset R&D $900.

If the company experiences a downturn in business, profit is halved in year 2 and there may be insufficient profit available to pay the required dividend (2a). There is little the company can do in operational terms (generating additional revenue or reducing costs), but it might be tempted to consider a change in its policy for the treatment of R&D.

It could be argued that a better form of presentation and a more accurate reflection of the events would result from spreading the R&D investment. That is, it would be more reasonable to spread the amount spent on R&D over the years when the new products and services result. It could also be argued that it would be unfair accounting treatment to burden one year's sales revenue with what is really ten years' investment in R&D.

The company opts to charge only one-tenth of the R&D spend against the year 2 sales revenue, and to continue writing it off over the next nine years. The balance, $1,000 - $100 = $900, is capitalised as an asset having future value to the company (2b).

The impact of this change in accounting presentation is that the company in year 2b shows a profit of $650, and so may pay the $250 dividend. It also exhibits a new asset, R&D valued at $900, in the balance sheet. Although it is not possible find fault with the book-keeping involved in this exercise, it might be possible to raise questions about the validity of displaying R&D as an asset in the balance sheet.

During the 1960s and 1970s, there were many examples of companies capitalising R&D and then discovering that under pressure it was impossible for it to be translated quickly into positive cash flow. In response to this, and to avoid the potential for misrepresentation or error in companies' financial reports, R&D became subject to accounting standards which enforced the prudence rule and required companies to write off their R&D through the income statement in the year it is incurred. German and US companies are expected to take R&D costs into the income statement in the year in which they are incurred. In Belgium, France and Italy, R&D may be either expensed or capitalised. In the UK, research costs must be expensed, but it is possible that development costs may be capitalised.

Although the example of R&D may now be only of historic interest, many of the same issues face companies today regarding such intangible assets as brand names (see Chapter 2). When a company is so desperate to show a profit that it throws the rule book away it is not unusual to see expenses being capitalised. The 1990s provides examples of companies:

- adding maintenance and repairs to fixed asset values;
- capitalising software that had dubious real value;
- capitalising internal software costs;
- capitalising marketing and advertising expenses.

Once this was done the cost was written off over a number of years or treated as a one-off non-recurring or special charge not affecting the current year's reported operating profit. With the CEO insisting " we have to hit our numbers", reducing real capital expenditure and capitalising operating expenses were key to WorldCom's creative accounting, contributing some $3.8bn to the overall $11bn fraud.

Interest

Interest paid by a company on borrowings and interest received on investments is shown either on the face of the income statement or in the notes. Often the income statement figure is for net interest payable, that is the interest payable less the interest received and the interest capitalised.

The total interest payable during the year should be divided into interest relating to short-term borrowings, such as bank loans, repayable on demand or within 12 months, and interest on loans falling due within five years.

Capitalising interest payments

If a company borrows money to complete a major project, such as building a new factory or hypermarket, it is possible to capitalise the interest payments and write them off under the company's normal depreciation policy rather than including them as a charge in the income statement. Although this is a reasonable policy because the interest cost has been incurred to allow the asset to be built, it reduces the costs charged to the income statement, thereby increasing the company's profit. The notes to the accounts should clearly indicate how much interest has been capitalised during the year.

When looking at the interest a company has to pay, perhaps for use in an interest cover measure, it is best to use the total interest payable figure. That a company has capitalised a proportion of its interest payments does not affect how much interest it has to pay.

Operating or finance leases

A further example of the distinction between capital and revenue items is found in the treatment of leases. Should lease payments be treated as an operating (income statement) expense or as the acquisition cost of a fixed asset shown in the balance sheet? Again the decision will affect reported profit for the year.

The main criterion is whether the rights and associated risks and rewards of ownership of the asset pass to the lessee. If they do, the lease is capitalised and taken into the balance sheet (a finance sheet). If they do not, the company is treated as renting the asset and the lease payments are included in the income statement (an operating lease).

There are rules and guidelines to help clarify the distinctions between operating and finance leases. In the UK and the United States, a lease is normally treated as a finance lease if a right to purchase option is included in the lease agreement, or if the present value of lease payments exceeds 90% of the fair value of the asset. Although there will be differences in the annual charge included in the income statement, the total amount charged over the life of the lease will be identical for both forms of lease and the cash flow impact will be the same.

Provisions, contingent liabilities and reserves

Once the profit after tax and dividend has been reached a company may decide to set aside a portion of it to pay for future liabilities – for example, through a deferred taxation account. Where the precise timing or amount is uncertain, it is prudent to make a provision to cover the likely cost.

Provisions are often shown as exceptional items in the income statement and may relate to the costs incurred by the company for rationalisation or restructuring. However, they can only be made by a company in relation to "obligations ... to transfer economic benefits as a result of past transactions or events" (FRS 12). They should not be created in respect of possible future liabilities or likely losses.

An annual report may contain reference to a contingent liability. Where an event is uncertain and the amount involved is difficult to estimate, under the rules of FRS 12, it cannot be included in the accounts. However, a company may wish to draw attention to it through a note in the annual report under the heading of "contingent liability".

A reserve is the setting aside of retained profit (see below) in the balance sheet and appears as part of shareholders' funds. There are two types of reserves: capital and revenue. Revenue reserves can be considered available for use in paying dividends. Capital reserves, which may be called legal or non-distributable, are considered undistributable and so cannot normally be used for this purpose.

Retained profit

After all costs and expenses, interest and dividend payments have been covered, the retained profit, net income or surplus is what is left. This is taken to the balance sheet to add to the accumulating shareholders' interests.

Earnings per share

Earnings per share (EPS) is the amount of profit a company has made for each ordinary share. It is calculated by dividing the profit attributable to shareholders by the average (defined as the weighted average for the year) number of ordinary shares in issue during the year. The actual number of shares used is given in the notes relating to the disclosure of EPS in the accounts. The proportion of any subsidiary company's profit due to minority interests is deducted from the after-tax profit to provide the attributable profit for the year, as are any dividends due to non-equity shareholders such as preference shareholders.

In the United States stock is equivalent to shares in the UK, but the shorthand EPS is used in both countries. If a company makes an after-tax loss, the calculation is completed but EPS appears as a negative figure.

$$\text{Earnings per share} = \text{after-tax profit} \div \text{number of shares in issue}$$

A company with $2,000 after-tax profit and 5,000 shares in issue has an EPS of 40¢ ($2,000 ÷ $5,000).

Dividends

The profit attributable to shareholders forms the potential source of dividend payments. The dividends the company has paid and the directors have proposed for the year are shown in the income statement as a single figure. The notes provide details of when the dividends are to be paid and the rate. When a dividend is declared as 10% this relates to the nominal value of the shares involved. A company with $1 or £1 shares paying a 10% dividend is offering 10¢ or 10p per share to shareholders.

It is becoming increasingly popular for companies to offer shareholders a scrip or stock dividend – the alternative of taking additional shares rather than cash dividends. This has the advantage of not reducing the company's cash balances and of offering shareholders the possibility of increased capital gains and future dividends.

The total of dividends paid and proposed is shown as a deduction from the after-tax profit for the year. This figure includes the dividend on the ordinary shares that the directors propose at the annual general meeting of the company as well as the dividends on any other types or classes of shares, such as preference shares. To identify the dividend relating to the ordinary shares, refer to the accompanying notes.

No profit, no dividend

Basic good housekeeping would suggest that a company with little or no profit should not be expected to pay a dividend. Technically, it is possible for a company with a loss for the year to pay a dividend. As long as it has sufficient distributable reserves in the balance sheet, and of course enough cash, a dividend can be declared.

Pro forma profits

Always make sure the profit figures you are using are taken from the published income statement. A recent trend is for companies to offer "pro forma" financial information to investors. In 2002 the International Organisation of Securities Commissions (IOSCO) recommended care when using non-GAAP figures:

> Investors should be aware than non-GAAP pro forma earning measures are not prepared in accordance with the accounting standards applied to financial statement and may omit or reclassify significant expenses.

In 2003 the FSA drew attention to the dangers of pro forma figures:

"Consider whether publishing non-GAAP numbers may give a misleading presentation of financial performance." In the United States the Sarbanes-Oxley Act of 2003 was supported by the SEC with firm rules covering all pro forma financial information released by listed companies.

4 The cash flow statement

A COMPANY'S INCOME STATEMENT can show a healthy profit for the year, but this does not guarantee that it has the cash necessary to survive. Profit is not cash. Profit is an accounting measure; cash is a physical item. In the 1970s and 1980s many apparently profitable companies failed because of a lack of cash. This increased pressure for financial reports to give more emphasis to a company's cash flows, liquidity and borrowings. Thus the cash flow statement became the third significant financial statement to be presented by companies in their annual reports. Cash flow statements were introduced in the United States in the late 1970s and the UK in the early 1990s.

No cash, no business

Profit is part fact, part opinion and occasionally part hope. Different assumptions, views and accounting treatment will produce different profits. Low profitability or loss-making operations may be distressing or embarrassing for management but not necessarily terminal for a company. Companies can survive without profit as long as they have cash available. Even a profitable company cannot survive without cash.

Every activity of a company is translated into cash at some time. Companies use it to pay employees and suppliers and customers use it to purchase products and services. It is necessary to allow investment in assets to support growth and to pay interest and dividends to providers of financial resources, and to pay taxes. At any time there is a single indisputable figure for cash, which can be physically counted and checked.

What is cash?

Cash is normally understood to be the notes and coins used in the day-to-day transactions of companies and individuals. For the purposes of accounting and financial analysis the definition of cash is slightly broader, including not only coins and notes but also money held in bank accounts. These cash or near-cash assets form part of a company's liquid assets. A starting point for assessing the strength of a company's cash position is to look at the changes in the amounts of cash held at the beginning and end of the year. All that is required is two consecutive balance sheets. An increase in cash held could be taken to be a good sign representing an improvement in liquidity. However, in making an assessment of a company's liquidity, any short-term borrowings, such as overdrafts in the UK, should be deducted from cash and bank balances to identify the net position.

Cash balances

For most purposes cash can be taken to include all cash and bank balances net of overdraft or other borrowings repayable on demand, in other words the cash a company has readily available for immediate use. Although cash is essential in the running of any business, it is, except for any interest it may earn, a non-productive asset that can be used to increase productive resources or to repay debt, thus reducing interest charges and improving profitability. A company with a shortage of cash may be in trouble. A company with a lot of cash may not be operating as profitably as it could be. But you have to be careful about reading too much into the cash balance given in the annual report. A large figure may simply reflect the setting aside of money to pay for machines in the following financial year.

What matters

Working capital

To consider only the movement in cash and liquid assets over a period of time does not provide sufficient basis for understanding the financial changes a business is experiencing. A better view of a company's financial position can be obtained if the scope of analysis is expanded to cover all current assets and current liabilities. Current assets are likely to be turned into cash, if they are not already in this form, within a fairly short period. Similarly, current liabilities will have to be paid in cash within 12 months of the balance sheet date, if not much sooner. By deducting current liabilities from current assets to produce net current assets or liabilities, you get what is commonly called the working capital of a company. Changes seen to be occurring within the working capital of a business can be important indicators of its performance and position.

As a business is managed there is a continual movement of financial resources or funds including cash, as Figure 4.1 shows. In a typical business, inventory is produced or purchased, suppliers deliver raw materials, operating costs and expenses are incurred and customers buy the products. All these transactions are completed either in cash or on credit

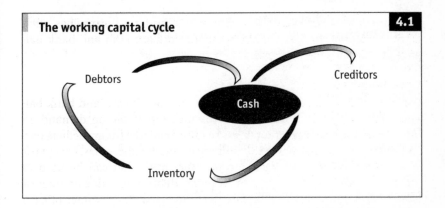

The working capital cycle

4.1

terms. Current assets and liabilities change to reflect the impact of the transactions made to enable the business to operate.

There are problems, however, in using working capital as the basis for analysing the financial changes of a business. Concentrating on working capital movements ignores other sections of the balance sheet, such as changes in fixed assets, shareholders' funds and long-term borrowings. Also it is possible for a company to control the level of current assets and liabilities at the time the balance sheet is drafted. Immediately before the end of the financial year customers can be chased for payment so the balance sheet shows a low level of debtors; payment for a major fixed asset can be delayed to allow higher than normal cash balances; and suppliers can be paid earlier or later than normal to adjust the level of credit.

Funds flow

For all businesses there are movements of cash resulting from transactions and events outside the area of working capital. There is more to a business than just the working capital cycle. Fixed assets may be bought or sold, dividends, interest and tax paid, loans raised or repaid and shares issued or repurchased. When these items are included, a better foundation is provided for the analysis of movements in a company's financial resources. If all the changes between two consecutive balance sheets are analysed, every financial movement will be covered. This is called funds flow analysis.

Funds can be defined as being any source of finance allowing a company to acquire assets. Cash raised from shareholders is a source of finance or funds that can be used in the business. Additional credit taken from suppliers, although not cash, acts as a source of funds, enabling the level of inventory held to increase. Any liability increasing during the year acts as a source of funds available for use on the other side of the balance sheet to increase assets.

Sources and uses

The balance sheet is the starting point for discovering what funds have been generated during the year and how these have been used in the business. The balance sheet equation, assets = liabilities, ensures that in any year a company cannot use more funds than it generates or generate more than it uses; in other words, sources = uses. If more funds are generated than can be immediately used for operational purposes, paying interest and dividends or repaying borrowings, the surplus will appear in the year-end cash balances. Holding more cash is a use of funds.

Sources of funds

A company considering making an investment can fund it by:

- using existing cash balances;
- generating cash from operations;
- raising capital from shareholders;
- borrowing money;
- changing credit terms;
- selling assets.

Sources of funds fall into two categories: internal and external. Internal sources are largely under the control of the company. A proportion of internal funds can be expected to be generated through the income statement. Shareholders can be an internal source of funds, but they also make demands on cash for payment of dividends. External sources consist of suppliers giving credit payment terms to the company and banks and other institutions providing short-, medium- or long-term finance.

In looking at the changes that have taken place between two balance sheets, a decrease in the value of an asset or an increase in a liability can be assumed to act as a source of funds to the business. However, common sense indicates that the revaluation of property during the year will show an increase in assets matched by an increase in liabilities (shareholders' funds); since this does not indicate any actual movement in financial resources it should be ignored.

Sources = increases in liabilities and/or decreases in assets

Uses of funds

The funds available to a company during the year can be used for:

- increasing current assets;
- decreasing current liabilities;
- purchasing fixed assets;
- repaying borrowings;
- repurchasing shares;
- covering operating losses.

A change in customer credit policy resulting in an increase in trade debtors at the end of the year is a use of funds. Customers are, in effect, being allowed to borrow more of the company's money. Until they pay for the goods or services received they are tying up financial resources that could be used elsewhere in the business. An increase in the value of an asset or a decrease in a liability, such as the purchase of a new machine, payments to suppliers or the repayment of a loan, can be assumed to have consumed funds.

Uses = increases in assets and/or decreases in liabilities

Funds flow statement

A statement displaying the changes in a company's financial position can be called:

- a funds flow statement;
- a statement of changes in financial position;
- a source and application of funds statement.

A funds flow statement is produced by comparing two consecutive balance sheets and identifying the changes that have occurred. This can be done by deducting, line by line, one balance sheet from the other. The differences represent an increase or a decrease in an asset or a liability. All the changes that have occurred during the year are thus identified as representing a source or a use of funds.

($)	Year 1		Year 2		Increase/ decrease
Fixed assets	200		250		+50
Depreciation	<u>100</u>	100	<u>125</u>	125	+25
Current assets					
Inventory	60		75		+15
Debtors	40		30		−10
Investment	0		10		+10
Cash	<u>10</u>	110	<u>15</u>	130	+5
		210		255	
Capital and reserves					
Share capital	100		100		
Retained profit	<u>65</u>	165	<u>75</u>	175	+10
Loan				20	+20
Current liabilities					
Creditors		<u>45</u>		<u>60</u>	+15
		210		255	

If the year 1 balance sheet is deducted from that of year 2, the changes represent either a source or a use of funds during the year.

Sources	$	Uses	$
Retained profit	10	Fixed assets	50
Depreciation	25	Inventory	15
Creditors	15	Investment	10
Loan	20	Cash	<u>5</u>
Debtors	<u>10</u>		
	80		80

The treatment of depreciation

In the example above, depreciation ($25) has been included as a source of funds. Although depreciation is charged in the income statement as an expense for the year, there is no cash movement. If the fixed assets on which the depreciation charge is based were paid for in cash at the time of their acquisition, there will be no further cash movements associated with them until their disposal. Depreciation is a non-cash expense.

It would be possible to show only the $25 net change after depreciation ($50 − $25) instead of the $50 increase in investment in fixed assets. However, this would conceal the true financial movements associated with fixed assets. The depreciation charge of $25 has been generated by the company from its operations and is available for reinvestment in fixed assets during the year, allowing the company not only to maintain its productive resources but also to increase them. It is better to view the changes that have taken place during the year as the company having spent $50 on additional fixed assets.

It is important to understand that although it is common practice to refer to depreciation as a source of funds, this is technically incorrect. A change in depreciation policy has no impact on cash. A company cannot generate funds by changing its depreciation policy. If it decided to increase the depreciation charge from $25 to $30, this would reduce the reported profit for the year by $5 but would not affect funds flow, which remains at $35 ($5 + $30).

Cash balance changes

It is helpful to adjust the presentation format of the funds flow statement to highlight the changes that have occurred in cash balances.

($)		
Opening cash balance		**10**
Sources		
Retained profit and depreciation	35	
Increase in creditors	15	
Loan	20	
Decrease in debtors	<u>10</u>	<u>80</u>
		90
Uses		
Increase in fixed assets	50	
Increase in inventory	15	
Increase in investment	<u>10</u>	<u>75</u>
Closing cash balance		**15**

Problems with funds flow statements

Until 1991 all UK companies had to provide a Statement of Source and

Application of Funds in their annual reports. The SSAP 10 accounting standard offered considerable flexibility on how the statement could be presented and what it contained. With companies adopting slightly different forms of presentation it proved hard to compare companies' funds flow directly. But difficulties with comparability were not the only problem; several major companies disclosed a profit in their annual report, only to go into liquidation or receivership soon after because of a lack of liquid assets. A company could report an increase in net current assets or working capital with debtors and inventory increasing during the year but cash depleted to a dangerous level.

($)	Year 1	Year 2
Inventory	20	30
Debtors	10	20
Cash	5	0
	35	50
Creditors	10	20
Working capital	25	30

The funds flow statement merely showed the changes taking place in the interval between the two balance sheets. It did not provide the additional information necessary to assess a company's ability to meet its obligations, including payments to suppliers, shareholders and others, as they fell due.

From funds flow to cash flow

Pressure for change grew as users of financial statements made clear their dissatisfaction with the level of disclosure. They wanted to see clearly where financial resources were being generated, how they were being applied in the business, and what changes in liquidity and borrowings had taken place. As a result, many major UK companies were by the end of the 1980s providing a cash flow statement, which covers only the actual cash movements experienced during the financial period, rather than a funds flow statement.

Cash flow

Reporting cash flow was the subject of the first Financial Reporting Standard (FRS 1) published by the UK Accounting Standards Board (ASB) in September 1991 and revised in 1996. Cash flow statements have been required in the United States since 1988.

The cash flow from sales revenue is not the same as the sales revenue appearing in the income statement. It is the actual cash received and does not, as under accrual accounting, include credit transactions with customers that have no cash impact during the year. Cash inflows from customers and cash outflows to suppliers are produced by adjusting the total amounts for the year by the credit element involved.

Cash inflow = sales + (opening debtors − closing debtors)
Cash outflow = purchases + (opening creditors − closing creditors)

	$		$
Sales revenue	100		
Opening debtors	40	Cash from opening debtors	40
	140		
Closing debtors	30	Cash from sales for year	70
Cash inflow	110	Cash inflow	110

Cash flow and profit

A company may be creative in arriving at its reported profit for the year, but it is much more difficult, if not impossible, for it to create cash. This is a reason for the shift in emphasis in recent years to seeing the cash flow statement as an integral and important part of the annual report.

The profit produced from operations (running the business) should be an important element of cash flow. If a loss is incurred, there is a positive internally generated operational cash flow only if the depreciation charge for the year exceeds the loss. Depreciation, a non-cash item, is added back to the profit for the year in the same way as in the funds flow statement.

There is little point in a company having profit but no cash – its long-term survival is likely to be difficult to manage. Equally, there is no advantage, apart from short-term survival, in having cash but no profit. A company may show a profit from making a credit sale to a customer but experience a reduction in cash balances.

For example, a $100 sale to a customer and the associated $70 cost is recorded when the transaction is completed and included in the income statement for the year, but there may have been no cash movement. If suppliers have been paid $35 cash of the $70 total cost of sale by the end of the year, but the customer has not paid the $100 owed, profit has increased by $30 and the cash balance has decreased by $35.

	$		$
Sales revenue	100	Cash inflow	0
Costs	70	Cash outflow	35
Profit	30	Cash flow	(35)

Capitalising expenses and cash flow

By deciding to capitalise some of its expenses, interest payments or product development costs, a company can move the charge from the income statement into the balance sheet, thereby improving reported profit. However, the cash movements associated with the year's expenses remain unchanged. Following the capitalisation of expenses it would be possible for the income statement to show a profit and the cash flow statement to show a negative cash flow from operations.

Cash flow and dividends and tax

Operating cash flow is what remains after paying the direct costs and expenses of the business. Ideally, it is sufficient to cover interest on borrowings and the company's tax liability, and then to provide the source of dividends paid to shareholders. Where a company incurs a loss, it is still possible to declare a dividend as long as there are sufficient revenue reserves in the balance sheet and cash available to make the payment. But a company that continues to deplete reserves and cash resources in order to pay dividends will eventually run into trouble.

A simple rule of good housekeeping is that companies should pay shareholders dividends only from sound and positive cash flow. They should not have to rely on selling fixed assets or borrowing more. A company making dividend payments from declining operating cash flows may satisfy the short-term needs of shareholders but not have sufficient funds to reinvest in the business to ensure future growth and continued profitability.

The income statement shows the dividends declared for the current year and the tax due on that year's profits. The cash outflow associated with these is the cash paid in the year to shareholders for dividends and to the government for tax. The tax paid in one year normally relates to the profits of previous years – there is a delay between generating the profit and paying the tax. Timing differences can be considerable and result, for most companies, in a difference between the figures for dividends and tax in the income statement and the actual cash payments for these appearing the cash flow statement. For reasons of clarity and simplicity, timing differences for payment of interest, tax, dividends and fixed asset investment are ignored in the examples used in this chapter.

Working capital and cash flow

Any change in the amount of inventory held and the credit given to customers or taken from suppliers has an impact on both reported profit and cash flow. Increasing the amount of credit taken from suppliers acts as a source and an increase in credit offered to customers acts as a use of available financial resources.

The relationship between current assets and current liabilities can be explored by looking at movements that have taken place within working capital. In the example below, financial resources ($30) have been used to allow an increase in inventory ($15) and investment and cash balances ($15) during the year. This has been covered partly by a reduction in year-end debtors of $10, representing a decrease in money owed to the company by customers, and partly by an increase in the amount owed to creditors ($15). The net change in working capital represents an increase during the year of $5. The cash flow from operations ($35) and the loan ($20) taken during the year equal $55, of which $50 was used to purchase fixed assets; the $5 remaining is used to finance the increase in working capital.

	$	$	$
Cash flow			
From operations	35		
Loan	20	55	
Investment in fixed assets		50	5
Increase in working capital			
Increase in inventory	15		
Increase in investment	10		
Increase in cash	5	30	
Decrease in debtors	10		
Increase in creditors	15	25	5

Presenting a statement of financial movements in this way helps explain the sources and uses of cash flow and separates the investment activity and capital structure changes from those of working capital and cash balances.

Cash flow statement

The cash flow statement provides an essential link between the income statement and the balance sheet, and is much more difficult for companies to manipulate. The detailed internal accounting records of a company are needed to prepare a statement of the actual cash movements. It is not possible, as was the case with a funds flow statement, to prepare a cash flow statement yourself from the income statement and balance sheet.

Typically, the cash flow statement is divided into sections with cash flows shown according to the activity giving rise to them. All cash movements are classified under standard headings. This provides a basis to assess which of the areas of activity are most significant to a company's cash flow and makes possible comparisons with other companies in similar businesses. The headings used vary internationally but those used in the UK are reasonably representative:

- Operating activities
- Dividends from joint ventures and associates
- Returns on investments and servicing of finance
- Tax
- Capital expenditure and financial investment
- Acquisitions and disposals
- Equity dividends paid
- Management of liquid resources
- Financing

The cash flow statement also discloses the actual amount of cash paid in interest during the year, whether or not some of this was capitalised ("returns on investments and servicing of finance"). It provides a basis to assess what proportion of cash flow available during the year is being used to cover the cost of borrowings. Any interest the company has received during the year on investments or loans is shown separately in the statement as part of the internally generated cash flow. Many companies highlight "free cash flow" (see Chapter 11) with a subtotal after "capital expenditure and financial investment". This is a useful figure showing how much cash remains after covering all operating costs and making the necessary investment in asset replacement. Free cash flow is available for dividend payments to shareholders and to finance expansion through acquisition. It is a good indicator of the ability of a company to generate cash.

Another important indicator of how well a company is being managed is the impact of cash flow on its borrowing requirements. The annual report provides a reconciliation between the balance sheet and the cash flow statement, with the opening and closing balance sheet figures for cash and borrowings linked to the movements for the year shown in the cash flow statement.

Cash flow from operating activities

The cash flow statement can be assumed to have taken all operating revenues net of sales taxes. In the example used to explain funds flow at the beginning of this chapter, retained profit for the year was $10. In presenting a cash flow statement additional detail is disclosed.

	$
Operating profit	40
Interest paid	10
Pre-tax profit	30
Tax	15
After-tax profit	15
Dividend	5
Retained profit	10

The statement starts with the net cash flow from operations: the cash inflow or outflow for the year resulting from the business or trading activities of the company. The net cash flow from operations mirrors the activities bringing about the profit or loss for the year disclosed in the income statement.

Companies should provide a detailed reconciliation between operating profit and operating cash flow. This anchors the cash flow statement to the income statement. Operating profit is then adjusted for depreciation, timing differences, working capital changes and any use made of provisions to provide operating cash flow.

Cash flow from operations should include the cash impact of all trading activities and the cash movement resulting from the achievement of the operating profit displayed in the income statement. The cash flow statement deals only with cash movements during the year; anything else is ignored.

To arrive at the net operating cash flow for the year, adjustments must be made to the operating profit to allow for changes in working capital as well as for any non-cash items, such as depreciation, included in the income statement. Operating cash flow can be reported using either the direct or the indirect method (sometimes referred to as net or gross).

The direct method – a summary of the year's cash receipts and payments – provides a better and more detailed representation of cash flows than the indirect method. In the indirect method, just a single figure for cash flow from operations is shown. Companies can either follow one of the recommended formats in the accounting standard or publish a detailed listing of major headings of costs and expenses incurred in arriving at the operating profit for the year.

	$
Operating profit	40
Depreciation	25
Increase in inventory	(15)
Decrease in debtors	10
Increase in creditors	15
Net cash inflow	75

The amount of cash flow generated from the income statement or the operations of the business is $75. American companies start their cash flow statements with net income (after-tax profit) rather than operating profit (pre-tax profit) as is the case in the UK. It is important to remember this difference if attempting to compare American and UK companies.

Net cash flow from operating activities	$75

It is impossible for any accounting standard to produce a set of rules tightly defining every possible event or transaction that a company might experience, so there may still be some allocation problems. For many items appearing in the cash flow statement a decision has been made about which heading they are to appear under: are they operating expenses or investments? However, the statement will show the impact of the transaction in cash terms.

Returns on investments and servicing of finance

This section of the cash flow statement gives cash inflows and outflows associated with investment income and payments to providers of financial resources. It shows the interest paid in the financial year and any dividends paid to non-equity shareholders; dividends paid to equity shareholders are shown under a separate heading. Any dividends the company has received that are not included in the operating profit will also be detailed in this section of the cash flow statement.

Returns on investment and servicing of finance	
Interest paid	$10

Taxation

This section of the cash flow statement gives the actual cash paid in the year in tax. This is not the same as the tax figure shown in the income statement, but in the example it is assumed that there are no timing differences. Any cash receipts derived from repayments or other dealings with the tax authorities are also shown in this section.

Tax paid	$15

Capital expenditure and financial investment

This section includes cash movements resulting from the acquisition or disposal of fixed assets and any current asset not dealt with as a part of liquid resources. The purchase or sale of a subsidiary is dealt with under a separate heading. Any loans made by or repaid to the company (financial investment) will be detailed in this section. The amount of cash used for investment in fixed assets and any cash received from the sale of fixed assets during the year is shown here. Non-cash events do not appear; for example, a company revaluing its property shows a change in the balance sheet but nothing in the cash flow statement.

There is a difference between the change in fixed asset investment shown in the balance sheet and that appearing in the cash flow statement. The cash flow statement identifies the actual amount of cash spent by the company during the year. The balance sheet figures are subject to timing differences. An asset may have been purchased but not paid for by the end of the financial year, so an increase in fixed assets is shown in the balance sheet but there is nothing in the cash flow statement.

A crucial role of management is to make investment decisions allocating the available financial resources to appropriate parts of the business with a view to providing future profitable growth. The cash flow statement shows the cash outflows associated with the investing activities of the company, and the cash inflow when assets are sold. It indicates the total amount spent on fixed assets but does not necessarily disclose in any detail precisely where or on what the cash was spent. The cash flow statement does not therefore provide a basis for assessing the quality of fixed asset investments being made.

Capital expenditure
Purchase of fixed assets $50

Acquisitions and disposals

If a subsidiary is acquired or disposed of during the year, only the cash paid or received is included in the cash flow statement and any cash out-flow figure is net of any cash gained with the subsidiary. When an acquisition is made by the issue of shares, with no cash involved, the only impact on the cash flow statement is the receipt of the subsidiary's cash balances. The price paid may be different from that appearing in the cash flow statement. There should be a note showing the actual amount of cash or overdraft being acquired or, in the case of the sale of a subsidiary, disposed of.

For example, a company uses a combination of shares and cash to acquire a subsidiary.

Consideration paid ($)			Assets acquired ($)		
Shares issued	80		Assets	50	
Cash	20	100	Goodwill	20	
			Cash	30	100

The subsidiary has been purchased and the net cash result is to increase group cash balances by $10; the parent company has paid out $20 to acquire $30 cash. It is only this net cash movement of $10 that is recorded in the cash flow statement. Additional notes should help explain acquisitions and disposals.

Not all of a company's transactions have an impact on the income statement; they may be detailed in the balance sheet. In the UK, companies write off goodwill against reserves on acquisition. The additional profit flowing from the acquisition is included in the group's profit for the year, but the cost of acquisition is ignored in the income statement. The cash flow statement can offer a much clearer indication of the true profitability of acquisitions as it shows the actual cash outflow and its impact on financing requirements.

The way in which acquisition and disposal cash flows are considered depends on the nature of the group being analysed. Some companies trade or deal in businesses, buying and selling companies regularly throughout the year. For them the profit and positive cash flow generated from the sale of a business can be accepted as a part of their continuing operations. For most companies this is not the case; selling a major subsidiary may generate a substantial cash benefit, but only once.

If possible, a view should be taken on whether the sale of a subsidiary or a major business investment is part of a carefully planned strategy or merely the result of painful necessity. It is not always possible to be certain of the reason for a disposal through reading the various management statements in the annual report. It is unlikely that a company will admit that a subsidiary was sold because it ran out of cash. More commonly, the terms rationalisation, refocusing, re-engineering and suchlike are used to explain and justify major business disposals.

Equity dividends paid

The cash outflow devoted to the payment of dividends to equity shareholders is shown under this heading in the cash flow statement.

Equity dividends paid $5

Management of liquid resources

For the purposes of the cash flow statement, a liquid resource is defined as any current asset investment that is readily convertible into cash. As part of its financial or treasury management operations aimed at getting some positive benefit from cash balances, a company may make short-term investments which are shown as part of the current assets in the balance sheet. Surplus cash is used to earn interest, the investments being planned to ensure that cash is available as and when required.

This section of the cash flow statement shows all changes in short-term investments that fall under the heading of cash, and is intended to clarify how short-term cash flows are being managed.

Purchase of listed investment $10

Financing

This section deals with cash flows resulting from the raising or repayment of finance. Apart from the internally generated sources of finance, a company has only two options: it can raise additional funds from shareholders through the issue of shares, or go outside the company and borrow the money from a bank or other financial institution. If any equity shares are issued or repurchased during the year, the cash movements will be shown here. The cash flow statement helps to identify how much money has been raised from shareholders and how much from external sources. Taken together with the internally generated cash flows, these give a clear picture of the way in which the company has been financed during the year.

Financing	
New secured loan	$20

Companies should provide a reconciliation between the appropriate opening and closing balance sheet figures and movements in equity or debt financing shown in the cash flow statement. For example, shares issued without cash payment affect the balance sheet but not the cash flow statement.

There will be a reconciliation of the cash movements in the year with the movement in net debt. Net debt is defined as all borrowings, including derivatives and obligations under finance leases, less cash and liquid resources. A positive position is called net funds. This is normally shown in the accompanying notes, starting with the figure for the increase or decrease in cash for the year shown at the end of the cash flow statement and ending with the year-end net debt or net funds.

Finance leases

The net book value of assets held under finance leases is not normally separately identified in the balance sheet but included in the figure of total fixed assets. Finance leases do not involve any cash outflow for capital. Where an asset is acquired under a finance lease during the year, the value should be deducted from fixed assets in order to disclose the actual cash outflow for additional fixed assets. This is shown as part of the cash outflows relating to financing activities under a separate heading, capital element of finance lease rental payments. The interest element of the lease agreement appears in the section of the statement dealing with returns on investments and servicing of finance.

Example cash flow statement

Using the same data as for the funds flow statement appearing earlier in this chapter, a cash flow statement can be produced incorporating the cash flow movements explained above.

	$
Net cash flow from operating activities	**75**
Returns on investment and servicing of finance	(10)
Taxation	(15)
Capital expenditure	(50)
Equity dividends paid	(5)
Cash outflow before management of liquid resources and financing	**(5)**
Management of liquid resources	(10)
Financing	20
Increase in cash	**5**

The balance left after capital expenditure gives an indication of free cash flow for the year. This shows whether or not sufficient cash flow is being generated to finance operations and necessary asset investment, excluding acquisitions, without the need to rely on outside borrowings or finance. In the example, this gives a figure of $0; when dividends of $5 are paid the net cash outflow before financing is -$5.

Changes in cash balances

The opening and closing cash balances do not appear in the cash flow statement. However, there should be a reconciliation linking the opening and closing cash balances shown in the balance sheet with the cash flow for the year. This reconciliation helps to clarify the financial changes that have occurred. In the example, the company had a neutral cash flow of $0 before paying a dividend of $5. The loan of $20 covers the cash outflow before management of liquid resources and financing (-$5) and allows closing cash balances to be $5 greater at the end of the year ($15) than they were at the beginning ($10).

Exceptional and extraordinary events

Every business is likely at some time to experience an exceptional or extraordinary event. Such events should be clearly identified within the appropriate section of the cash flow statement. In most circumstances this is the operating activities section.

A major reorganisation by a company may result in significant cash outflows to cover redundancy payments or the cost of closing or relocating operating units. The cash outflows can be shown under the operating activities or the capital expenditure and acquisitions and disposals headings. Common practice is to show just the net cash movement as part of operating activities with additional details in the accompanying notes.

Foreign currency and cash flow

Most companies transact business in foreign currencies and many have subsidiaries in other countries. To prepare the financial statements, all transactions must be translated into the reporting company's currency. When foreign assets or liabilities are translated into a holding company's currency at the balance sheet date exchange rate differences will occur.

For example, a company sells $100 worth of goods to an overseas customer when the exchange rate is $1 = 4x, and at the end of the year the rate moves to $1 = 5x. If the customer pays cash during the financial year, any gain or loss resulting from exchange rate movements is automatically included in the operating profit for that year and no adjustment is required in the cash flow statement.

If at the end of the year the customer has not paid the invoice, there is no cash flow involved. However, the transaction has been recorded and included as part of the income for the year in the income statement at an exchange rate of $1 = 4x. An adjustment is required to the closing debtors figure.

The income statement and balance sheet of a foreign subsidiary can be translated into the currency of the holding company using one of two methods: the temporal method or the closing rate (net investment) method. The temporal method uses the exchange rate ruling at the time of the transaction or an average for the year if this is not materially different. Using this method the consolidated accounts treat all the transactions of the foreign subsidiary as if they were undertaken by the parent company.

The closing rate (net investment) method, which is the most common, uses the exchange rate ruling at the balance sheet date or an average rate for the year. If borrowings are made in a foreign currency, the reconciliation of cash movements to net debt accompanying the cash flow statement should show the effect of any exchange rate movements. If the $20 loan in the example cash flow statement is a long-term loan of 80x at an exchange rate of $1 = 4x, and at the balance sheet date the rate is

$1 = 5x$, an adjustment of $4 is necessary. The 80x loan at $1 = 5x$ is the equivalent of $16 not $20.

The treatment of exchange rate differences is complex. When looking at the cash flow statement all you need to remember is that it deals only with actual cash movements. Any exchange rate differences that have not had a cash impact during the year are ignored.

Summary

- To complete a full analysis and assessment of a company the cash flow statement must be used in conjunction with the income statement, which deals with the profit or loss made from running the business, and the balance sheet, which shows the financial position at the end of the year.
- The cash flow statement covers the same period as the income statement, setting out the changes in cash balances and borrowing that have taken place between the opening and closing balance sheets. It is extremely useful in assessing a company's liquidity, viability and financial adaptability. An increase in reported profit need not be supported by sound and positive cash flow.
- A reasonable starting point is to see if the company is showing a continuing and positive cash flow from its operations. Is there stability? Has the increase in cash flow over the previous year at least matched the rate of inflation?
- The cash flow statement shows whether a company is generating or consuming cash. Has it proved capable of producing sufficient cash from the business or has it used up all available liquid resources and had to raise additional funds?
- A change in the relationship betweeen operating cash flow (cash flow statement) and net income (income statement) can act as a warning signal. If cash flow begins to lag behind income, ask why? One explanation may be that sales revenue is being massaged. Perhaps, to generate sales, customers are being given excessively generous credit terms. Net income increases in the year but, as debtors rise, cash flow does not follow.
- Remember, at any point in the cash flow statement, a company is free to create a subtotal and to highlight the figure. This does not mean that the figure is truly indicative of performance or position. Make sure your attention is not being distracted from

more important evidence contained within the statement.

◾ If a business is absorbing large amounts of cash, this will be evident in the cash flow statement. A forecast can be made of how long the company could support the continuing cash outflow.

◾ The quality of a company's cash flow depends partly on management's competence and partly upon the nature of the business and its areas of operation. Even exceptional management may achieve only low profitability and poor cash flows in a declining business sector. Its quality must also be judged on the basis of how much cash comes from continuing operations: the more the better.

◾ Study changes in cash balances and in each element of working capital. If, for example, inventory and customer credit levels are increasing, the company may be in trouble; the inducement of extra credit is not leading to additional sales. The company may be in danger of overtrading.

◾ Where is the cash flow coming from? In most groups, individual companies and business sectors have different cash flow patterns, but there should be at least one business capable of generating positive cash flows to help finance others with negative cash flows develop and survive. Showing cash flows as part of a company's segmental reporting would be useful.

◾ Other useful indicators of company performance are whether more or less cash is being held at the end of the year than at the beginning, or whether the company's borrowings have increased or decreased during the year.

◾ The cash flow statement can show whether the company has the necessary liquid resources to pay a cash dividend and whether it is likely to generate sufficient cash to meet its obligations, including loan repayments, as they fall due.

◾ The current year's cash flow statement can be used as a basis for forecasting future years' cash flow. Depreciation is simple to calculate and forecast for future years. Rates are known and assumptions about future investment in additional assets can be allowed for to provide a fairly accurate estimate for future years' depreciation charges.

◾ The profit contribution to cash flow is less easy to predict accurately. For most businesses, it is the least certain element in a cash flow forecast. However, an estimate can be made based on the trend shown for previous years.

5 Other statements

IN ADDITION TO THE INCOME STATEMENT, balance sheet and cash flow statement, the annual report contains the following.

- ◪ Statement of total recognised gains and losses
- ◪ Note of historic cost profit and losses
- ◪ A reconciliation of movements in shareholders' funds

Statement of total recognised gains and losses

Financial reporting is concerned with all profits and losses that have taken place or been realised during the financial period. The prudence requirement in annual report presentation suggests that some changes in the value of assets representing potential profit or loss although not realised should be recognised, so that a fair representation of a company's performance and position can be presented.

Shareholders would lack information if profits or losses were taken directly to the reserves in the balance sheet rather than through the income statement. If a company could choose either to charge an expense on the face of income statement or deduct it from reserves in the balance sheet, and hide the fact in small print notes at the back of the annuual report, creativity would rule. FRS 3 "Reporting financial performance", issued in 1992, clarified the presentation of the income statement. It added the statement of total recognised gains and losses (STRGL) to the set of company accounts. The STRGL is intended to provide complete information concerning the impact of the company's operating activities on shareholders' funds as distinct from those of capital transactions – these being shown in the reconciliation of movements in shareholders' funds (see below).

All gains and losses for the year, including those dealt with in the income statement, are disclosed in the STRGL. It is probable that the STRGL will soon be incorporated into the income statement rather than remain a separate item in the annual report.

The STRGL starts with the after-tax profit attributable to shareholders (profit for the financial year), and adjustments are made for unrealised gains or losses that have not been taken into account in arriving at the profit for the year shown in the income statement. It ends with the total recognised gains or losses relating to the year.

It is not unusual for an asset to increase or decrease in value during the year. Details of this, if material, should be included in the annual report. The asset should be revalued in the light of current knowledge (FRS 15, IAS 16) and the changes shown as an unrealised surplus or deficit on revaluation in the STRGL. Another item that is often found in the STRGL is the figure for exchange differences on foreign currency translation.

The STRGL shows all the gains and losses recognised in the financial period. When the asset is disposed of the profit or loss is calculated as the difference between the sale price and the revalued figure, which forms part of the balance sheet value of fixed assets, not the original balance sheet value. This calculation provides the figure for profit or loss that appears in the income statement in the year of disposal.

Note of historic cost profit and losses

UK companies are allowed to revalue fixed assets, but in other countries such as the United States this is not possible. If companies are allowed selectively to adjust historic cost profit by revaluing all or part of their assets, it can be difficult to compare their performance. It can be argued that profit based on historic cost offers the best foundation for effective comparison of one company with another.

In the UK, if a company revalues any assets or otherwise modifies their traditional historic cost in the balance sheet, a note providing details of what the traditional historic-cost based profit or loss for the year would have been is included in the annual report. The main difference between the profit or loss based on historic cost and that shown in the income statement stems from adjustments to the depreciation charge.

The note starts with the profit on ordinary activities before tax appearing in the income statement and makes an adjustment for the difference between the historic cost depreciation charge and the actual depreciation charged in the income statement. It ends with the historic cost profit on ordinary activities before tax.

This is intended to help compare performance among companies where some may and some may not have revalued their assets. It also allows the profit or loss on the sale of assets to be judged on the basis of their original cost rather than on any revaluation figure produced by the company.

Reconciliation of movements in shareholders' funds

All changes in shareholders' funds that have taken place during the year are shown in this reconciliation, which explains the changes between the opening and closing balance sheets. Changes in shareholders' funds may arise from:

- profit or loss for the year;
- recognised gains or losses;
- dividends paid;
- share issue or redemption;
- goodwill.

The reconciliation starts with the shareholders' funds at the beginning of the financial year. To this is added the after-tax profit attributable to shareholders (profit for the financial year). Dividends paid to shareholders are deducted, and other adjustments are made for items such as goodwill or a share issue, to produce the figure for shareholders' funds at the end of the year as shown in the balance sheet.

Interim reports and preliminary announcements

The annual report is not the only financial statement available to assist in the analysis of a company's performance and position. Listed companies are required to publish interim reports – six monthly in the UK, quarterly in the United States. An interim report, published within 90 days of the period end, is intended to bridge the gap between annual reports and to keep shareholders up-to-date. It can be a useful aid in trend analysis.

The interim report contains a management commentary similar to that of the operating and financial review (OFR), explaining experience since the last published report and perhaps offering some indication as to the likely future prospects. This is linked to a summarised income statement (including earnings per share and segmental details), balance sheet and cash flow statement.

The stock exchange expects companies to make a preliminary announcement of annual results and dividends within 120 days of the financial year-end, with most companies complying within 90 days. The preliminary announcement contains similar information to that of the interim report, and, ideally, there should be some linkage to the final quarter or second half of the year. It acts as a quick overview of the annual report and normally forms the basis for media comment on the company's performance.

Access to the preliminary announcement was a major advantage for analysts as it was not sent to shareholders. The internet now makes it possible for anyone to have almost as speedy access to this information as the professionals by using a company's website.

2
ASSESSING THE FACTS

6 Guidelines for financial analysis

THIS CHAPTER GIVES SOME GENERAL GUIDELINES on the calculation and interpretation of the ratios covered later. Perhaps the most
important rule to remember is to keep it simple.

Comparability and consistency

The figures used in analysis of a company or for the comparison of a
number of companies must as far as possible be truly comparable. In
calculating rates of return there is no point taking the pre-tax profit of
one company and comparing it with the post-tax profit of another. A
company capitalising interest may appear to have a better profit
performance than one that does not do so. If, rather than the interest
figure appearing in the income statement, the total interest payment for
the year is used for both companies, there may be no difference in their
profitability.

It is essential to make sure that consistent figures are used in the ratios
being developed. Companies may change the ways in which they present their financial data and define individual items in the financial
statements. Always check that the analysis has been adjusted to take
account of such changes; the notes to the financial statements should
give details of these as well as other crucial matters.

Never rely on a single ratio

It is inadvisable to judge a company on the basis of a single ratio. Either
the previous year's ratio should be calculated to gain an impression of
how what is being considered is changing and what is the trend, or the
ratio of one company should be compared with that of companies operating in the same business or of a comparable size. The tables of ratios
in Part 3 offer some benchmarks for the sector and country against
which individual companies may be assessed.

The more years the better

Do not judge a company on the basis of a single year's figures. Three
or, ideally, five years' figures should be analysed in order to get a
clear view of the consistency of a company's performance and to

highlight any movements in the ratios that require explanation or investigation.

It does not require a great intellect to use creative accounting methods to produce a one-off high level of profitability for a company. The real art is in maintaining such an illusion. Once accounts are being manipulated a company is walking a tightrope, and each year more oscillations are generated guaranteeing that at some time in the near future it is going to cry for help or fall off.

Year ends

One problem in comparing companies is that they are unlikely to have the same financial year end. In most countries there are three popular dates: March/April, September/October and December/January. A company's choice of year end depends on such things as the date it was founded, fiscal legislation, or the nature of its business. Companies involved in seasonal businesses are unlikely to want to prepare year-end accounts at the peak of their trading cycle, so few retailers have December 31st as their financial year end.

Differences in year ends and the timing of the publication of results often create problems in producing tables for cross-country and cross-company comparison. The best that can normally be done is to bring together companies reporting within the 12-month period, although this may span two calendar years. This may result in some distortions because of seasonality, but at least it provides an acceptable common time base.

How many weeks in the year?

Care should also taken to make sure that the income statement is for a standard 52-week year. A company may have adjusted its year end and so have more or less than 12 months' trading contained in the accounts. For example, a change may follow a merger or acquisition where one company moves to bring its year end into line with the other. In such cases, the data used in the analysis can be adjusted back to 52 weeks or 12 months by dividing the data by the actual number of weeks or months covered in the income statement and then multiplying by either 52 or 12. However, bear in mind that such an adjustment may result in a distortion.

Average, median or mode?

It is often advisable to top and tail league tables of companies operating in a selected sector to provide some guidelines on average performance or position. Extremes of performance or position, although of considerable importance to the companies concerned, are best ignored when trying to determine averages or standards for a set of companies or a business sector. Otherwise an extreme case can distort any average being calculated.

In many cases, it is preferable to use the median rather than the average as the benchmark. If ten companies are being compared and the indicator being used gives a figure of 10 for nine companies and 100 for one company, the average (190/10) is 19. This results in nine out of the ten companies being below average.

A better guide may be the median or the middle or mid-point figure in a table showing the ranking of companies or ratios. Where there are an odd number of items the median is the middle figure. In the example below the median of the first line is 7.

2	5	7	9	12
	6	8	10	11

The median can be calculated from the formula $(n + 1) \div 2$, where n is the number of items in the group. With 5 items this provides $(5 + 1) \div 2 = 3$, the third item in the list. With an even number of items the formula identifies the position of the median between the two mid-point figures $(4 + 1) \div 2 = 2.5$. The median is halfway between 8 and 10 = 9.

An alternative measure is to take the mode, that is, the figure that occurs most often in the table. The mode is best identified by eye rather than by calculation, and of course it is possible for a table to be bimodal (with two modes).

Investigate variations

When the ratios of a company cause it to stand out among others in the same sector it is important to try to discover the reasons for the variation. It may be that the company is unique and setting standards of performance or financial structure for the rest of the sector. However, care should be taken that its uniqueness is not merely the result of the application of accounting practices different from those of other companies.

Similarly, any sudden and dramatic shift in a company's performance or position should be investigated. A significant improvement in reported profit may be the result of a one-off sale of an asset or changes in the accounting treatment of items in the financial statements.

In financial analysis it is safest and usually most productive not to give the benefit of the doubt. When a company displays markedly different characteristics from others in the same sector, it is best to assume that this is not a positive signal until further investigation proves otherwise.

Graphs and charts

For most people a graph offers the best means of displaying a series of financial data and information. Setting out five years' turnover and profit or profit margin and the return on total assets in a graph provides an ideal way of identifying trends and annual movement and is certainly more effective than a table packed with figures containing the same data. Standard software packages make it easy to turn a set of figures into a graph, bar chart or pie chart.

Check the integrity

Companies have been making increasing use of graphic displays in corporate reports. But what kind of picture is being presented? It is a simple matter to disguise or distort a trend in, for example, profit growth by picking a scale for a graph that delivers the message you want to give. The two bar charts in Figure 6.1 display exactly the same annual profits. If you take the trouble to measure the bars with a ruler, both charts show the final year profit is four times that of the first year. However, for most people the one on the right appears to indicate the better performance.

Never rely on someone else's analysis

It is safest never to rely entirely on someone else's analysis, particularly if this is offered by the company being studied. Always base the company assessment and calculations on the original financial data available in the financial statements.

Percentage rules

A useful aid to interpreting a financial statement is to express the figures in percentage terms, particularly when studying one company's data for a number of years or data for several companies. Percentages simplify things wonderfully, reducing figures that may be presented in billions, millions or thousands to a single comparable measure. Furthermore, they make it easier to spot trends or differences, as the following example of a cash flow statement shows.

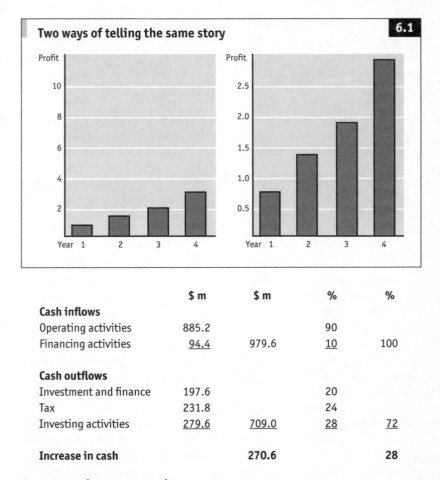

	$ m	$ m	%	%
Cash inflows				
Operating activities	885.2		90	
Financing activities	94.4	979.6	10	100
Cash outflows				
Investment and finance	197.6		20	
Tax	231.8		24	
Investing activities	279.6	709.0	28	72
Increase in cash		270.6		28

Common size presentation

Similarly, a percentage-like presentation approach, known as common size presentation, makes it easier to analyse and compare the contribution each source of finance makes towards the financing of the total assets employed by companies. Often it is useful to present all the important items in an income statement as percentages of sales revenue. An added advantage to the application of common size presentation is that where companies are reporting in different currencies all currency differences are automatically removed.

If total assets are expressed as 100, sources of finance can be shown in relation to this, as the following example shows.

($)	Year 1	Year 2	Year 3
Fixed assets	1,515	1,580	1,729
Current assets	1,573	1,704	1,692
Total assets	3,088	3,284	3,421
Capital and reserves	926	1,314	1,711
Long-term loans	618	656	343
Current liabilities	1,544	1,314	1,367
Total liabilities	3,088	3,284	3,421

The process is simple. Each source of finance is divided by total assets and multiplied by 100. For example, in year 3, capital and reserves of $1,711 divided by total assets of $3,421 and multiplied by 100 gives 50%. The balance sheets can now be represented as follows.

(%)	Year 1	Year 2	Year 3
Capital and reserves	30	40	50
Long-term borrowing	20	20	10
Current liabilities	50	40	40
Total assets	100	100	100

The three sources of finance can be clearly identified, and it is much easier to identify changes and trends from this presentation than from the three years' balance sheets.

Any changes in gearing can quickly be spotted when the common size presentation is used and debt/equity ratios can easily be calculated. This offers an alternative means of both calculating and interpreting gearing. From the first year's balance sheet, total debt of $2,162 divided by shareholders' funds of $926 gives a debt/equity ratio of 2.3:1. The same calculation can be completed directly from the common size presentation. In year 1, total debt (70) divided by shareholders' funds (30) produces the ratio 2.3:1 or 233%. By year 3 this can be seen to have reduced to 1:1 or 100%. The long-term debt ratio could be calculated in the same way, with long-term debt (20) divided by long-term debt and equity (20+30) giving a ratio of 0.4:1 or 40% in year 1 moving to 0.33:1 or 33% in year 3.

This presentation format can be used to explain how one side of the balance sheet, total assets, is being financed. For every $1 of assets employed in year 1 shareholders contributed 30¢, and by year 3 this had become 50¢. What remains of each $1 has been provided from external sources, debt and current liabilities; in year 1 this was 70¢ and year 3 it was 50¢.

($m)	—Turnover—		—Op. profit—		—Net assets—	
	Year 1	Year 2	Year 1	Year 2	Year 1	Year 2
Class of business						
Consumer goods	956	998	65	71	408	421
Office equipment	488	532	15	22	188	201
Medical equipment	694	725	72	84	484	526
Electronic systems	355	501	−6	9	125	201
	2,493	**2,756**	**146**	**186**	**1,205**	**1,349**
Geographic analysis by location						
UK	860	877	61	63	451	434
Rest of Europe	485	498	32	34	274	255
North America	484	508	39	42	185	287
South America	307	486	−6	19	159	196
Asia/Australasia	259	333	19	26	136	177
Others	98	54	1	2	0	0
	2,493	**2,756**	**146**	**186**	**1,250**	**1,349**

(%)	—Turnover—		—Op. profit—		—Net assets—	
	Year 1	Year 2	Year 1	Year 2	Year 1	Year 2
Class of business						
Consumer goods	38	36	44	38	34	31
Office equipment	20	19	10	12	16	15
Medical equipment	28	26	49	45	40	39
Electronic systems	14	18	−4	5	10	15
	100	**100**	**100**	**100**	**100**	**100**
Geographic analysis by location						
UK	34	32	42	34	37	32
Rest of Europe	19	18	22	18	23	19
North America	19	18	27	23	15	21
South America	12	18	−4	10	13	14
Asia/Australasia	10	12	13	14	11	13
Others	4	2	1	1	0	0
	100	**100**	**100**	**100**	**100**	**100**

This approach can also be used to analyse a five-year record, segmental report or one of a company's financial statements, as in the example.

Index numbers

The use of index numbers is another way of shedding light on the performance of a company. The result – a trend statement – offers a more reliable means of identifying trends in performance or position than a common size statement, as the following example of a company's five-year financial record shows.

($)	Year 1	Year 2	Year 3	Year 4	Year 5
Turnover	5,200	5,500	6,100	6,300	6,600
Pre-tax profit	350	400	475	490	520

If the figure for each year is divided by that of the base year and the result multiplied by 100, a series of index numbers is produced. The year 2 turnover ($5,500) divided by that of year 1 ($5,200) and multiplied by 100 gives 106.

	Year 1	Year 2	Year 3	Year 4	Year 5
Turnover	100	106	117	121	127
Pre-tax profit	100	114	136	140	149

In interpreting index numbers it must be remembered that they relate directly to the first year. Turnover in year 2 increased by $300 ($5,500 – 5,200), which was a 6% increase and was reflected in the index number movement from 100 to 106. However, it is incorrect to assume that the turnover increase in year 5 was also 6% (127 – 121). Turnover in year 5 increased by $300, which was less than a 5% increase on the $6,300 of year 4. The turnover in year 5 represents a 27% increase on that in year 1. Of course, if year 2 was used as the base (100) a different picture would be presented.

Growth rates and trends

Assessing the rate at which change is occurring can be useful in financial analysis. To measure the percentage change from one year to the next the calculation is:

$$100 \times [(\text{Year 2} - \text{Year 1}) \div \text{Year 1}]$$

Turnover and profit growth for the second and the last year are as follows.

	Year 1 − Year 2	Year 4 − Year 5
Turnover	$(5,500 - 5,200) \div 5,200 = 5.8\%$	$(6,600 - 6,300) \div 6,300 = 4.8\%$
Pre-tax profit	$(400 - 350) \div 350 = 14.3\%$	$(520 - 490) \div 490 = 6.1\%$

The company has an apparently steady growth in turnover. Where there is a significant level of inflation, growth patterns can be distorted. To overcome this problem an appropriate measure of inflation, such as the retail price index, can be used to adjust turnover. To express turnover for any year in year 5 dollars, that year's turnover is multiplied by the year 5 index divided by that year's index. For example, to express year 1 turnover in year 5 dollars the calculation is:

$$\$5,200 \times (140 \div 100) = \$5,200 \times 1.4 = \$7,280$$

The adjusted figures provide a better basis for interpreting the real underlying growth patterns. Based on the adjusted figures for the five-year period, profit increased by 6% and turnover decreased by 9%.

	Year 1	Year 2	Year 3	Year 4	Year 5
Turnover ($)	5,200	5,500	6,100	6,300	6,600
Inflation index	100	110	120	130	140
Adjusted turnover ($)	7,280	7,000	7,117	6,785	6,600

Compound growth rates

To assess the growth trend over a number of years the compound growth rate can be calculated. There are statistical formulas for calculating it, but as in most cases all that is required is a broad indicator of the rate, the table on the next page can be used for most situations.

From the five-year financial record table appearing in an annual report it is possible to calculate growth over four years. If using the figures in the example above, the final year figure is divided by that of the first year, and the resultant factor can be read from the table to discover the approximate compound growth rate over the four-year period:

Turnover $6,600 \div \$5,200 = 1.27$ Pre-tax profit $520 \div \$350 = 1.49$

Looking at the four-year column in the table, the closest figure to 1.27 is 6% and to 1.49 is 10%. Thus over the period turnover has grown at the rate of just over 6% per year and pre-tax profit at just over 10% per year.

	2 years	3 years	4 years
1%	1.02	1.03	1.04
2%	1.04	1.06	1.08
3%	1.06	1.09	1.13
4%	1.08	1.12	1.17
5%	1.11	1.16	1.22
6%	1.12	1.19	1.26
8%	1.17	1.26	1.36
10%	1.21	1.33	1.46
12%	1.25	1.40	1.57
14%	1.30	1.48	1.69
16%	1.35	1.56	1.81
18%	1.39	1.64	1.94
20%	1.44	1.73	2.07
25%	1.56	1.95	2.44
30%	1.69	2.20	2.86
40%	1.96	2.74	3.82
50%	2.25	3.37	5.06
60%	2.56	4.10	6.55
70%	2.89	4.91	8.35
80%	3.24	5.83	10.00
90%	3.61	6.86	13.00
100%	4.00	8.00	16.00

If the growth for the last three years is required, the calculations would be $6,600 ÷ $5,500 = 1.2 and $520 ÷ $400 = 1.3. Moving down the three-year column, this indicates a turnover growth of just over 6% and profit growth of just under 10% over the last three years.

It should be noted that a compound growth rate is based only on the first and last years. The company providing the five-year record could have made a $600 profit or loss in year 3 and the compound growth rate would not be affected.

Foreign currencies

Analysing a number of companies based in the same country avoids any problems associated with currency. Making an international comparison is inevitably more difficult. There is little point in trying to compare a US company's $96,000 profit per employee with a French company's €90,000 and a UK company's £60,000. The best way to deal with this problem is to translate all the figures involved into one currency. However, there are potential difficulties in doing this, the most obvious being which exchange rate to use. Two alternatives are the exchange rate ruling at the balance sheet date of each company or the average exchange rate for the year. The simplest method, although by no means the most accurate or representative, is to take all the currencies involved and use the exchange rates of the day the analysis is being completed to translate the figures into a single currency base.

If the three example companies are being compared from a UK base, the figures can be adjusted to show the ratio in sterling equivalents.

	Rate	£
$96,000	1.6	60,000
€90,000	1.5	60,000
£60,000	1.0	60,000

The three companies can now be directly compared in a currency that the person preparing the analysis is used to working with. Thus international comparisons can be made of the size, efficiency and performance of companies. However, care must be taken in adopting this approach, particularly when the analysis is looking back over a number of years. The revaluation of one country's currency against those of others would almost certainly result in a dramatic shift in the translated values for any ratios being used in the year in which this took place.

Using databases

If a commercial database is available as the source of company data and information, this will offer not only ease of access to the financial statements but also the advantage that each one is set out in a standard format. This can be particularly attractive when companies operating in several countries are being compared. The figures will be in a consistent form and the accompanying text translated into a common language, considerably reducing the stress of analysis. Note, however, that commercial databases take the figures provided by companies in their financial statements at face value when producing ratios. If you suspect creative accounting has been employed, you will need to look at the information in the annual report. Datastream is a financial database that is widely available and useful, but not necessarily the most immediately user-friendly.

It should be accepted that databases occasionally change the format of their financial data presentation. Adding or removing a line in the income statement or balance sheet can throw out any spreadsheet calculations if the raw data are imported directly into the spreadsheet. Always check to ensure that the data input is consistent before completing or using any form of analysis. (See Chapter 11.)

7 Measuring profitability

THIS CHAPTER IS CONCERNED with the analysis of company profitability. It starts by concentrating on the data contained within the income statement profit and loss account and then broadens out to include the balance sheet and other sources of financial data and relevant information.

What is profit?

One definition of profit is that it represents the surplus of income over expenditure. In accounting, where income is greater than expenditure a profit is produced, and where expenditure is greater than income a loss results. Hence the operating statement dealing with revenue and expenditure is termed the profit and loss account in the UK and the income statement in most other countries.

Defining and measuring profit provides one of several areas of argument between accountants and economists. Economists direct their attention to what may happen in the future – the present value of future income. Accountants are more concerned with what has happened in the past – revenue less expenses. An economist may prove to be accurate in forecasting *what* will actually happen but is less likely to be able to state precisely *when* it will happen. An accountant, however, might argue that in most cases an economist only has to define profit whereas an accountant actually has to quantify it each year as a single figure in a set of accounts.

Different perspectives

The term profit may mean different things, not only to economists and accountants but also to a company's various interest groups, each of which view the profit a company makes from a different perspective.

◗ **Shareholders** may be most concerned about the ability of a company to maintain or improve the value of their investment and future income stream. They look to the company to generate sufficient profit to provide for dividend payments and an increase in the market value of the shares they own. In most annual reports the company's shareholders are provided with a detailed statement of the changes that have taken place during the year in their investment in the company (see Chapter 5).

■ **Lenders** of money may be expected to be most interested in evidence to support the company's ability to continue to pay the interest on borrowed funds as this falls due.

■ **Customers** may be concerned to assess the levels of profit being made, particularly if there is regulation of the business sector intended to offer some level of customer protection. Now that increasing emphasis is put on high standards of customer service and satisfaction, there is little advantage in making excessive short-term profits at the long-term expense of the customer.

■ **Competitors** are most interested in comparing their own performance and efficiency with that of other companies operating in the same business sector.

■ **Management and other employees** are usually most interested in the profit being generated from their section of the business and in assessing their employment prospects. Senior executives are expected to focus on the overall levels of profitability being provided by the company's main operating units, its strategic business units (SBUs). Their interest should be focused on the future potential rather than the historic performance of the company.

■ **Business and investment analysts** may be expected by their clients or employers to provide an indication of whether a particular company's shares are worth holding or buying for future gain, or are best sold immediately. They will study the current year's profit and compare it with previous years and that of other companies, and set this against their assessment for the future of the business sector to forecast profit trends.

The fundamentals of capital maintenance

Profit can be defined as the difference between the capital shown in the balance sheet at the start and that shown at the end of an accounting period. If this profit were distributed to shareholders as dividend, the financial capital of the company would be unchanged (financial capital maintenance). All companies are required to maintain their financial capital. It is also reasonable to expect a company to maintain its ability to produce the goods or services upon which its business depends by providing for necessary fixed asset replacement (operating capital maintenance).

Economists and accountants agree that in arriving at a figure for profit, account must be taken of the assets being used or capital employed by the company to generate that profit. Before a profit can be declared, the "using up" of part of the assets or capital employed in the business must be charged as part of the overall costs and expenses for the year. This, as discussed in Chapter 3, is fundamental to accounting theory and company law, and is normally achieved through the charging of depreciation. It can be seen as the setting aside of funds for the eventual replacement of the company's assets when this becomes necessary.

If a company were not to comply with the capital maintenance requirement and paid tax to the government on, and dividends to its shareholders out of, the amount it had not charged as depreciation, it would not be retaining sufficient funds to maintain the asset base of its operations. This would be reflected on the other side of the balance sheet in a reduction in the shareholders' stake in the business. As a result, the capital employed and potentially the ability to meet the liabilities of creditors and those lending money to the company would be eroded.

In short, a company that fails to make consistent and reasonable or prudent provision each year for depreciation will overstate its real profitability and store up trouble for the future. It is therefore important to ensure that not only the requirement of capital maintenance but also all the basic principles of income statement preparation (see Chapter 3) are followed by a company in arriving at its stated profit.

Starting considerations

The starting point for analysing and assessing profitability is most likely to be the annual report, which provides on a regular basis data on a company's activities. The income statement sets out the company's income and expenditure. The result will be a profit where total income is greater than total expenditure and a loss where the reverse is the case.

$$Profit = total\ income - total\ cost$$

This equation appears to offer a simple definition of profit. But how is cost calculated? It is worth remembering the story of the executive who, exasperated at never receiving a clear answer to any question he asked his accountant, demanded, "What is 1 plus 1?". The accountant smiled and replied, "Are you buying or selling?" Because it is rarely possible to provide a clear and unambiguous definition of the cost of any product or service, it is difficult to define profit and therefore to interpret the figure a company declares as its profit.

For the purposes of the ratios and analysis covered in this chapter, it is assumed that the income or sales revenue figures used exclude all sales taxes or equivalents. In the UK it is normal in the profit and loss account to give sales revenue exclusive or net of value-added tax (VAT).

Sales revenue during the year is often divided into income generated from continuing and from discontinued business operations. This division continues in the statement of profit for the year. The intention is to show consistently each year where the company has been generating income and profit, and to make it easy to see how much the businesses that will contribute subsequent profits (or losses) have contributed in the year being reported. A company that has sold a profit source and not reinvested in another one will not only report the monies received from the sale as part of its overall profit but also be giving up the income that source would have contributed to future profits.

Measuring sticks

It is possible to prepare a table listing, in order of the monetary value of their profit for the year, companies operating within a business sector. This list, with the largest numerical profit at the top and the smallest at the bottom, would tell you which of the chosen companies was making the largest profit. It might also be useful in revealing the total profit made by the selected companies. However, such a list would not necessarily tell you which of the companies was the most profitable. To discover this, a number of ratios can help.

Profit margin ratios

In the income statement, the profit margin can be used to begin the analysis of a company's profitability. It is calculated by dividing profit by sales revenue and expressing the result as a percentage.

$$\% \text{ profit margin} = 100 \times (\text{profit} \div \text{sales revenue})$$

Gross profit margin

Working down the income statement, the first profit normally displayed is the gross profit, which is produced by deducting the cost of sales from sales revenue for the year. It is normally safe to assume that the cost of sales includes all the direct materials and services provided by suppliers, direct employee remuneration and all direct overheads. However, it is essential to read the notes providing additional details of the figures appearing in the income statement.

Unfortunately there is, as yet, little real consistency in how different companies present crucial information. For example, some companies deduct the remuneration of all shop-floor employees in arriving at gross profit and some do not. When several companies are being analysed, it will probably be necessary to make a number of adjustments to the figures provided in the accounts before it is possible to be confident that profitability ratios are truly comparable.

$$\% \text{ gross profit margin} = 100 \times (\text{gross profit} \div \text{sales revenue})$$

The gross profit margin, often simply referred to as the gross margin, offers a reasonable indication of the basic profitability of a business and is useful when comparing the performance of companies operating within the same sector. When one company has a totally different level of gross margin, it is worth trying to discover why.

Movements in the level of profit margins may be caused by many factors. For example, gross margin is influenced by changes in the mix of products or services being marketed by a company and is directly affected by price increases or decreases. Similarly, changes in production efficiency or materials purchasing affect the cost of sales, which in turn have an impact on gross margin. The potential for incorrect inventory valuation to distort profit, and thereby gross margin, was discussed in Chapter 2.

Operating profit margin

Operating profit usually follows gross profit in the income statement. It normally allows for all of a company's expenses of distribution, administration, research and development and general overheads.

Care must be taken to ensure there is a consistent treatment of any turnover and profit relating to joint ventures and associates. If the total turnover figure is being used, then the total operating profit – including the share of joint ventures' and associates' profit – should be matched with this.

The operating profit margin offers an assessment of the profitability of a company after taking into account all the normal costs of producing and supplying goods or services and the income from selling them, but excluding financing costs, such as interest payments on bank loans, or investment income, such as interest earned on bank deposits.

% operating margin = 100 × (operating profit ÷ sales revenue)

If a company has a consistent level of gross margin but a declining operating profit margin, it is worth investigating why. One explanation could be efficient purchasing and basic cost control but poor control of general overheads, which are increasing without any compensating improvement in sales revenue.

At this stage you should turn to the notes that accompany the figures for sales revenue and operating profit in the income statement. As described in Chapter 3, these notes offer a valuable source of information on exactly where a company is generating revenue and, linked to this, what level of profit is being made in each business sector and geographic area of operation.

Because comparative figures are given for the previous year in the notes, it is possible to identify movements not only within a sector but also among the various geographic areas where a company has an interest. With some additional historic data any significant trends can be identified. Often it is possible to make comparisons with other companies operating in the same sector and location.

Pre-tax profit margin

Moving down the income statement, the next step is to deduct the remaining expenses and charges from operating profit to produce the pre-tax profit (PTP) for the year. When the pre-tax profit margin is calculated, this shows the level of profitability of a company after all operating costs and expenses except tax and dividends to shareholders have been allowed for.

% pre-tax profit margin = 100 × (pre-tax profit ÷ sales revenue)

A company maintaining a stable operating profit margin but a declining pre-tax profit margin may have raised finance for investment upon which it pays interest, but the investment has yet to be translated into either reduced costs or increased revenue. The interest charge is deducted in arriving at the pre-tax profit for the year, but no income has yet been generated from the investment of the finance raised.

After-tax profit and retained profit margins

It is possible to calculate both the after-tax profit margin and the retained profit margin from the income statement, but such ratios do not offer any significant additional help in the overall appreciation of a company's profitability.

The efficiency ratios

The next step in analysing a company's profitability is to combine information from the income statement and the balance sheet in ways that enable you to measure how efficiently a company is using its assets or capital employed.

($)	A	B	C
Revenue	100	100	100
Profit	20	20	27
Assets	100	125	150

For example, companies A and B have a 20% profit margin and C has a 27% profit margin. On the basis of this measure, C appears to be the most profitable company and it is impossible to distinguish between A and B. The following ratios can be used as part of a more detailed analysis.

Rate of return on assets or capital employed

The overall rate of return on capital or assets can be calculated by dividing profit, taken from the income statement, by assets or capital employed, as shown in the balance sheet, and expressing the result as a percentage.

$$\text{\% rate of return on assets} = 100 \times (\text{profit} \div \text{assets})$$

$$\text{\% rate of return on capital} = 100 \times (\text{profit} \div \text{capital})$$

If this ratio is produced for the three companies their rates of return on assets are seen to be:

A	B	C
20%	16%	18%

Company C has the highest profit margin (27%), but it has a greater investment in assets than A or B. Company A has the same profit margin (20%) as B, but it has a lower asset base and so shows a higher rate of return. Linking the assets employed in the business to the profit being generated by them offers a more realistic measure of profitability than the use of profit margin ratios alone. Company A with a 20% return on assets is now identified as the most profitable of the three.

Which profit? What assets?

When dealing with profitability ratios it is important to recognise that there is no single method of calculating rates of return and that the same term may be used to refer to quite different things. A rate of return on assets (ROA) may have been produced using the gross, operating, pre-tax or after-tax profit. It is not usual to use gross profit in a rate of return measure, but there is no reason why this should not be done for a number of companies to provide the basis for performance comparisons and the analysis of a business sector.

Which profit measure to use?

As with any art, financial analysis is subject to fad and fashion. A ratio is adopted, rises in repute, declines and is replaced. One measure of profit currently enjoying favour is that of earnings before interest, taxation, depreciation and amortisation (EBITDA). It is argued that this measure strips out all the incidentals to highlight the "real" profitability of a business and is not biased by capital structure, tax systems or depreciation policies. It can be used to produce an EBITDA earnings per share figure (see pages 141–2).

The holy grail of financial analysis is the discovery of a single fool-proof measure of company performance. EBITDA can be useful as part of a detailed analysis of a company, but there are flaws in its claimed perfection. EBITDA ignores the cost of fixed assets employed in a business, yet surely these are as much an operating cost as anything else. As a measure of profitability it is a long way from the bottom line of the income statement, and so ignores not only depreciation but also interest and tax. A company delivering an after-tax loss from a huge investment in fixed assets financed by equally substantial borrowings could look quite healthy on an EBITDA basis.

Whichever profit is selected, the end result will be the return on assets, but each of the possible profits will produce a different level of return. For each ratio the denominator has remained constant but a different numerator has been used. Before making use of a pre-calculated rate of return figure always check which profit has been used to produce the ratio.

Similar problems can arise in selecting the denominator for the ROA ratio. This could equally well be the total, operating or net assets employed. Whichever figures are used, the end ratio is correctly described as a ROA for the company in question. If the three companies in the example above had used different definitions of profit and of assets, it would not be of any practical benefit to try to draw any conclusions by comparing their rates of return. For this reason, rate of return ratios given in annual reports or by analysts should not be taken at their face value.

In short, in calculating comparative rates of return it is essential that there is consistency in both the numerator and the denominator in the equation. In other words, you should ensure that each company's ROA is calculated in the same way.

Averaging assets

As soon as a figure for assets or capital is taken from the balance sheet for use in the development of a performance measure there is a problem. The balance sheet provides the financial picture of a company on the final day of its financial year. The income statement is a statement of the company's ability to generate revenue and profit throughout the financial year. The income statement is dynamic, covering the whole year; the balance sheet is static, showing the position only at the end of the year. The year-end balance sheet incorporates the retained profit appearing at the foot of the current year's income statement. Any finance raised during the year for investment in operating assets, even in the last few days of the year, appears in the balance sheet as a source of finance and an asset. For the purposes of rate of return ratios, there is a mismatch between the income statement and the balance sheet.

To overcome this, an average figure for assets or capital is often used in calculating rates of return. This clearly should produce a more accurate ratio, but, for most purposes, it is probably not worth the time and effort involved. Moreover, it may be difficult to get the necessary data for earlier years.

One instance where more detailed analysis is required, with perhaps an average asset or capital figure or other appropriate adjustment, is when a company has experienced major changes during the year. For example, it may have raised capital or made a major acquisition or disposal.

Rate of return on total assets

A useful ratio in analysing company profitability is the rate of return on total assets (ROTA). Total assets, as set out in the balance sheet, represent the total amount of physical and financial resources a company had available for use during the year to generate the profit shown in the income statement. To arrive at the figure for total assets in the UK, it is necessary to add together fixed and current assets; in most other countries total assets is highlighted in the balance sheet.

Irrespective of the way in which assets are financed (by using shareholders' funds, debt or short-term borrowing), or of how the total capital and debt is employed (in fixed assets, investments, intangibles or current assets), total assets represents the total resources available to a company to undertake its business. It is therefore appropriate to look at a company's ability to generate a profit on the basis of the total assets it has employed. Using an alternative to total assets as the denominator can make true comparisons difficult, as companies use different means of financing their business.

% return on total assets = 100 × (pre-interest and tax profit ÷ total assets)

When total assets is used, the numerator should be the pre-interest and tax profit (PITP) or earnings before interest and tax (EBIT). This is to find the true return on assets before the cost of financing through interest payments on borrowings used to finance any part of those assets is deducted. By the same logic, interest or income received from financial investments, which form a part of total assets, is included in this profit figure.

Return on total tangible assets

As intangible assets are often considered of less certain value than tangible assets, is possible to argue that only the tangible assets employed in a company should be taken into account when measuring its rate of return. To arrive at a figure for tangible assets that can be used to determine the return on total tangible assets (ROTTA), deduct the intangibles set out in the fixed asset section of the balance sheet from total assets.

Return on (net) operating assets

To make further practical use of the segment details provided in the annual report, it is worth calculating the rate of return on operating assets (ROOA) or the return on net operating assets (RONOA). The figure for operating profit can be taken straight from the profit and loss account or, for each business sector, from the segment notes. It represents the profit made by the company after allowing for all normal business costs and expenses but before any interest, tax or unusual, exceptional and extraordinary items.

Net operating assets

Net operating assets are the assets employed to support the running of a business, assuming that short-term creditors are used to finance short-term assets.

In the UK, most companies' balance sheets contain a separately identified figure for total assets less current liabilities (see Chapter 2). This approach assumes that current liabilities have been used to finance current assets and the net assets (referred to as net current assets) when added to fixed assets provide an indication of the total long-term capital and debt invested in the business. This figure can be used as the denominator for measuring the return on net operating assets.

Net operating assets = operating fixed assets + net current operating assets

Operating fixed assets

Within the fixed asset section of the balance sheet the tangible fixed assets are shown at their net book value after provision for depreciation; intangibles and investments are also separately valued and displayed. Intangible assets are included in this definition of operating fixed assets, but, because operating profit is before any interest or other non-operational income or expenditure, investments within the fixed asset heading should in theory be deducted if they represent a significant proportion of a company's asset base. In practice, making such adjustments normally introduces as many problems as it solves. When in doubt keep the analysis simple and consistent.

Net current operating assets

In arriving at the figure for net current operating assets, cash and short-term investment within current assets are excluded as are any short-term borrowings or debt repayments appearing within current liabilities. These items are financial rather than operating assets. The intention is to show the profitability of running the business excluding any financial asset or liability and allied income or expense.

NOA equals NOCE

The net operating assets (NOA) equal the net operating capital employed (NOCE) of a company.

Operating fixed assets	Shareholders' capital and reserves
Inventory + debtors	Long-term borrowings and creditors
Less creditors	*Less* fixed asset investments
	+/- net cash balances
Net operating assets =	**Net operating capital employed**

Breaking down ROONA

If the return on operating assets is calculated using at least the two years' figures available from the annual report of a company, this may be linked with the information on operating assets set out in the segment notes quantifying the investment in each sector and geographic area. From this analysis some indication is provided of how effectively the company is using its available operating assets in each sector, and when comparison is made with other companies some benchmarks of performance can be developed.

The shareholders' return

So far the analysis of rates of return has concentrated on the operational side of a business in measuring the level of profit generated on the assets of a company. Shareholders are the principal stakeholders in a company; they own the company, and can be presumed to have invested their money with a view to receiving some benefits or returns. They want to profit from their investment.

Shareholders should use the profitability ratios described so far in this chapter to monitor a company's performance and to compare it with others in their portfolios or against business sector averages.

The after-tax profit should be used in developing measures of shareholders' return. After a company has covered all costs, expenses and tax, and provided for minority interests in the profit, what remains, often called profit attributable to shareholders, is available for dividends. The after-tax profit can be paid out in dividends to shareholders or retained to finance future growth and development.

It is possible to develop an after-tax rate of return on assets, which can be useful when considering the track record of one company but is of less value for comparing companies. As each company has its unique tax position – for example, one may own freehold property and another leasehold property, or they may be operating in different countries – it is difficult to draw any firm conclusions on performance in addition to those provided by the pre-tax profit ratios. But although after-tax profit may be of less interest as a basis for comparing companies' perform-ance, it is crucial to every company's shareholders. It represents the end result of management's activities in running the company on their behalf throughout the year.

Which figure to take from the balance sheet to represent the share-holders' stake or investment in the business is more problematic. In most balance sheets the shareholders' total funds is set out as capital and reserves. Preference shares or other non-voting capital are often found within the figure for total shareholders' funds. Strictly, these should be removed in the calculation of shareholder returns, because it is only the ordinary shareholders, the owners of the company, that are being con-sidered here, not other providers of long-term finance and capital.

The figure for shareholders' funds may have several different labels attached to it.

Net assets = total assets − (current liabilities + debt)
Capital employed = net assets
Shareholders' funds = capital employed
Shareholders' funds = capital employed = net assets

Once the shareholders' investment has been identified it is possible, using the after-tax profit, to calculate an appropriate rate of return. This rate of return may be defined as:

- return on capital (ROC)
- return on capital employed (ROCE)
- return on shareholders' funds (ROSF)
- return on equity (ROE)
- return on investment (ROI)
- return on net assets (RONA)

Earnings per share

Shareholders often make use of earnings per share (EPS) as a measure of the overall profitability of a company. EPS is to be found in the annual report either at the foot of the income statement (see Chapter 3) or in a separate note giving earnings and share price movements. As with any pre-calculated ratio appearing in an annual report, care should be taken to discover precisely how it has been derived. In most cases, it is probably worth doing the simple arithmetic yourself to ensure consistency if making comparisons with other businesses.

EPS is calculated by dividing the after-tax profit for the year, after minority interests' and any non-voting share dividends have been deducted, by the weighted average of the number of ordinary (equity) shares in issue during the year (FRS 14, IAS 33, FAS 128). The result is shown as pence or cents per share.

Earnings per share = after-tax profit ÷ number of shares in issue

EPS shows the profit a company has earned on each ordinary share or unit of common stock it has in issue after allowing for all costs, expenses, financial charges and tax.

Anti-massage measures

One problem with interpreting EPS can be in the treatment of extraordinary, exceptional, or one-off gains or losses that arise, for example, on the sale or closure of part of a business. These can result in a dramatic rise or fall in earnings per share. FRS 3, issued in 1992 to combat these problems, in effect made all costs and expenses "ordinary", and they must be deducted before arriving at the profit used in the EPS calculation. Companies are still free to focus attention on their own "'pro forma", "normalised", "adjusted" or "underlying" figure for EPS, but they must provide a reconciliation with FRS 3 earnings per share.

Recognising that there was a need for a useful and understandable EPS figure, but that "to attempt to define a single earnings figure for all purposes is bound to fail", the Institute of Investment Management and Research (IIMR) has recommended that EPS be calculated to exclude all:

- gains or losses from the termination of a business operation or the sale of a fixed asset;
- trading profits and losses including exceptional items;
- acquired and discontinued activities.

The intention is to exclude all capital items and focus on the profit generated from running the business – "headline earnings". You should always check, however, as a company can use its own definition of "headline earnings".

Long-term adjustments

The number of shares a company has in issue is set out in the notes to the accounts. For the earnings per share calculation, the weighted average number of shares in issue throughout the year is taken as the denominator. Where a company offers five-year or ten-year historic performance statistics, the necessary adjustments for changes in the number of shares in issue will have been made to allow year-on-year comparisons.

The dilution factor

Sometimes the earnings per share figure is referred to as being "diluted". This arises if a company has issued securities which have the right to convert into ordinary shares at some point in the future (see Chapter 2). The diluted EPS is calculated assuming that this conversion has taken place. The diluted earnings figure shows the position if all the possible options were taken up and shares issued. When a loan is converted into shares there will be a saving in interest payable. Profit after tax increases, as does the number of shares used in the diluted EPS calculation.

A company may offer individuals the right to acquire shares in the future at some agreed price formula; often a significant factor in arriving at the diluted EPS is share options for directors and other employees.

False conclusions

It is important to recognise that it is not possible to compare two companies' earnings per share and draw any useful conclusions.

	A	B
After-tax profit ($)	100	100
Share capital ($)	100	100
Number of shares	1,000	200
EPS	**0.10**	**0.50**

The two companies have an identical after-tax profit for the year and value of issued share capital. Company A has 1,000 shares of 10¢ each in issue and company B has 200 shares of 50¢ each in issue. It is wrong to assume by looking at the EPS that company B is more profitable or a better performer than company A. The difference in EPS may be simply because the companies have different share capital structures.

Useful conclusions

The only effective way to compare companies' earnings per share is to use the compound growth rate. Looking at the rate at which earnings have been growing over a number of years allows comparison of the ability of companies to improve their earnings.

Dividend cover

Having arrived at the after-tax profit for the year, the next step is for the directors to declare the dividend they propose to be paid to shareholders. The final dividend will not be paid until after the company's annual general meeting at which the shareholders vote on the directors' proposal; it is unusual for the dividend proposed to be rejected at the AGM.

If the dividend per share is deducted from the earnings per share, what remains is the retained profit per share for the year.

Earnings per share − dividend per share = retained profit per share

The retained profit per share is an important element in the assessment of the financial performance and position of a company. For any company it is expected that a continuing and significant source of funds is its current operations (the income statement). Retained earnings is the self-generated finance of a company. A healthy and consistent level of retained profit being reinvested in the business is an indication that rather than relying on borrowing money or issuing more shares, a company is generating the required financial resources internally.

A ratio measuring the availability of funds to pay dividends which also provides some indication of the safety of the level of the dividends is the dividend cover ratio. The higher it is the better or safer is the position of a company. A company paying shareholders a $10 dividend from $20 after-tax profit has a dividend cover of 2. The company had $2 of profit available for every $1 of dividend distributed to shareholders; 50% of the earnings per share is paid out in dividend.

Every major company should have a clear policy on dividend payments and dividend cover. Sometimes this is described in the annual report. The five-year or ten-year record of earnings and dividends given in the annual report can be used to assess a company's historic practice.

Benchmarks

It is not usual for a company to pay dividends from anything other than after-tax profit for the year, otherwise the capital maintenance requirement discussed at the beginning of this chapter would be breached. Thus a dividend cover ratio of 1:1 showing that a company is distributing all of its profit to shareholders and retaining nothing to support the future development of the business can be taken as a guide for the uppermost limit of prudent dividend policy. It would certainly be unusual, if not unacceptable, for a company consistently to operate on less than 1:1 dividend cover.

$$\text{Dividend cover} = \text{after-tax profit} \div \text{dividends}$$
$$= \text{earnings per share} \div \text{dividend per share}$$

Mind the gap

In a typical five-year statement, a company shows both the earnings and dividend per share for each year. It is worth bringing these two lines together to see the relationship. The gap – the difference between earnings and dividend per share – indicates how much the company is generating from its operations to plough back into the business for future growth. The larger this figure the better it is for the company. A company that is retaining little or no profit must inevitably be looking to its shareholders or outside sources for additional capital to finance any major investment programme or activity.

Dividend politics

In most countries, when a company's profit declines it is expected that the dividend will be reduced; this is common-sense good housekeeping. In the UK in the early 1990s this rule did not appear to hold. The dividend cover for many companies declined rapidly as profits fell during the recession, but dividends were maintained.

There are at least two possible explanations for this. It could be claimed that company directors were taking a long-term view in deciding what dividend it was appropriate for their shareholders to receive, allowing for the inevitable fact of business life that as years passed there would be peaks and troughs in the actual profit generated. The possibility of short-term fluctuations in dividend cover was accepted to provide long-term regularity and security of dividend payment to shareholders. Alternatively, it could be that company directors, particularly chairmen and CEOs, were worried that if they did not deliver the level of dividend their major shareholders, the institutional investors, were relying on the share price of the company might fall, and they might be faced with personal job insecurity. Institutional shareholders rely on the dividend streams from their investments to support their own businesses. The management of a company failing to perform with respect to dividend is likely, at least, to be open to criticism, and possibly the target for direct attention and action. Directors of family owned or controlled companies may find themselves under pressure to continue paying dividends that allow shareholders to maintain their lifestyle but may not necessarily be in the best long-term interests of the company.

The Du Pont pyramid of ratios

The use of the rate of return ratio as a measure of company profitability and performance is widespread and effective. If people had to opt for only one measure of a company's performance, most would choose the rate of return. Yet simply to take the profit for the year and express it as a percentage of the assets or capital employed in a business is a fairly blunt or broad approach to measuring profitability. A single figure from the income statement is linked to a single figure from the balance sheet. If this exercise is completed for two companies and the returns of both are similar, what conclusions can be drawn?

	A	B
Sales revenue ($)	300	100
Profit ($)	25	40
Assets ($)	125	200
Return on assets (%)	20	20

Both company A and company B have a 20% rate of return on assets.

To gain an understanding of the level of a company's profitability and how the profit is being made, there is much to recommend the use of the Du Pont approach, named after the US company credited with pioneering work in this area. Sometimes this is referred to as the construction of a pyramid of ratios, because all the ratios can be presented as a pyramid with the rate of return as the summit (see page 168).

Assessing the rate of return

In assessing the rate of return for a company, two separate questions are being addressed. First, the ability of the company to make a profit from its operations; and second, the efficiency with which it is utilising its available assets and capital to produce that profit.

Take the profit margin   To answer the first, the level of profitability of a company's operations, the profit margin offers an appropriate and easily identifiable measure. If the profit margin is calculated for the two companies in the above example, for A it is 8.3% and for B it is 40%. On this basis company B is the more profitable with a profit margin almost five times greater than that of company A.

Introduce the asset or capital turn   A new measure, the asset or capital turn, must be identified to answer the second question and obtain a view of a company's efficiency in the use of its assets or capital. The only reason for a company to maintain assets is to support the conduct of its business and to assist the generation of current and future profits. The success of this intention, in accounting terms, can be measured through the level of sales revenue. The greater the level of sales revenue being generated from the use of the assets employed in the business, the greater is the level of effective utilisation of those assets.

$$\text{Asset turn} = \text{sales revenue} \div \text{assets}$$
$$\text{Capital turn} = \text{sales revenue} \div \text{capital}$$

If this ratio is calculated for the two example companies, it can be seen that they have quite different levels of ability to generate sales revenues from their assets.

A $300 ÷ £125 = 2.4
B $100 ÷ £200 = 0.5

Company A is turning over the assets employed 2.4 times each year, whereas company B manages to turn its assets over only once every two years. Company A has proved capable of generating $2.4 of sales revenue for each $1 of assets employed while company B has managed to generate only $0.50. If one company were a retailer and the other a heavy goods manufacturer, there would be little point in pursuing the comparison. However, if it is assumed that both the companies are operating in the same business sector, the conclusions of comparative performance and profitability would be justified and explanations for the differences sought through further analysis.

Bringing the two together

It is now possible to take these two companies and examine the differing means by which they have achieved an identical 20% rate of return. Company A has the lower profit margin but the higher asset turn. If the two ratios are brought together, it can be seen clearly how the rate of return is being produced.

% rate of return on assets = % profit margin $\times$ asset turn

A   8.3% $\times$ 2.4 = 20%
B   40% $\times$ 0.5 = 20%

Now draw a chart   The combination of the profit margin and asset turn ratios to give the return on assets may be displayed in a chart, or pyramid of ratios. The use of the supporting ratios to those of a company's profit margin and asset turn is discussed in Chapter 8.

The presentation in Figure 7.1 of the rate of return as the combining of the two component ratios is a useful basis for the assessment and comparison of companies' performance. It is essential to calculate what is the overall rate of return of a company, ideally completing this for a number of years to see the trend and to allow direct comparison with other companies. It is also important to try to discover precisely how a company is achieving its level of profitability. What is the relationship between the profit margin and the asset turn? Is it consistent, and if not, why is it changing?

Using the ratios

The relationship between the two component ratios can be visualised as a seesaw with profit margin at one end and asset turn at the other. Company B in the example has a higher profit margin but a lower asset turn than A.

Although both companies have an identical 20% rate of return, it is the result of a different balancing act between the two ratios. A company trying to improve its rate of return can do so only by adjusting either or both of the two component ratios. Can it improve the profit margin through improved cost efficiency or increased prices or a combination of the two? Is it possible to improve the ability to generate sales revenue from the same or fewer assets – for example, through lower inventory levels – or can investment be made to provide additional sales revenue at lower cost without harming the asset turn?

Return on assets

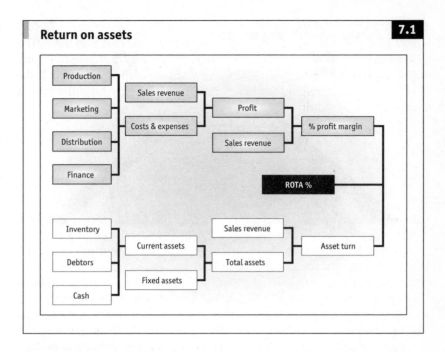

A company concentrating on only one of the two component ratios in an attempt to improve its rate of return is likely to run into difficulties. An example, based on a real-life situation, can illustrate the issues involved. If the average return on assets for the sector is 20% (10% profit margin and 2.0 asset turn), company X, at the bottom of the league table for profitability for the sector, decides that performance must be improved. A small investment is made to increase capacity and, with a view to improving sales volume, the profit margin is reduced.

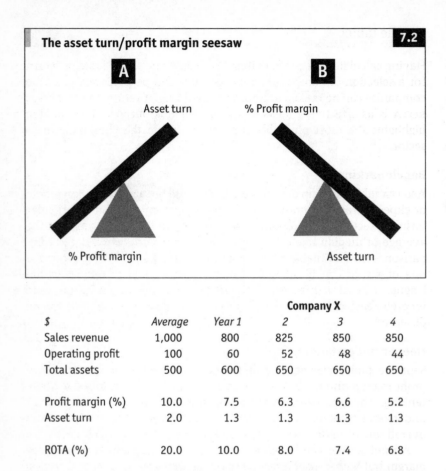

The asset turn/profit margin seesaw — 7.2

			Company X		
$	*Average*	*Year 1*	*2*	*3*	*4*
Sales revenue	1,000	800	825	850	850
Operating profit	100	60	52	48	44
Total assets	500	600	650	650	650
Profit margin (%)	10.0	7.5	6.3	6.6	5.2
Asset turn	2.0	1.3	1.3	1.3	1.3
ROTA (%)	20.0	10.0	8.0	7.4	6.8

Prices are cut – the easy bit – and the margin falls from 7.5% to 5.2%. One end of the seesaw has been pushed down, but what happens if the other end refuses to come up and there is not as great an increase in sales as anticipated? The result is a decline in profitability. If the asset turn remains at 1.3, with a profit margin of 5.2%, ROTA drops to under 7% in year 4. Maintaining the original 10% ROTA requires either a profit margin of 7.6% (7.6% × 1.3 = 10%), or an asset turn of 1.9 (5.2% × 1.9 = 10%).

League tables

Having calculated the profit margin, asset turn and overall rate of return for a selection of companies, a league table can be prepared. First, the companies can be ranked according to their rate of return. In most cases ROTA is as effective a measure as any for this purpose. This ranking highlights the most profitable companies within the chosen business sector.

Benchmarking

A ROTA table can help determine what should be taken as an acceptable or expected rate of return for a company operating within a particular business sector. The mid-point in the table provides an indication of the average or median rate of return for the sector. A benchmark for comparison is now available. Companies producing higher than the average rate of return can be identified, as can those that are trailing in the league. If at least three years' figures are used in the table, the trend whereby each company arrived at its current place in the ranking can be observed.

Deeper understanding

Separate tables can be prepared ranking the selected companies by profit margin and asset turn. These will help in interpreting the ROTA ranking. The two component ratios will also contribute to a deeper understanding of the way in which each company has generated its overall rate of return. Is the seesaw tipping the right way?

A food retailer can be expected to have a comparatively low profit margin but higher asset turn than most other types of retail companies. Discount retailers operate on the basis that low prices (low profit margins) result in more sales and produce a high asset turn: "pile it high and sell it cheap". In the ROTA listings the discount retailers, as is to be expected, are towards the top end of asset turn ranking but lower down for profit margin. Similarly, a company manufacturing a simple unchanging product, for example nuts and bolts, may be able to edge its prices up in return for excellent customer service and quality, but as any other form of product differentiation is difficult it is likely to be operating on low profit margins.

A quality department store may be able to charge high prices to achieve a good profit margin, but it will also find it necessary to provide a pleasing environment for its customers (such as carpets, wide aisles and escalators) which requires capital investment and reduces the asset turn. A manufacturer of a premium product may be able to generate high profit margins but be forced to invest in expensive machinery and facilities necessary for its production.

The rate of return of a company may be viewed as resulting from its pricing policy as much as from internal efficiencies or levels of asset utilisation. Equally, it could be argued that rate of return is directly dependent on the quality of a company's financial management. If major assets are not purchased but rented, or just-in-time inventory control is introduced, the asset turn is improved. Although one factor may, at one time, be more significant than others, it is dangerous to take this in isolation as "explaining" rate of return. The two ends of the seesaw should be examined independently, but they should also be recognised as being directly and inseparably linked in the rate of return measure.

Like-for-like sales

Business sectors often use their own indices to prepare league tables, and these can be mistaken for profitability measures. The retail sector places considerable emphasis on "like-for-like" sales growth as an indicator of performance. The aim is to present a measure of year-on-year sales growth that is not distorted by sales from stores opened in the current year – these being excluded from the calculation. The assumption is that this truly indicates the underlying revenue growth, and so provides a comparative performance measure.

Immediately after the peak selling season like-for-like sales are given considerable emphasis in retail performance analysis – the higher the figure the better is the company rating. It is unwise to take too much notice of such analysis, and it is certainly a mistake to assume it has anything to do with profitability. A company selling at a loss is more likely to generate a higher like-for-like sales growth than one striving to maintain or increase profit margins.

Internally, the like-for-like sales ratio can be of great benefit to management. If calculated in a consistent manner it can indicate, period by period, how the business and its individual units are performing. However, it is unlikely that any two companies will calculate the ratio in exactly the same manner, so be careful in using it as the basis for comparison. There is no accounting standard or even firm guidance on presenting like-for-like figures. A soon as companies realise the importance analysts attach to a particular measure they do their best to deliver the right figures.

Value-added statement

Some companies provide a statement of value added in the annual report. Value added is produced by deducting from sales revenue or income all costs and expenses due to a company's suppliers of goods and services. The difference is the value the company has added to the goods and services it received.

Value added = sales revenue − purchases and services

If the annual report contains sufficient data, you can prepare a simple value-added statement, which can be used to reinforce the ratio analysis discussed earlier in this chapter. Having arrived at the total of the value added for the year, the next step is to see how this was divided up among the company's internal and external interest groups. If sales revenue is expressed as 100, representing 100 pence or cents or 100%, the proportion of revenue being allotted to each interest group can be shown.

Sales revenue		100
Suppliers	50	
Employees	20	
Interest	5	
Tax	5	
Shareholders	5	85
Retained profit		15

Presenting income and expenditure in this way is still popular with many companies as a means of explaining to their employees the quite complex financial information contained in the annual report. The value-added statement has proved to be a useful and practical means of communicating financial information to employees who find the annual report somewhat impenetrable.

A value-added statement can be displayed as a bar chart or pie chart. A pie chart can effectively represent the $1 or £1 coin and show how each unit of income or sales revenue received by the company in the year was shared out: how much went to suppliers, employees, shareholders and government, and how much was left as retained profit for reinvestment into the business at the end of the year.

Dispensing with profit

All the figures set out in the income statement can be incorporated in a value-added statement. For example, a single figure for profit for the year is sufficient in a value-added statement rather than the five or six years that appear in a typical published income statement. Companies often found that if they provided employees with the published income statement, one of the first questions that arose was which of the five or six profits shown should be used as a measure of profitability, and therefore as a basis for wage negotiations. Indeed, the word profit need not appear in a value-added statement. What is left after all interest groups have received their share of the value added (the retained profit) may simply be referred to as "amount retained for investment".

If a value-added statement is prepared for a number of companies operating in the same business sector, it may be used for comparison and the development of benchmarks.

Summary

- ◪ Profit is not the same thing as profitability.
- ◪ Profitability can only be measured using a ratio that combines profit with at least one other figure from the income statement, the balance sheet, or from somewhere else in the annual report.
- ◪ The preparation of profitability league tables comparing companies operating in the same sector makes it easy to see how companies are performing against the median benchmark.
- ◪ Never rely solely on one year's figures; three to five years' figures should be compared and an explanation sought for any big changes between one year and another.
- ◪ The most effective starting point in comparing the performance of a set of companies operating in the same business sector is to use the gross profit margin. This shows the level of a company's profitability after covering all the direct costs and expenses of running the business. For companies undertaking the same type of business, some common levels of gross profit margin are to be expected.
- ◪ Whichever profit figure is used, ensure that any "one-off" profits or losses – exceptional or extraordinary items – are removed. It is a company's continuing and sustainable operating profit that should form the basis of any profitability assessment.

■ Avoid using a company's own profitability indices, such as EBITDA. A company is free to be selective as to how a ratio is calculated and presented. Where a company uses non-GAAP measures this should be fully explained.

■ To provide a comprehensive measure of profitability, you must determine how efficiently a company is using its assets to generate its profit. If only one measure of profitability is used, it should be that of rate of return. The rate of return on total assets (ROTA) ratio (profit before interest and tax expressed as a percentage of total assets) is the best to use. The figures needed to calculate it are easy to gather from a typical annual report. It can be used to make direct comparisons between companies as it is not subject to distortion resulting from differing forms of financial structures, the profit is before any financial charges and the denominator is not affected by the way in which the assets have been financed. The use of ROTA is particularly recommended when companies operating in different countries are being compared because it overcomes many of the problems of obtaining comparable figures.

■ To understand a company better, see how it is achieving its rate of return by looking at the asset turn as well as the gross margin.

■ The segment notes in the annual report offer a valuable additional source of data to help assess a company's profit performance, as well as providing an appreciation of trends and shifts in the balance of its activities. Segment data are normally shown on an operating profit and operating asset basis. This allows the calculation of the return on operating assets for each business and geographic sector.

■ Shareholders are obviously interested in the profitability of their company but can be expected to focus on the after-tax profit and the dividend they receive. A key measure for shareholders is earnings per share (EPS). This is calculated using the after-tax profit, with a few adjustments, as the numerator and the weighted average number of shares in issue as the denominator.

■ Shareholders and analysts are interested in what remains after the dividends have been paid out of the after-tax profit (the retained profit available for investment). This is an important indicator of the ability of a company to self-finance its operations. The more profit a company can reinvest in the business, after satisfying shareholder dividend requirements, the better.

◪ Also of interest is the dividend cover ratio, that is, how many times the amount paid out in dividends the profit is. When the ratio is calculated for several years it gives a useful insight into a company's dividend policy and also how well a company has done in any particular year.

8 Measuring efficiency

THE EFFICIENCY OF A COMPANY can be defined as the relationship between the output of products or services and the input of resources necessary for their delivery. Quantified as a ratio of output to input, the efficiency of one company can be measured over time and compared with that of others. One of the main responsibilities of management is to make efficient use of the human, physical and financial resources available to a company. This chapter considers various means of measuring, assessing and comparing companies' efficiency of utilisation of each of these three categories of resources.

Practical control of efficiency in companies must be carried out internally. It is the focus of management accounting rather than financial accounting and external reporting. In most cases information about the internal control systems of companies is not available to outsiders.

Human resource management

The total employee cost and number of people employed for the current and previous year will be found in the income statement and the notes in a company's annual report.

Problems of definition
It may seem unlikely that it should be difficult to define the number of employees of a company, but unfortunately it is true. In the annual report a company may define the number of employees as being any of the following:

- the average number employed during the year;
- the number employed at the end of the year;
- the total number of full-time and part-time employees;
- the number of full-time equivalent employees.

A full-time equivalent (FTE) is produced by dividing the total number of hours worked by all employees by the standard number of hours in the selected working period: a week, a month or a year. This definition is popular in the retail, hotel and catering sectors and in other organisations where large numbers of part-time workers are employed.

When a number of companies are being studied in order to assess the comparative efficiency in the use of human resources, it is important as far as possible to use a common basis for the definition of the number of employees. In most cases, the figure for employees given in the annual report will be either the average number employed during the year or the number employed at the year end. A straight comparison between two companies based on an analysis where one provides a figure for average employees during the year and the other for year-end total employees is potentially misleading. However, when comparing a number of companies, particularly if they are located in different countries, there is often no other option.

Average remuneration per employee

Most companies provide a figure for the total wages and salaries paid during the year either in the income statement or in the accompanying notes. If total remuneration is divided by the number of employees, the result is the average remuneration per employee.

Average remuneration = total wages and salaries ÷ number of employees

Where there are significant variations in average remuneration between companies in the same sector, the first check (and this applies to all the ratios of efficiency in this section) is to see if there is a difference in the definition of the number of employees. If this is not the explanation, further investigation is required to discover the reasons for the variation. One company may be operating in a different segment of the market or be based in a higher- or lower-cost employment area than another. It is not appropriate to use this ratio as a measure of efficiency to compare companies in different countries, but it may be of use in deciding where to locate a business.

The figure given for the total employee costs can be assumed to include the remuneration of a company's directors since they are employees. Directors normally receive above-average pay, but it is unusual for this to result in the distortion of the average remuneration ratio for a major company – and you can subtract directors' remuneration as it is given separately (see page 164).

Interpreting the figures

A company seen to be offering its employees well below what appears to be the norm for the sector or the national average wage for the country in which it is based may be efficient in the control of employee cost, but whether such a policy will prove to be in the best long-term interests of all concerned is questionable. In recent years, many companies defending their executive remuneration packages have reaffirmed their belief that "if you pay peanuts you get monkeys". There is no reason to assume that this is not equally true for the shop or factory floor.

When a business sector is being investigated it may be useful to have some indication of the total numbers employed in it and the position of companies as employers. This can be achieved by preparing a table ranking the companies according to numbers of employees and calculating the total. From this the importance of an individual company as an employer within a sector, or of a sector as a source of employment within a country, can be highlighted. If employee figures for a number of years are available, then any employment trends by company or by sector can be identified.

The long-term view

Companies often choose to provide employee statistics as part of their five-year or ten-year record of financial performance. Where this information is available it can be used to study a company's record as an employer. Over a number of years a company can be expected to show some consistency in its number of employees. If a company increases the number one year and reduces it the next, it may be exhibiting weakness. Management may not be in control of the business and may be unable to plot and follow a medium-term, let alone a long-term, action plan. In a company that relies on highly skilled employees to deliver its products or services, a hire-and-fire employment policy usually has a negative impact not only on employee loyalty and productivity but also, eventually, on the company's financial performance.

Other sources of information

In addition to a company's annual report, newspapers, magazines and journals can be useful sources of information. Large changes, either up or down, in the employee numbers of a company are often the subject of informed comment. Trade journals that cater for the business sector a company is in can also be helpful.

Sales revenue per employee

Having looked at the number of employees and their average remuneration, the next step is to consider employees' contribution to the generation of sales revenue and profit. If sales revenue is divided by the number of employees, the ratio of sales revenue per employee is produced. This is a measure of the ability of a company to generate sales revenue on the basis of its employees.

Revenue per employee = sales revenue ÷ number of employees

This ratio should be calculated for a number of years to see the trend for a selected company. It is particularly useful when used to compare a number of companies operating in the same business sector. Companies can be ranked in order of their sales per employee, and, if the data is available for a number of years, their relative and changing positions in the league table can be assessed.

Interpreting the figures

Differences between companies in the sales per employee ratio can often be explained by differences in their focus within a sector. A discount food retailer is likely to have higher sales per employee than a department store, and the rate for a fashionable boutique may be even higher. A labour-intensive goods manufacturer will have lower sales per employee than one with a highly automated plant. A construction company that subcontracts much of its work to other companies rather than undertaking this itself will have a much higher sales per employee ratio than one that does not subcontract. When studying a business sector, it is important to look at variations among companies in the level of this and other ratios and to try to explain any trends exhibited, both for individual companies and for the sector as a whole. A company may then be seen in the context of its business sector to be setting, following or matching the general standards of performance and trends.

A company that cannot generate sales revenue per employee of at least double the average wage applying in its country of operation can be assumed to be if not already in trouble then certainly heading for it. A company only just managing to earn enough revenue to cover its wage bill and associated employment costs will not be producing exciting rates of return.

Profit per employee

Most businesses can be expected to strive to produce the highest level of revenue per employee possible, but it is profit rather than revenue that may be seen as the only true measure of efficiency. There is little point in generating revenue if this does not in turn produce profit. The ratio of profit per employee is a measure of the ability of a company to produce profit based on employees.

Profit per employee = profit ÷ number of employees

Chapter 7 discussed the importance of the selection of an appropriate profit from the income statement to produce a meaningful profit margin. The same issues are involved in the decision about which profit to use in the ratio of profit per employee. It is probably most effective to concentrate on the gross and operating profits per employee as measures of how efficiently a company is using its employees and the employees' contribution to its overall performance and success.

Interpreting the figures

As with the ratio of sales per employee, the trends for both individual companies and the business sector should be studied. Individual company performance in profit per employee can be compared with the average or standard for the sector and year-by-year movements assessed. Significant one-off shifts in this ratio should be investigated to discover if they are the result of a change in the efficiency of a company or some other action or event – such as an acquisition or disposal of a labour-intensive subsidiary. Where possible, it is most effective to concentrate on the continuing business operations of a company and to ignore any exceptional profits.

Value added per employee

Chapter 7 dealt with the use of a value-added statement to investigate a company's cost and expense structure and the way in which the corporate cake is divided among various interest groups. Value added can be defined as the difference between the revenue received by a company and the amount it paid for goods and services. It is easy to produce a figure for the value added per employee, and, as with profit per employee, the higher the ratio the better is a company's performance.

Value added per employee = value added ÷ number of employees

Employee cost per unit of revenue or unit of value added

A third measure relevant to efficiency in the utilisation of employees can be produced by dividing the total employee cost by sales revenue and presenting it as a percentage. This produces the employee cost per unit of sales revenue.

Employee cost per unit of revenue = 100 × (employee costs ÷ sales revenue)

Value added may be used in place of sales revenue to produce a ratio of employee cost per unit of value added to indicate the proportion of value added of a company being devoted to employees.

The employee cost to sales ratio shows what proportion of each unit of sales revenue generated during the year was taken up by employee remuneration and allied expenses. Broadly, the lower the ratio the better it is for the company. If less of each unit of revenue is devoted to employee remuneration, there will be more available for other purposes.

	$	$
Sales revenue	100	100
Employee cost	30	20
Employee cost per unit of revenue	**0.30**	**0.20**

Interpreting the figures

For every $1 of sales revenue generated during the year, company A puts 30¢ and company B puts 20¢ towards employee remuneration and allied expenses. If the amount set aside for employment expenses is taken as a measure of efficiency, company B appears to be performing better than company A. There may be a number of reasons for the variation between the two. Company B may employ fewer people or pay a lower rate to its employees, or it may be operating in a different segment of the market and be able to charge a higher price for its products or services.

Relating employee cost to revenue is a useful way of comparing companies operating in the same business. If the ratio is calculated for a representative number of companies, an average or median can be found for the sector against which individual companies can be measured and compared over time.

Where the ratio of employee cost to sales revenue is used for international comparison, major variations can be expected because wage levels differ and social security and other benefit charges may be included in the total employee cost. It is therefore not recommended that too much weight be placed on this ratio for comparison of companies operating in different countries.

Tangible fixed assets per employee

In many businesses the investment in tangible fixed assets provided to assist employees is an important factor in gaining an overview of the efficiency of a company's activities. If heavy engineering companies or car manufacturers are being analysed, it is useful to assess their ability to generate sales revenue and profit per employee and to maintain control over total employment costs; but measurement of investment in assets used in the production process to support employees' activities is equally important in assessing each company's efficiency in human resource management.

If the total of tangible fixed assets shown in the balance sheet is divided by the number of employees, the ratio of tangible fixed assets per employee is produced.

Tangible fixed assets per employee = tangible fixed assets ÷ number of employees

Interpreting the figures

This ratio provides a basis for comparing companies with respect to the investment they have made in assets necessary for their production activities. For example, a car manufacturer can be expected to require continued and substantial investment in robotics to maintain the quality and level of output and, perhaps, to allow a reduction in employee numbers. This will be reflected in the asset per employee ratio. A company undertaking the necessary investment can be expected to display a higher figure for the ratio than one that is not.

The use of this ratio may also be appropriate when analysing some service organisations. For example, when studying the passenger transport sector the amount of fixed assets per employee may be used to compare one company with another to assess the supporting investment in trains, planes, ships, buses or coaches. The ratio can also be employed to highlight for further investigation the variation between companies operating in the same line of business but in different countries.

Inevitably there will be problems of comparison, as some companies may own their factories and plant and machinery and others may rent or lease these assets. However, when the fixed asset per employee ratio is prepared for a number of companies operating in the same business, it provides a useful measure of the comparative levels of investment in assets used in the production process. The average or median ratio for all of the companies being studied gives a base against which to assess individual companies and, over a number of years, to observe any trends that are developing in a business sector.

Operating or net assets per employee

If a company provides detailed segmental information that includes the allocation of employees between sectors and geographic locations, the ratios described above can be adapted to provide measures for each unit. It should also be possible to calculate the operating assets or net assets per employee from the segmental information provided. If it is possible to prepare these ratios for a number of years, movements in the allocation of a company's employees between businesses and countries, as well as the supporting investment in productive assets, can be observed.

Directors' remuneration

In the UK especially there has been widespread criticism of what have been described as "fat cat" remuneration packages given to some directors. The annual report contains details of the remuneration or emoluments of a company's directors. The figure for directors' remuneration or emoluments can be taken to cover all of their salary, profit share, bonus payments and other benefits. Include in directors' remuneration not only bonuses for good performance but also any one-off payments for redundancy, contract severance or "golden goodbyes". Whether a board member takes the money as a result of competence or incompetence, it is an expense to the shareholders. Shareholders appear to be becoming increasingly irritated by payments made to directors that bear no relationship – except inverse – to company performance or investor returns.

As a contribution to showing how well directors are doing for shareholders, a performance graph – ideally for the last five years – is included in the report on directors' remuneration. This illustrates the trend in total shareholder return against a selected index – for example, the FTSE 100. Total shareholder return consists of the change in the market price of shares together with all income (dividends) which are assumed to have been reinvested in additional shares.

Plus dividends

It is important to remember that this figure does not include any dividends received by directors on shares they own in the company. To gain a fuller picture of the total income that flows to directors from the company, the number of shares they own should be multiplied by the dividend paid. This can be done quite easily, as the annual report should contain a table listing directors' names and the number of shares owned or in which they have a beneficial interest.

The cost of the board

It is worth calculating the cost of the board of directors as a whole. The total remuneration package of each director, consisting of salary and fees plus any bonuses or other benefits, should appear in the annual report. If the total of these is added to the total number of directors' shares multiplied by the dividend paid, a reasonably accurate figure of the cost of the board of directors is produced. This figure can be expressed as a percentage of sales revenue or profit, as was suggested for the total employee cost, to produce ratios that can be used to compare the practice of different companies. Where one company is seen to provide much higher directors' remuneration than similar companies, you may want to find out why this is the case.

Average director's remuneration

If the total figure for directors' remuneration shown in the accounts is divided by the number of directors, a figure for the average director's remuneration is produced. The current year's figure can be compared with that of previous years to test for consistency and trends. It can also be compared with that of similar companies.

Share options

Directors and other employees of a company are often given share options. Share option schemes are considered a standard means of motivating and rewarding a company's management. An individual is offered the right to purchase a company's shares at some time in the future at a predetermined price. For example, a director may be offered the right to purchase 1,000 shares in two years' time at $2 each. If in two years the share price reaches $4 and the director exercises the right to purchase, a "profit" of $2,000 is made (although if shares are then sold there may be a capital gains tax liability). Shareholders have a right to expect a company to inform them not only of what share option schemes are in operation but also of what options have been taken up by executives and at what prices. Where this information is available it can be incorporated in the analysis of directors' rewards suggested above.

Who controls the board?

Ultimately, shareholders – although in practice this means the institutional investors who have substantial shareholdings – can overturn the directors' remuneration policy. Indirect pressure from government, public opinion, professional bodies and stock exchanges may also influence board policy. However, there are many instances where boards have shown themselves to be thick-skinned when it comes to the remuneration of board members.

Of course, if media reports of the remuneration of a company's directors do not tie up with the information given in the annual report, further investigation is required. If the media have their facts correct, and the board is not being straight with shareholders on directors' remuneration, can you trust other information in the annual report?

Physical resource management

The decision of how to measure the efficiency of a company's use of its available physical resources – the assets employed – must be based on an understanding of the nature of its business. Different types of businesses demand different measures.

Starting point

A useful first step towards such understanding is to turn to the income statement to discover the broad cost structure of the company being analysed. The income statement provides outline details of a company's costs and expenses. The way the information is set out depends upon the nature of the business. For example, retail and manufacturing companies may set them out as follows.

Retail	Manufacturing
Cost of sales	Cost of sales
Staff costs	Distribution expenses
Occupancy costs	Administration expenses
Maintenance and renewals	Research and development

If each cost and expense heading is expressed as a percentage of sales revenue for the year and a number of years are considered or a number of companies are compared, trends and variations can quickly be highlighted for further investigation.

Sales revenue		100	
Cost of sales		<u>65</u>	
		35	% gross profit margin
Distribution	12		
Administration	8		
Research & development	1		
Other expenses	<u>4</u>	<u>25</u>	
		10	% operating profit margin

Analysing the rate of return

A single overall measure of a company's efficiency can be taken as the rate of return it produces on the assets employed. Rate of return ratios were discussed in Chapter 7. The target for almost any business is to make efficient use of assets to produce sales revenue from which profit is made. Dividing sales revenue by the assets employed in the business produces the asset turn ratio (see page 147). This ratio is for most companies an eminently suitable measure of their efficiency in managing their assets.

Asset turn = sales revenue ÷ assets

A company displaying a low asset turn when compared with similar companies may be assumed to have some unproductive assets, some overvalued assets or inadequate management skills, or a combination of the three. The asset turn ratio is simple to produce, combining sales revenue from the income statement with the denominator – total assets, net assets, capital employed or whichever one is chosen. (Chapter 7 discussed the selection of an appropriate asset or capital employed figure from the balance sheet.) If calculated for a number of years, it offers some insight into the continuing efficiency of a company. When a number of companies operating in the same business sector are being studied, this ratio is an excellent basis on which to make judgments of comparative efficiency in the use of assets to generate sales and profit.

The overall rate of return of a company is produced from the combination of profit margin and asset or capital turn. The one multiplied by the other provides the ratio.

$$\% \text{ rate of return} = \% \text{ profit margin} \times \text{asset or capital turn}$$

The use of the Du Pont or pyramid approach to presenting rates of return is discussed on pages 146–50. The two main component ratios of profit margin and asset turn can be further subdivided to offer insight into the way in which the rate of return is produced and the efficiency of a company at various stages of its production activities.

This pyramid of ratios can be helpful in analysing a company and in identifying which aspects of a business most affect its overall profitability. For example, it enables you to assess the impact on the rate of return of a decline in the inventory turn.

Ideally, it is the continuing business operations of a company that should be the focus of this analysis. In practice, however, where several companies operating from various country bases are being studied it is probably easier to take the total of both continued and discontinued operations for a year-by-year comparison.

For any company, the act of adding or removing businesses from its portfolio of operations can be significant, as can when in the financial year this is done. The accounting treatment of acquisitions, in particular, can influence the profit displayed for the year. Whether a proportion of the full year's profit or the total profit of the acquired company is brought into the income statement can have a direct influence on apparent profitability. The level of provisions made against acquisitions may also be important. The potential for a company to massage its profits for the year by the careful selection of an appropriate accounting treatment of an acquisition should not be ignored. These factors are covered in Chapter 2 as part of the discussion on the treatment of goodwill.

Once the figures have been translated into a table, it is easy to see whether there is a consistent approach by which a company is, over a number of years, managing to achieve its profit margins. If similar data can be collected for similar companies, benchmarks can be selected for the measurement of comparative performance.

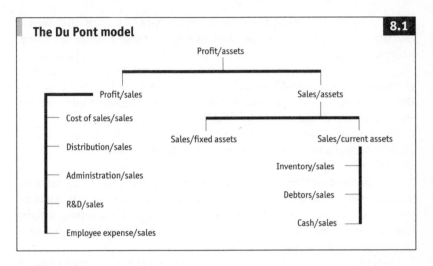

The Du Pont model 8.1

Profit/assets

Profit/sales   Sales/assets

Cost of sales/sales

Sales/fixed assets   Sales/current assets

Distribution/sales

Inventory/sales

Administration/sales

Debtors/sales

R&D/sales

Cash/sales

Employee expense/sales

Additional measures

A company may, in its annual report, provide additional information on the company's operations and performance. Needless to say, a company that has nothing to boast about will not often provide anything beyond the minimum required.

In the case of companies that provide more information than that stipulated by legislation or accounting rules and practice, note that they may adopt any form of presentation they wish and the figures published are not necessarily subject to the normal independent check and verification by an auditor. Furthermore, the provision of additional operating details in one year's annual report does not commit a company to provide the same details in other years or, if it does, to ensure that the figures are presented on a consistent and therefore comparable basis.

Many retail companies give details of the number and size of their outlets and total sales area. These provide a basis for calculating ratios of sales and profit per square foot or square metre of selling space. For any retailer, a practical measure of its efficiency is that of its ability to generate sales and profit per unit of sales space, and operating targets are often set to try to improve both of these ratios.

Such measures are an excellent means of assessing one company's performance over a number of years and of comparing several companies. But differences between companies may be explained partly because they are in different sectors of the business. For example, a food retailer can be expected to sell more per square metre than a department store but to be operating at a lower profit margin and therefore probably a lower profit ratio.

Output or level of service ratios

Other businesses may provide statistics on their output or levels of service. A transport company may publish the number of passengers carried or the passenger miles travelled in a year. These figures can be used as the denominator in ratios to assist the study of a company's historic performance and to compare one company with another.

The cost and profit per passenger or per passenger mile can be calculated in a similar way to provide another measure of how efficiently companies deliver transport services. The staff cost of one company can be linked to the number of passengers, or ideally passenger miles, to allow comparison with previous years and with other transport companies. Transport companies in other countries may usefully be included in the analysis to produce the average amount paid by a passenger.

An electricity generating or supply company may provide details of the amount of electricity (MW) produced during the year. A motor manufacturer may disclose how many cars or tractors were produced during the year. Whenever a suitable common denominator for a business sector can be determined, this should be used as the basis for the preparation of a series of ratios to measure efficiency and performance.

Other sources of additional information

Additional information on a company or business sector can usefully be obtained from sources other than annual reports. Newspapers, journals, magazines and government and trade publications may offer data and information that can effectively be incorporated in performance and efficiency measures.

It is often possible to obtain national statistics relevant to a business sector - for total retail sales, total amount of electricity generated, number of cars and trucks manufactured and sold, for example. Even if the financial year end of a company does not match the calendar or fiscal year on which the statistics are based, it is still worth estimating the market share of a company to see how this has changed over the years.

Declining assets

Some indication of the age of assets employed in the business may help in the assessment of the efficiency of a company. Details may be provided in the notes accompanying the balance sheet; there should at least be a statement on when the assets were last valued. A general guide to the expected future effective working life of assets can be arrived at by dividing the balance sheet value of the tangible fixed assets by the depreciation charged for the year in the income statement. The resulting figure indicates how many years it will be before the assets are completely written off and may be taken as a measure of their estimated future useful working life.

Estimated life of assets = tangible fixed assets ÷ depreciation

If tangible assets are shown in the balance sheet at $100 and the income statement includes $10 for depreciation, this implies a ten-year useful working life for the assets. Of course, there are many factors and events that can render this ratio ineffective. A company may acquire a major asset at the end of the year and decide not to make any depreciation charge for it in the accounts. It may revalue all or part of its assets, or it may change its depreciation policy. But this quick and simple ratio provides a starting point for more detailed analysis of tangible fixed assets.

In the income statement notes a company should provide details of its depreciation policy, giving for each class of asset the rate and method of depreciation being charged. The most common depreciation methods were discussed in Chapter 2. Depreciation policy can have a significant impact on reported profit.

Asset replacement rate

The rate at which a company is replacing its assets can provide an indication of its ability to keep pace with technological change – an important factor for most companies and crucial for many. One means of determining the rate is to divide the tangible fixed assets shown in the balance sheet by the amount of capital expenditure for the year.

Asset replacement rate = gross tangible fixed assets ÷ capital expenditure

The figures for the gross, undepreciated value of tangible fixed assets and capital expenditure are given in the notes in the annual report. Alternatively, although it is not ideal, the capital expenditure figure in the cash flow statement can be used. A company with gross tangible assets of $1,000 and capital expenditure for the year of $125 can be assumed to be replacing its assets approximately every eight years. Ideally, this ratio should be calculated for a number of years so the trend and consistency can be studied, and one company can be compared with others to see whether it is above or below the average or standard levels for the business sector.

Capital expenditure turnover

The way a company's capital expenditure is maintained or moving in relation to sales revenue can be measured by dividing sales revenue by capital expenditure to produce a ratio of capital expenditure turnover.

Capital expenditure turnover = sales revenue ÷ capital expenditure

If the ratio is decreasing, this may indicate that a company is increasing its investment in tangible assets to support the continuing generation of sales revenue. An increasing ratio may indicate a reduction in investment owing to a lack of available funds or a lack of confidence in the business's prospects.

The asset ownership ratio

In studying the tangible assets of a company, it is worth seeing what proportion of the fixed assets is owned and what proportion is leased. Is the foundation of growth to be on owned or leased assets? What may be the implications of this policy and what is the practice of other companies in the same business sector? The notes in the accounts give details not only of the division between owned and leased assets but also of that between long and short leases and operating and finance leases. This additional information may be of use when looking at the trend exhibited by a company over a number of years as it grows and develops.

Leasehold proportion = 100 × (leased assets ÷ total tangible fixed assets)

Research and development

A crucial function that often acts as a direct link between a company's physical and human resources is research and development (R&D). The successful and profitable move from basic research to the development of commercially viable products and services is normally achieved through the application of the talents of highly skilled employees using sophisticated machines and instrumentation.

As described in Chapter 3, for most companies in most countries the total amount of R&D is written off in the year in which the expense is incurred; it is not usual to capitalise all or part of the R&D expense. If a company incurring an R&D expense of $100 follows the generally accepted accounting practice of writing the total amount off through the income statement, a loss may be disclosed as in company A below.

	A	B
Income statement		
R&D	100	10
(Loss) profit	(Loss)	Profit
Balance sheet		
R&D	n/a	90

The income statement is charged with the total $100 of R&D expenditure and none is capitalised into the balance sheet. If the company were allowed to spread the R&D expense over a ten-year period, arguing that this was the time period over which the benefits from the investment would be gained, the position would be that of company B. Nothing has really changed, but a loss has been turned into a profit of $10 and the balance sheet value of the company is $90 larger because a new asset of R&D has appeared reflecting the capitalisation of the balance of the expense, which will be written off over the next nine years. This might be acceptable if there was no uncertainty about the survival of the company over the nine years, but were the company to run into problems immediately after the publication of its annual report, it is debatable whether the R&D asset in the balance sheet could be sold for $90. R&D is an intangible asset and accountants generally consider that its real value is too subjective for quantification in the accounts. Referring to Chapter 2, the rule of "when in doubt write it off" applies.

A simple test of the effectiveness of a company's R&D investment is to see whether or not it produces results. There is no commercial benefit to a company in investing resources in interesting research projects if these do not result in products and services reaching the marketplace. There is equally no point in a company investing large sums in R&D when there is no call for this from its customers. For retail companies only a limited amount of R&D is worthwhile, but for their suppliers more substantial investment in this area may be essential. Sectors in which sizeable and continuing investment in R&D is crucial include pharmaceuticals, defence and information technology.

A company's annual report contains details of the amount spent on R&D and may also provide information on new products developed and launched, together with details of any breakthroughs that have taken place. All this is of at least some help in assessing the effectiveness of a company's R&D programme.

R&D to sales ratio

One way of determining the consistency of a company's policy on R&D is to divide the amount spent on it by sales revenue. The result multiplied by 100 gives the R&D to sales ratio.

$$\text{R\&D to sales} = 100 \times (\text{R\&D expense} \div \text{sales revenue})$$

For most companies, a reasonably constant level of investment in R&D is to be expected. A decline in the ratio may be because R&D expenditure is constant but sales revenue is rising, but a sudden reduction in the ratio may be an indication of corporate malaise. An easy way to "improve" profit when business is tough is to cut expenditure on things like R&D. As discussed in Chapter 11, such action may bring short-term profit, but it may also damage long-term prospects.

Problems with percentages

Although this ratio removes any necessity for currency conversion where international comparisons are being made, it does not overcome the size differences of companies. If two companies invest 1% of their sales revenue in R&D, the ratio would not distinguish between them. However, if one company had sales of $10m and the other had sales of $1m, then the amounts being invested in R&D by each are quite different. For example, a big computer company may spend more on R&D than the total sales revenue of some of its smaller competitors.

Another problem is that many companies set their R&D budget as a regular percentage of sales revenue. This has the merit of consistency, but it may lead to difficulties. If revenue is declining, owing to a lack of competitive edge in a company's products, reducing spending on R&D in line with the set R&D to sales ratio is likely to exacerbate the decline.

Additional sources of information

Well-informed media coverage and reports from analysts who are experts in the relevant sector will help in assessing a company's R&D performance. However, a simple but effective rule for anyone thinking of investing in a company is: "If you can't see it, don't buy it." Before investing money in a company, try to get some first-hand knowledge of its products or services. Are the company's products and the range offered as good as, if not better than, those of competitors? Do the company's staff give the impression of competence and enthusiasm? If you are not impressed, why should anyone else be?

When you have invested in a company, regular physical checks on its products and services are as important as the financial analysis suggested in this book. This may seem like hard work, but it can be interesting and it is definitely a safer approach.

Financial resource management

Chapters 9 and 10 deal with many aspects of financial management efficiency, but there are some that are properly covered here.

The treasury function

The role of a company's treasury department has increased in importance in recent years, mainly as a result of the increase in international business and the complexity of cash flows. Not long ago, a finance director might have spent a few minutes now and then considering the implications of currency movements for a company. Today, every major company has full-time professional staff overseeing the management of finance and cash flows.

For a company with its head office in the UK and a subsidiary operating in the United States, a shift in the exchange rate between the pound and the dollar can have a dramatic impact on group profitability. If the subsidiary has a profit of $100 and this is "sent" to head office when the exchange rate is $1.55, £64.52 is incorporated into the group accounts. If the exchange rate was $1.65 or $1.45, the profit would become £60.60 or £68.96. Thus the equivalent of a 10% change in the apparent profits of the subsidiary can be brought about simply by fluctuations in the exchange rate. The accounting treatment of international transactions is discussed in Chapters 2 and 3. Any company should do its best to avoid undue exposure to the risks of exchange rate movements. In recent years, there have been some notable examples of companies that have lost large amounts of money because they were in effect betting on how currencies would move in relation to each other rather than hedging their risk from exchange rate fluctuations. Managing currency transactions is a core responsibility of the treasury department.

Interest cover ratio

One financial efficiency measure for a company is its ability to pay the interest on its borrowings from operating profits. When profit before interest and tax (PBIT) or earnings before interest and tax (EBIT) is divided by the amount of interest paid, the resulting interest cover ratio shows how many times a company's profit covers the interest payments it has to make.

$$\text{Interest cover} = \text{pre-interest and tax profit} \div \text{interest}$$

The higher the figure the safer is the company. A company with an interest cover ratio of 2 could suffer a 50% drop in profit and still meet its interest payments. A company with a ratio of less than 1 would have to dip into its cash reserves or sell assets or raise additional finance to meet its interest payment commitments if there was any reduction in profit.

Summary

- Efficiency is normally associated with the control of costs and expenses and with the productive use of all the available resources of a company to deliver its products or services to the market place at a competitive price.
- The efficiency of a business can be measured in various ways. It can be argued that the acid test of efficiency is profit. The development of a suitable set of performance measures linked to profitability is described in Chapter 7. However, a company may be highly efficient in managing its costs and expenses but face factors beyond its control that limit its ability to generate profitable revenues. There may be a recession or oversupply, or there may be a price war within the sector. In such circumstances, the lower profitability of the company may not indicate a lack of efficiency.

  After you have gathered relevant data for as many years as possible, a useful first step is to reduce the income statement to a common factor basis by expressing costs and profits as a percentage of sales revenue (see Chapter 6).

	Year 1 ($)	Year 2 ($)	Year 1 (%)	Year 2 (%)
Sales revenue	7,200	8,500	100	100
Cost of sales	4,680	6,125	65	72
Gross profit	2,520	2,375	35	28

Using this approach makes it much easier to pick out changes and trends, either from year to year for one company or when comparing one company with another, particularly if they are operating in different countries. The profit margin ratio strips out problems of size and currency.

◼ Profit per employee is probably the best measure of the efficiency of use of the human resource element of a company.

◼ The rate of return ratio is the best single ratio to use as a measure of the overall efficiency of a company (see Chapter 7). An efficient company is more likely to produce a profit than an inefficient one, and is thus more likely to produce consistently higher rates of return.

◼ In assessing the ability of a company to make use of its available resources, the asset turn ratio is ideal. It is quick and simple to calculate. Sales revenue is taken from the income statement and a figure for assets taken from the balance sheet; one divided by the other produces the asset turn for a company. If each time a company makes a sale it takes a profit, the more sales are generated the more profit is produced. The higher the asset turn the better is the productive use being made of the assets employed in the business and the better is the eventual overall rate of return.

◼ Financial management can be encapsulated in the interest cover ratio. This displays the cost of a company's external borrowings as a proportion of pre-interest and tax profit for the year. The more a company finances operations from external sources on which interest is paid or the higher the interest rates being charged the lower is the ratio.

9 Working capital and liquidity

THIS CHAPTER CONCENTRATES on the ways of assessing the short-term financial position and health of a company. Although the terms solvency and liquidity are often used to refer to the same thing, each focuses on a different aspect of financial viability. Solvency (discussed in Chapter 10) is a measure of the ability of a company to meet its various financial obligations as they fall due, whether they are loan repayments or creditors' invoices. Liquidity is directly related to cash flows and the nature of a company's short-term assets; that is, whether there is an appropriate amount of cash on hand or readily available. You may have $1m invested in stocks and shares but not enough cash in your pocket to buy a bus ticket. You may be solvent but far from being liquid.

A simple check on the short-term financial viability of a company might be first to ensure a profit was made for the year, and then turn to the balance sheet to see if there was a large cash balance at the end of the year. If the company made a profit and shows positive cash balances, you might think all is surely well. Unfortunately, you might be wrong; positive cash balances at the year end, even when combined with profit, do not guarantee corporate survival in the short term, let alone the long term.

The balance sheet is a snapshot of a company's assets and liabilities at the end of the financial year. It does not claim to be representative of the position during the rest of the year. The income statement matches income and expenditure for the year. Income and therefore the profit for the year includes credit sales income and credit expenditure as well as cash transactions. A company might show a profit for the year but have numerous creditors, perhaps its major supplier of raw materials, requiring payment in cash within the next few weeks. It is also possible for a company to manipulate the year-end cash position. If towards the end of the financial year the company puts more emphasis and effort into collecting cash from customers and slows payment to creditors, this will result in an increase in cash balances.

Creditors provide finance to support a company and debtors tie up its financial resources. A company extending more credit to its customers than it, in turn, can take in credit from its suppliers may be profitable, but it is also running down its cash resources. This is called overtrading and is a common problem among small and rapidly growing companies. It is crucial for any business to maintain an adequate cash balance between credit given to customers and credit taken from suppliers.

Working capital and cash flow

The relationship between short-term assets and liabilities was discussed in Chapter 2. In UK balance sheets current liabilities are set against current assets to highlight net current assets or net current liabilities. The net current assets figure is often referred to as the working capital of a company to emphasise the fact that it is a continually changing amount.

Current assets and liabilities change not only from day to day but also from minute to minute as a company conducts its business. Cash is used to pay the invoices of suppliers for the production of goods that are then sold, usually on credit, to customers, who in return pay cash to the company. The cash cycles around the business on a continuing basis (see Figure 9.1 on the next page). On each turn of the cycle the company makes a profit, the goods or services being sold for more than the cost of their production, resulting in more cash available to expand the business and for the purchase or production of goods for sale.

The key to a company's short-term financial viability is to be found in the study of working capital. Current assets consist of cash or near-cash items listed under four main headings: inventory (or stock), prepayments, debtors and cash. In the standard balance sheet presentation these are set out in order of liquidity, with cash being the ultimate form of liquidity:

- Inventory: finished goods, work in progress, raw materials
- Prepayments: advance payment of expenses
- Debtors (accounts receivable): trade and other
- Cash: cash and bank balances, short-term deposits and investments

Current liabilities are the total amount of creditors due for payment within one year, indicating how much the company will have to pay in cash in the near future. Short-term borrowings also appear as part of current liabilities. Typically, five items appear in the balance sheet under this heading:

- Creditors (accounts payable): trade and other

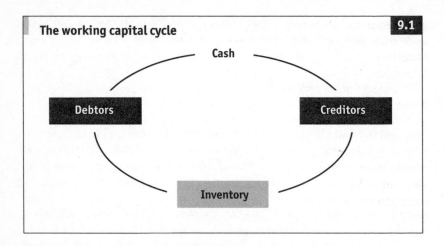

The working capital cycle — 9.1

- Accruals: expenses not paid at the end of the year
- Bank loans: short-term loans and other borrowings
- Tax: amounts due for payment with the coming year
- Dividends: dividends declared but not yet paid to shareholders

Inventory

The least liquid current asset is inventory (or stock). When inventory is sold to customers, it moves up the current asset liquidity ranking to become part of debtors and lastly to become completely liquid as a part of cash and bank balances when customers pay their invoices.

For many companies the total figure for inventory in the balance sheet is further subdivided in the notes to give the amounts held as raw materials, work-in-progress and finished goods. For practical purposes it is safe to assume that finished goods represent a more liquid asset than work in progress, which in turn is likely to prove easier to turn quickly into cash than raw materials.

Most companies can be expected to sell their inventory and turn it into cash at least once each year. If this is not the case, there should be a good reason for the company to hold that item or amount of inventory. If inventory is not turning into cash, valuable financial resources are being tied up for no profitable return.

Debtors

After inventory, the next most liquid item appearing within current assets is debtors. These are divided into debtors where the cash is expected to be received by the company within 12 months of the balance sheet date and those where the cash is expected later. Often it is necessary to refer to the notes to discover the precise make-up of the total figure.

If a group of companies is being analysed, the amount disclosed for debtors may include amounts owed by subsidiary companies. These are also divided into the amount due within one year of the balance sheet date and the amount due later.

It is reasonable to assume that debtors due within one year are mainly trade debtors; that is, customers owing money for goods or services provided during the year and expected to pay the cash due to the company under the normal terms of trade. If customers are offered 30 days' credit, they are expected to pay cash to the company within 30 days of accepting delivery of the goods or services provided.

To give the impression of income growth, a company may pursue a creative approach to sales revenue recognition – for example, counting future income in the current income statement. That something is amiss will be indicated by the much greater growth in trade debtors than in turnover. A company may opt to push inventory out to dealers on a sale or return basis and treat this as sales revenue for the year. In effect, the company is turning inventory into debtors. The income statement will show revenue and profit increasing, but here will be a mismatch evident when the growth trends of inventory and debtors are compared.

Faced with an unacceptably large level of credit extended to customers, a company may factor or securitise trade debtors. This will result in a reduction in the level of debtors shown in the balance sheet – the true level is disguised. Always read the notes provided in the accounts for trade debtors. For a normal, healthy company, the growth in levels of turnover, inventory and trade debtors can be expected to be compatible. Any significant differences should be studied.

Debtors shown in the balance sheet may be assumed to be good debts. Customers owing the company money are expected to pay their bills when they fall due. Any known or estimated bad debts will have been written off through the income statement. Bad debts can be either deducted from sales revenue to reduce income for the year or charged as an expense in arriving at the profit for the year. Almost every type of business experiences bad debts. Customers may become bankrupt, flee the country or otherwise disappear; or there may be fraud.

Bad debts may be written off individually as they are incurred or there may be a regular percentage of sales revenue written off each year. Often a percentage charge is made, based on historic experience for the particular company and the sector in which it operates. If there is a substantial or material bad debt, the company may make reference to this in the annual report. If a major customer is declared bankrupt, this should be drawn to shareholders' attention in the annual report, even if the company hopes eventually to recoup all or most of the debt.

Prepayments and accruals

Sometimes a company will show prepayments or payments in advance as an item within current assets. Prepayments are money the company has paid in the current year for goods or services to be received in a future year. For example, a company may pay the rent on property three months in advance. For most forms of analysis, prepayments are treated as being as liquid as debtors.

Current liabilities often contain an amount for accruals. These may be considered the reverse of prepayments. Accruals are expenses relating to the current year that have yet to be settled in cash. Trade creditors are the suppliers' outstanding invoices for goods and services delivered during the year. Accruals relate to other operating expenses, such as power and light, paid in arrears rather than in advance.

Cash

Cash is as liquid as it is possible to be. It consists of money in the company's hands or bank accounts. Cash is immediately available to provide funds to pay creditors or to make investments.

Why do companies need to hold cash? Cash as an asset is worthless unless it is invested in productive assets or interest-bearing accounts. Companies hold cash for the same reasons as individuals. John Maynard Keynes, a successful investment analyst as well as a notable economist, identified three reasons for keeping cash rather than investing it in other assets:

- Transaction
- Precaution
- Speculation

The transactions and the precautionary motives should, ideally, dictate the appropriate size of a company's cash and bank balances. A company with no cash cannot continue in business. It would be unable to pay suppliers or employees. Cash is essential to fulfil the everyday routine transactions of the business. A company with insufficient cash in hand has no cushion to cover unbudgeted costs. Just as individuals try to keep some cash readily available, so companies need cash at short notice for the equivalent corporate experience.

Speculation, the third reason for holding cash, is generally less relevant to companies, since directors are on the whole not encouraged to gamble with shareholders' money. For individuals, surplus cash used for investment with a view to the longer-term, perhaps planning for retirement, can be said to be precautionary, whereas that used to buy lottery tickets, back horses or play poker is definitely for short-term speculation – money that may be lost but life can still continue.

One important aspect of the internal financial management of a company is to achieve the delicate balancing act of having precisely the right amount of cash available at any time. To have too much is wasteful; to have too little is dangerous.

How much money a company needs depends on what it does. A company that can confidently look forward to regular cash inflows, such as a food retailer, has less need to maintain substantial cash balances than a company with more discrete or uneven cash inflows, such as a construction company or a heavy goods manufacturer.

The only way to assess whether a particular company's cash balances are adequate is to compare them with those of previous years and those of other companies in the same kind of business. The ratios described later provide useful measures by which you can make comparisons.

In assessing a company's liquidity, it must be remembered that the timing of the balance sheet may have significant implications for the level of cash balances. A retail company producing accounts in January, following the Christmas sales period, might be expected to show little stock but a high cash balance. The company would be more liquid at the end of January than in December.

Short-term investments

Companies often invest cash which is not immediately required for running the business in short-term marketable securities or even overnight on money markets. Such investments appear as part of current assets in the balance sheet and are assumed to be readily turned into cash. For financial analysis purposes they are treated as being as liquid as cash.

Current liabilities

Many of the ratios that measure and assess a company's liquidity and solvency use the total figure for current liabilities. For most purposes this is perfectly acceptable, but it will produce somewhat cautious results. For example, dividends often appear as part of current liabilities. However, the final dividend for the year, which is included as a charge in the income statement, will not actually be paid to shareholders until after the company's annual general meeting (AGM) when the directors' dividend proposals are accepted. If a company were running into difficulties in paying suppliers and others, it is not unreasonable to assume it would reconsider its plans to pay shareholders a dividend.

Loans and other borrowings that fall due for repayment in the coming year are correctly shown as part of current liabilities in the balance sheet. Other short-term bank borrowing may also appear within current liabilities. Often, as with an overdraft in the UK, this is because they are repayable on demand. It may be argued that it is overcautious to include them among "creditors falling due within one year" when calculating liquidity or solvency ratios.

Intra-group trading

Intra-group trading by subsidiary companies may give rise to debtors and creditors appearing in current assets and liabilities at the year end. If a more sophisticated and refined analysis is required, these might be either netted off to produce a net debtor or creditor figure, or excluded completely. For most purposes, they may be treated in the same way as trade debtors and creditors.

Measuring liquidity

Cash and debtors are defined as the liquid or quick assets of a company. A liquid asset is already cash or capable of being turned into cash within a fairly short time. To look only at the total of current assets in the balance sheet is not a sufficient guide to the liquidity of a company.

($)	A	B	C
Inventory	50	25	25
Debtors	25	50	25
Cash	<u>25</u>	<u>25</u>	<u>50</u>
	100	100	100
Current liabilities	80	80	80
Operating profit	40	40	20
Depreciation	10	10	5

Although the three companies in the example have identical current assets of $100, their liquidity is quite different. Company C is the most liquid. At the year end it has $50 in cash and can expect to receive $25 in the near future from customers. Although company B has the same amount of liquid assets as C ($75), it is not as liquid as it has less cash immediately available. Company A is the least liquid with 50% of current assets being held as inventory, which will probably take much longer to turn into cash than debtors.

Current ratio

A simple guide to the ability of a company to meet its short-term obligations is to link current assets and liabilities in what is commonly termed the current ratio. This appears to have been developed by bankers towards the end of the 19th century as one of their first and, as it proved, one of their last contributions to financial analysis. It links total current assets and total current liabilities.

$$\text{Current ratio} = \text{current assets} \div \text{current liabilities}$$

Current assets consist of cash balances, short-term deposits and investments, debtors, prepaid expenses and inventory. Current liabilities include creditors, short-term bank borrowing, dividends and tax due within the coming year. The combination of the two in the current ratio provides a somewhat crude guide to the solvency rather than the liquidity of the company at the year end.

For the three companies in the example there would be no difference in the current ratio. As each company has $80 total current liabilities the ratio is:

$$\$100 \div \$80 = \$1.25$$

For every $1 of current liabilities, each company is maintaining at the year end $1.25 of current assets. If the company paid all its short-term creditors, it would have $0.25 left for every $1 of current asset used. As a rough guide, for most companies, to exhibit at least a 1.5:1 relationship between current assets and liabilities can be taken as an indication of the ability to meet short-term creditors without recourse to special borrowing or the sale of any assets, except those appearing as current in the balance sheet.

Liquid ratio

However, its inability to distinguish the short-term financial positions of the three companies highlights the comparative uselessness of the current ratio. A stricter approach is to exclude the year-end inventory from current assets to arrive at what are called liquid assets – those being cash or as near cash as makes no difference. This ratio is sometimes called the acid test, but it is more often termed the liquid or quick ratio.

Liquid ratio = liquid assets ÷ current liabilities

For the three companies the liquid ratio is as follows.

($)	A	B & C
Liquid assets	50	75
Current liabilities	80	80
Liquid ratio	**0.62**	**0.94**

The liquid ratio is easy to calculate from the balance sheet and there are two reasons to support its use. First, it is difficult to know precisely what physically is included in the figure for inventory disclosed in the balance sheet. Second, even good inventory often proves difficult to turn quickly into cash. Where inventory consists mainly of finished goods ready for sale, valued at the lower of cost or net realisable value, a company trying to turn such inventory quickly into cash would be unlikely to achieve this value; potential buyers can usually sense when a seller is desperate to sell and will hold out for the lowest possible price. Thus a prudent approach to assessing the ability of a company to meet its short-term liabilities assumes inventory will not provide a ready source of cash.

Company A is now identified as being potentially less liquid than companies B and C. There is still no revealed difference between B and

C. Both have an identical liquid ratio of 0.94:1. For most businesses, to have $0.94 readily available in cash or near cash for every $1 of current liability would be seen as very safe. Such a company could, without selling any inventory or borrowing money, immediately cover all but 6% of its short-term liabilities. A potential supplier, having first checked that the previous year's accounts disclosed a similar position, might justifiably feel confident in extending credit to such a company.

Whether the fact that company A has a liquid ratio of 0.62 would make suppliers unwilling to deal with it would depend on further knowledge and analysis. But clearly, through the use of the liquid ratio, company A is now isolated as being in a different short-term financial position from B and C.

Current liquidity ratio

Although the liquid ratio appears to be an improvement on the current ratio, it has still proved impossible to distinguish between companies B and C in the example. A further refinement is to consider current liabilities not only with current and liquid assets but also with a company's cash flow generating capability.

The simplest definition of cash flow is profit without any deduction for depreciation. Depreciation is merely a book-keeping entry and does not involve a physical movement of cash. If depreciation is added back to the trading or operating profit shown in the income statement, the resulting figure provides a rough indication of the cash flow being generated by the company during the year. On this basis, the cash flow for A and B is $50 and for C is $25.

A company wishing to pay creditors will first make use of its liquid assets. If it is assumed that inventory is not capable of being turned rapidly into cash, then, before borrowing money to pay creditors, the company will rely on cash being made available from its operations. The current liquidity ratio calculates how many days, at the normal level of cash flow generation, would be required to complete the payment of creditors.

Current liquidity ratio = 365 × (current liabilities − liquid assets) ÷ cash flow from operations

For the three companies in the example:

($)	A	B	C
Current liabilities	80	80	80
Less			
Liquid assets	<u>50</u>	<u>75</u>	<u>75</u>
	30	5	5
Divided by			
Cash flow	<u>50</u>	<u>50</u>	<u>25</u>
	0.6	0.1	0.2
x 365			
Days	**219**	**36**	**73**

If the only sources of finance other than liquid assets proved to be cash flow from operations, it would take company A 219 days, more than seven months, to complete payment of its current liabilities, whereas company B would require 36 days and company C 73 days. Assuming all three companies were operating in the same business sector, creditors assessing them would rightly feel least confident of company A.

Ratios in perspective

To explore further how the short-term financial position and viability of different companies can be analysed and compared, here is another example.

($m)	Department store group (D)	Food retailer (E)	Heavy goods manufacturer (F)	Restaurant chain (G)
Inventory	75	38	193	10
Other	30	20	80	40
Trade debtors	80	5	162	30
Cash	<u>120</u>	<u>15</u>	<u>215</u>	<u>190</u>
Current assets	305	78	650	270
Trade creditors	35	76	70	75
Other creditors	<u>165</u>	<u>104</u>	<u>300</u>	<u>285</u>
Current liabilities	200	180	370	360
Operating profit	130	60	160	300
Depreciation	20	25	35	20

From this the ratios covered so far in this chapter can be calculated.

	D	E	F	G
Current ratio	1.53	0.43	1.76	0.75
Liquid ratio	1.15	0.22	1.24	0.72
Current liquidity ratio	−73	601	−163	114

Companies D, F and G show a current ratio of close to, or better than 1:1. For every $1 of current liability at the year end they have $1, or more, available in current assets. The food retailer (E) and the restaurant chain (G) can be expected to operate with a lower current ratio than the department store group (D) or the heavy goods manufacturer (F). Their business is based on the sale of food with lower investment in inventory than for the other businesses represented in the example; nor do they normally offer long credit terms to their customers.

The differences between companies' financial positions are reinforced by the use of the liquid ratio. The manufacturer (F), with $1.24 in liquid assets for every $1 of current liability, shows the highest level of short-term solvency. As a potential creditor, possibly considering becoming a supplier, to company F, the 1.24:1 cover would provide reasonable confidence that invoices would be paid in full and on time.

However, before committing to a working relationship with F it would be necessary to compare this company with others in the same business to discover if 1.24:1 was typical. If a potential supplier to company E studied other food retailers, it would be seen that between 0.10:1 and 0.50:1 is typical. Thus on the basis of this ratio alone dealing with company E would appear reasonably safe.

As both the department store (D) and the manufacturer (F) have liquid ratios of more than 1:1, they will show a negative current liquidity ratio. They could pay all of their short-term liabilities from liquid assets and still have some left over. In practice, having seen the negative values for the liquid ratio, potential creditors would not find it worth calculating the current liquidity ratio for these companies since this would not give them a better appreciation of their likely financial exposure in dealing with the companies.

The food retailer (E) discloses the highest figure for the current liquidity ratio. If the company used all its readily available liquid assets to pay current liabilities and there were no other immediately available sources of cash, it would require a further 20 months (602 days) of operating cash flow to complete payment. Before drawing any conclusions about the acceptability of this and any other ratio, it is necessary to obtain some benchmarks for comparison. If the food retailer's 602 days is compared with the department store's -73 days, it is clear that they have different short-term financial positions, and that, although they are both retailers, they are in completely different businesses.

The food retailer can confidently expect a more consistent and regular pattern of future daily sales than the department store. Customers make purchases more regularly in food supermarkets than in department stores. A creditor to company E can be reasonably confident that the next day some $2.7m, the average daily sales figure (see page 192), will pass through the cash tills in the supermarket. The sales of the department store, although also averaging $2.7m per day, are more likely to be skewed in terms of their cash impact towards Christmas or other seasonal events.

Creditors of the food retailer need not be concerned about the 602-day current liquidity ratio. In the UK and the United States, current liquidity ratios of up to 1,200 days (four years) for food retailers are quite normal. In continental Europe, largely because of different working relationships with suppliers, ratios two or three times greater than this are common.

The key to interpreting this ratio, as with all others, is to obtain a sound basis for comparison. Different countries, as well as different business sectors, often have different solvency, liquidity and cash flow experiences and expectations.

Working capital to sales ratio

A useful indicator of the adequacy and consistent management of working capital is to relate it to sales revenue. For this measure, working capital, ignoring cash and investments, is defined as follows.

Working capital = inventory + trade debtors − trade creditors

For the four companies in the example the figures are as follows.

($m)	Department store group (D)	Food retailer (E)	Heavy goods manufacturer (F)	Restaurant chain (G)
Inventory	75	38	193	10
Trade debtors	80	5	162	30
Trade creditors	35	76	70	75
Working capital	120	-33	285	-35
Sales revenue	1,000	1,000	1,000	1,000
Working capital to sales revenue (%)	**12.0**	**-3.3**	**28.5**	**-3.5**

A negative figure for working capital denotes the fact that the company had, at the year end, more trade creditors than inventory and trade debtors. This is acceptable, providing creditors have confidence in the continuing ability of a company to pay its bills when they fall due. Normally, such confidence is directly linked to the company's business sector and its proven record of cash flow generation. What is acceptable for the food retailer and the restaurant chain is not acceptable for the heavy goods manufacturer, because its cash inflow over the next few days is much less certain.

As a general rule, the lower the percentage disclosed for this ratio the better it is for the business. If the department store group were to increase turnover by $1m, this ratio suggests that an additional $120,000 of working capital would be required. For the heavy goods manufacturer, an additional $285,000 would be required to support same $1m sales increase. However, for the food retailer and restaurant chain, for which the ratio is negative, an increase in sales revenue would appear to lead to a decrease in their working capital. This might well be the case for a company experiencing steady growth and maintaining creditors' confidence.

Debtors to creditors ratio

More detailed analysis can be completed using specific ratios focusing on particular aspects of the working capital management and structure of companies. For example, the relationship between credit given to customers and credit taken from suppliers can be assessed and compared by linking trade debtors and creditors.

Trade debtors ÷ trade creditors

For the four companies in the example the figures are as follows.

	D	E	F	G
Debtors ÷ creditors	2.3	0.1	2.3	0.4

This ratio shows that for every 100 units of credit taken from suppliers, company D, the department store, and company F, the heavy goods manufacturer, were extending 230 units of credit to their customers. Company G, the restaurant chain, gives only 40 units of credit to its customers for every 100 units of credit it receives from suppliers. Further evidence of the aggressive use of suppliers' finance by company E, the food retailer, is provided as this ratio shows that for every 100 units of supplier credit the company extends only 10 units to its customers.

In normal circumstances, this ratio should remain reasonably constant from year to year. Large and erratic shifts either way may signal a change in credit policy or business conditions.

Average daily sales and costs

Another useful indicator of a company's short-term cash flows and financial position is its average daily sales (ADS) and average daily costs (ADC). You can divide the total sales and cost of sales by 240 to more closely represent the number of working days in the year, but, given the broad nature of the analysis, it is as effective to use 365 days as the denominator.

The cost of sales is found in the income statement in most annual reports. The figure normally includes purchases but not always staff wages and associated expenses. If there is difficulty in obtaining a truly comparable cost of sales figure for all the companies being analysed, then, by deducting the operating or trading profit from sales revenue, you will get an approximation of cost of sales.

($m)	D	E	F	G
Turnover	1,000	1,000	1,000	1,000
Average daily sales	*2.74*	*2.74*	*2.74*	*2.74*
Cost of sales	650	920	840	620
Average daily cost	*1.78*	*2.52*	*2.30*	*1.70*

Although comparing the ADS and ADC gives a broad idea of how much more a company receives than it spends each day, the reality is that companies whose trade is seasonal will spend much more than an average amount to build up stock before their peak periods for sales. They will also receive more than average from sales during peak periods.

The cash cycle

When combined with other information from the balance sheet, ADS and ADC can help you understand the way in which the cash is flowing around the business in the cash cycle or working capital cycle ratio.

Inventory

To discover how long a company's cash is tied up in inventory, the balance sheet figure for inventory is divided by ADC to give the number of days that inventory appears to be held on average by the company. The ADC figure is used because inventory is valued at the lower of cost or net realisable value so there is no profit element involved. To use ADS would result in the number of days being understated.

($m)	D	E	F	G
Inventory	75	38	193	10
ADC	1.78	2.52	2.30	1.70
Days' inventory	**42**	**15**	**84**	**6**

The longer inventory is held, the longer financial resources are tied up in a non-profit-generating item; the lower the number of days inventory shown, the faster is the turnover of the inventory. Each time inventory is turned the company makes a profit and generates cash.

In the example, the companies hold, on average, 37 days of inventory. As you would expect, the heavy goods manufacturer (F) has the highest level and the restaurant chain (G), with fresh food, the lowest. The crucial factor is how these levels compare with those of other similar businesses.

An alternative way of looking at the efficiency of inventory levels is to calculate the inventory turnover for the year; this can be done by dividing the annual cost of sales by year-end inventory. The higher the resulting figure the more effective is a company's management of inventory. However, a company with a high inventory turnover may be maintaining inventory levels too low to meet demand satisfactorily, with the result that customers go elsewhere.

($m)	D	E	F	G
Cost of sales	650	920	840	620
Inventory	75	38	193	10
Inventory turnover	**9**	**24**	**4**	**62**

These figures provide an alternative view of how effectively companies are managing inventory.

Trade debtors

To discover the level of credit being offered to customers (trade debtors), average daily sales (ADS) is used as the denominator. The figure for trade debtors is usually found in the notes to the accounts and not on the face of the balance sheet.

($m)	D	E	F	G
Trade debtors	80	5	162	30
Average daily sales	*2.74*	*2.74*	*2.74*	*2.74*
Days' debtors	**29**	**2**	**59**	**11**

In the example, the average figure for what is sometimes called the credit period is 25 days. In effect, the companies are lending customers money for that period until cash is received, and they must provide the necessary finance to support this.

In the case of the department store group (company D), it can be assumed that cash is used to purchase inventory, which is displayed for 42 days before it is bought by a customer, who does not actually pay for it for another 29 days. The time from taking the cash out of the bank to receiving it back, plus a profit margin, is 71 days. The faster the cycle, the better it is for the company.

For example, if the ADC for the department store is $1.8m and it proved possible to reduce the level of inventory by one day, the cash cycle would speed up, the profit margin would be achieved one day earlier and more profit would be made in the year. Also the assets employed in the business would decrease by $1.8m, being one day's less inventory. If the time taken to collect cash from its customers could be reduced by one day, there would be a reduction of assets employed in the business of $2.7m and a corresponding increase in rate of return.

Cutting inventory or debtor levels reduces the level of assets employed in the business and increases profit, thus raising the return on total assets (see page 138). There is a direct link between the efficient management of cash flows and the overall profitability of a business.

Trade creditors

Trade creditors represent the amount of money the company owes its suppliers for goods and services delivered during the year. These are normally found, as are trade debtors, not on the face of the balance sheet but in the notes to the accounts. As trade creditors are shown at cost in the balance sheet, they are divided by average daily cost (ADC).

($m)	D	E	F	G
Trade creditors	35	76	70	75
Average daily cost	*1.78*	*2.52*	*2.30*	*1.70*
Days' credit taken	**20**	**30**	**30**	**44**

In the example, the average length of credit the companies are taking from their suppliers (the reverse of credit given to customers) is 31 days.

Calculating the cycle

Cash flows out of the bank into inventory, from inventory into customers' hands then back into the bank. The suppliers of the inventory are paid cash and the cash cycle is now complete. The three ratios can now be combined to give the cash cycle or working capital cycle.

Cash cycle = days' inventory − days' trade creditors + days' trade debtors

	D	E	F	G
Days' inventory	42	15	84	6
Less				
Days' credit taken	20	30	30	44
	22	−15	54	−38
Plus				
Days' credit given	29	2	59	11
Days' cash cycle	**51**	**−13**	**113**	**−27**

The average cash cycle is 31 days. The two extremes are the heavy goods manufacturer (F) with a cash cycle of 113 days and the restaurant

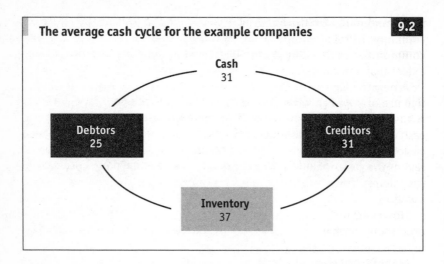

The average cash cycle for the example companies 9.2

Cash
31

Debtors
25

Creditors
31

Inventory
37

chain (G) with −27 days. It is possible now to return to the simple representation of the cash flow cycle shown earlier in this chapter and apply the average figures produced from the analysis (see Figure 9.2).

The average cash cycle experienced by the companies was for cash to be tied up in inventory for 37 days; after goods had been sold to customers it took a further 25 days for the cash to be received. The average company therefore required 62 days' finance to cover inventory holding and credit extended to customers. As the average company took 31 days' credit from its suppliers, it had to finance only 31 days of the cash cycle itself. Suppliers provided 31 out of the required 62 days' finance for the average company's investment in working capital.

The cash cycle can provide an indication of the short-term financial implications of sales growth. If the average cash cycle of 31 days is used this suggests that for every $100 of sales $8.5 working capital is required.

$$31 \div 365 \times 100 = 8.5$$

If it was planned to increase sales by $1m, some $85,000 additional working capital must be found to support the growth.

Using creditors for finance
The use of creditors to finance this operating cycle is normal. The degree to which short-term creditors' money is used depends partly on what is normal or acceptable within a business sector, and so acceptable to sup-

pliers, and partly on the financial management policy of the individual company. In retail companies, particularly food retailers, it is not uncommon for trade creditors to be used to finance the business to the extent that a negative number of days is disclosed for the cash cycle.

A negative figure for the cash cycle indicates an aggressive and positive use of suppliers' money to finance the operations of the company. A cash cycle of -10 days could be interpreted as the company taking cash out of the bank, holding it for 10 days as inventory and selling it to customers who pay within 1 day: a total of 11 days. Then the company retains the cash, including the profit margin, in the business, or invests it for interest, for a further 10 days before paying suppliers the money owed.

However, most businesses do not have negative cash cycles. Food processing companies supplying retailers, for example, can be expected to have comparably high cash cycles.

Manufacturers can be expected to hold much more inventory than retailers. In the case of company F, there is some 84 days' inventory including raw materials, work in progress and finished goods. Manufacturers are not cash businesses like many retailers, and they are unable to collect cash from their customers as quickly. Company F, on average, is offering customers 59 days' credit, twice as long as the department store group (D). This fact is supported by the average days' credit being taken by the retailers. The credit taken by the retailer is often the credit given by the manufacturer. Lastly, manufacturers are unlikely to be able to take much more credit from their suppliers than can retailers. The heavy goods manufacturer (F) takes some 30 days credit from its suppliers, as does the food retailer (E).

The heavy goods manufacturer therefore experiences a cash cycle of 113 days, representing the finance the company must provide for working capital. Different types of businesses produce different standards of ratios.

It could be argued that the cash cycle should be produced by taking the average of opening and closing inventory, debtors and creditors. This is found by adding the current and previous year's figure for each item and dividing the result by two. Given the broad nature of the analysis being undertaken, it is probably just as effective to use the year-end figures set out in the most recent balance sheet.

Assessing the cash position

Current assets include the year-end cash balances of the company. At the same time, current liabilities may show some short-term bank borrowing. It may seem odd that a company can have positive cash balances on one side of the balance sheet and short-term bank borrowing on the other. Such a situation is quite normal, particularly when dealing with a group of companies. If subsidiary companies are, while under the control of the holding company, operating independent bank accounts, one may have a short-term bank loan and another may have positive cash balances. In the assessment of liquidity, short-term bank borrowing should be set against positive cash balances to provide a net cash figure.

It is not normally possible to gain detailed information concerning a company's banking arrangements from the annual report. Moreover, the level of short-term borrowing shown at the year end as part of current liabilities may not be representative of the rest of the year.

What constitutes a good cash position?

Too little cash might indicate potential problems in paying short-term creditors. Too much cash, as an idle resource, may indicate poor financial management. Cash itself is no use unless it is being used to generate additional income for the company. Cash balances may produce interest when deposited in a bank, but a company should be able to generate more net income by investing the money in its own business.

Too much cash may make a company an attractive proposition to a predator. A company that is profitable and well regarded in the marketplace, with an appropriately high share price, may not have substantial cash balances. All available cash may be reinvested in the business to generate more profit. Such a company may regard a less profitable but cash-rich company as an attractive target for acquisition.

Various ratios can be used to gain some indication of the adequacy of a company's cash position. It is useful to have some idea of what proportion of current assets are being held in the form of cash and short-term investments. Short-term investments may be treated as the equivalent of cash.

For the example companies, the percentage of cash to total current assets is as follows.

	D	E	F	G
Current assets ($m)	305	78	650	270
Cash ($m)	120	15	215	190
Cash holding (%)	**39**	**19**	**33**	**70**

The more liquid a company is, the higher is the proportion of current assets in cash or near-cash items. The restaurant chain (G) held almost twice as much cash, represented as a proportion of current assets, at the year end as the department store group (D). The heavy goods manufacturer (F) and food retailer (E) maintained lower levels of liquidity.

It might also be of interest to see what proportion of a company's total assets is held in liquid form as either cash or short-term investments.

	D	E	F	G
Cash ($m)	120	15	215	190
Total assets ($m)	850	600	980	1,130
Cash holding (%)	**14**	**2**	**22**	**17**

Under this measure, there is little difference to be observed between D, F and G. For every $1 of total assets, company F had more than 22¢ retained in very liquid assets. Company E is the least liquid, holding just over 2% of total assets as cash or short-term investments.

The speed with which cash circulates within a company can be assessed by linking sales revenue for the year with year-end, or average, cash balances.

	D	E	F	G
Sales revenue ($m)	1,000	1,000	1,000	1,000
Cash balance ($m)	120	15	215	190
Cash turn	**8.3**	**66.7**	**4.6**	**5.3**

The higher the figure for cash turn the faster the cash circulation and the better it is for the company; each time it completes the circuit the company's profit margin is added. Once again, different levels of cash turn are expected and acceptable for different types of business. The food retailer has the most rapid cash turnover (66.7 times in the year) and the heavy goods manufacturer the slowest (4.6 times).

Defensive interval

Another useful measure of the adequacy of liquid resources is the defensive interval. If an extreme position is taken and it is assumed that a company, for whatever reason, ceases to have any cash inflows or sources of credit, its survival would be limited to the length of time that existing cash balances and short-term investments could support operations before the company was forced to rely on another source of finance to meet its obligations. This ratio, the defensive interval, is calculated by dividing cash and investments by ADC.

Cash and investments ÷ average daily cost

The more liquid a company the longer is the defensive interval.

	D	E	F	G
Cash ($m)	120	15	215	190
Average daily cost ($m)	1.8	2.5	2.3	1.7
Defensive interval	**67**	**6**	**93**	**112**

The previous ratios showed the restaurant group (G) to be the most liquid company, so it should come first when the defensive period is calculated. If all other sources of finance were closed to company G, it would theoretically be able to maintain its basic operations for almost four months (112 days) before running out of liquid resources. The food retailer (E) would, on the basis of a similar calculation, have cash flow problems within one week.

Another way of calculating the defensive interval is to use the average daily operating cash outflow of a company. If operating profit is deducted from sales revenue and depreciation is added back, a rough indication of total operating cash outflows is produced. Alternatively, the cash flow statement can be checked to see if it provides details of cash payments to suppliers and for employees' remuneration.

Lastly, when assessing liquidity, the figure for cash shown in a company's balance sheet will truly reflect the cash in hand or in the bank at the end of the year. It does not necessarily provide information on what currencies are involved or where the cash is actually held.

Profit and cash flow

There need be no short-term relationship between the profit a company displays in the income statement and the amount of cash it has available at the year end. There are a number of reasons for this. For example, a charge is made each year in the income statement for depreciation that does not affect cash balances. Differences between changes in cash position and reported earnings normally result from the following:

- Operating activities. There may be timing differences between the impact of cash flowing in or out of the business and that of transactions appearing in the income statement. Non-cash expenses such as depreciation are recognised in the income statement.
- Investing activities. Capital investment – purchasing fixed assets – or corporate acquisition or disinvestments may be contained within the balance sheets but not the income statement.
- Financing activities. Raising capital or repaying loans will change the cash position but not the profit in the income statement.

The working capital cycle discussed earlier can be disrupted if it is necessary for a company to use financial resources outside the current asset and current liabilities area. When a company makes capital investments, or pays dividends to shareholders, interest on borrowings or tax, the amount of cash within the working capital area is reduced.

Cash flow measures

The cash flow statement offers a most valuable source of information about the financial management of a company. A typical cash flow statement provides details on types of cash inflows and outflows for the year, linking them to disclose the net change in the cash position at the end of the year (see Chapter 4).

In Chapter 7 operating profit was used to calculate profit margin and rate of return on assets (ROA). It is useful to replace operating profit with operating cash flow to produce the cash flow margin and cash flow return on assets (CFROA).

($m)	D	E	F	G
Sales revenue	1,000	1,000	1,000	1,000
Operating profit	130	60	160	300
Depreciation	20	25	35	20
Operating cash flow	150	85	195	320
Cash flow margin (%)	**15.0**	**8.5**	**19.5**	**32.0**
($m)				
Total assets	850	600	980	1,130
Cash flow return (%)	**17.6**	**14.2**	**19.9**	**28.3**

The figure of operating cash flow is difficult to manipulate, and CFROA focuses attention on the ability of a company to produce a positive cash return on assets employed. The restaurant chain (G) has the highest cash flow margin and cash flow rate of return.

It is helpful to express the figures in the cash flow statement in percentage terms, especially when comparing several years or several companies. It also helps to highlight trends (see Chapter 6).

For any company, it is to be expected that the main source of cash is its normal business activities. A high level of internally generated cash is to be expected of a mature and successful company, whereas a younger and rapidly growing company is likely to have a different balance between sources of cash inflow. The way in which a company finances its operations depends partly on the type of business being undertaken and partly on its stage of growth and maturity.

A further area for exploration within the cash flow statement is to assess what a company is doing with its available cash. Is the cash being used to pay tax and dividends or for reinvestment in the business in fixed assets? A comparison with previous years' figures will reveal whether the company has a consistent policy on the level of investment (see Chapter 12).

The cash flow statement can also be used to spot signs of potential problems. Companies suffering from growth pangs or overtrading can be expected to show an increase in the level of debtors linked to sales revenue as more customers are offered extended credit terms. At the same time, credit taken from suppliers increases to an even greater extent as the company finds it difficult to make the necessary payments on time. During this process cash balances and short-term investments decline rapidly as cash is used up. Any major changes observed in the levels of inventory, debtors, creditors and liquid balances shown in the cash flow statement may reflect either the careful management of working capital or a lack of control by the company.

Lastly, the cash flow statement can be used to help decide whether the costs of capital and borrowings are consistent and of an appropriate level. Each year the proportion of cash flow being used to pay dividends to shareholders and interest on borrowings should be checked.

Summary

- Reading the annual report and discovering that a company made a profit for the year and has several million in cash in the bank at the year end is not sufficient evidence that the company is safe.
- The balance sheet and cash flow statement offer the key to understanding the short-term financial position of a company. The year-end short-term assets and liabilities are set out in the balance sheet; details of the major sources of cash inflow and the uses made of these during the year are to be found in the cash flow statement. This statement also shows, normally as its starting point, the amount of cash generated from the company's operations during the year through the income statement.
- The liquid ratio (quick ratio) is the simplest and probably most effective measure of a company's short-term financial position. It is assumed that inventory will not prove an immediate source of cash so it is ignored. It is easy to calculate this ratio for the current and previous year directly from the balance sheet. The result gives a simple indication of the liquidity of a company and to what extent this is consistent between the two years. The higher the ratio the greater confidence you can have in the short-term survival of the company. A 1:1 ratio indicates that for every $1 of its short-term creditors and borrowings the company is maintaining $1 in cash or assets that can realistically be turned into cash in the near future.
- As with all ratios, before interpreting the figures, it is essential to compare the subject company with others either in the same industry sector or of similar size or business mix. A low liquid ratio may be perfectly acceptable for a food retailer but not for a construction firm.

◾ The liquid ratio is no guide to the profitability or cash flow generation of the company. A profitable company with a healthy cash flow is less likely to suffer short-term financial problems than one with a less positive performance. Yet both companies might have an identical liquid ratio. The current liquidity ratio provides a useful means of combining a company's liquidity with its cash flow generating capability. The lower the number of days in the current liquidity ratio the safer the company is likely to be from short-term liquidity and solvency problems. As a rough rule for most businesses, warning bells should sound if the ratio is seen to be moving to over 1,500 days (four years).

◾ The liquid and current liquidity ratios provide a fairly straightforward indication of the short-term position of a company. But to gain real insight into a company's liquidity and financial management the cash flow statement should be carefully studied for at least the two years provided in the latest annual report. If the cash inflow from operations (profit plus depreciation) is not consistently the major source of funds for the company, try to find out why and then decide whether it is reasonable to assume that this state of affairs can continue.

◾ The cash cycle helps you see how a company is managing cash flows through investment in inventory, credit provided to customers and credit taken from suppliers. The faster the cash circulates through the business the lower is the amount of the capital tied up in operating assets and, as every time the cash completes the circuit a profit is taken, the higher is the rate of return achieved.

10 Capital and valuation

ANOTHER IMPORTANT ASPECT in the overall assessment of a company's financial position is its capital structure and the way in which this is viewed by providers of finance. This chapter analyses sources of finance and the performance measures applied by investors.

A useful first step in the analysis of a company's financial position is to use the balance sheet as a basis for seeing how a company is financed: the proportions of the total capital employed provided by shareholders and other sources of finance.

Equity and debt

A balance sheet has three broad classifications of liabilities: shareholders' funds, long-term loans and creditors, and current liabilities. These reflect the three potential sources of finance open to any company. Finance can be raised from shareholders, through long-term or short-term borrowing, or through the management of working capital.

The shareholders' contribution to the finances of a company is given a variety of names:

- shareholders' funds
- net worth
- capital and reserves
- equity

Equity is the term most commonly used to identify the ordinary shareholders' investment in a company. The balance sheet figure for share capital and reserves may include preference shares and other non-ordinary shares a company has in issue, but such shares should not be included in the definition of equity. Equity represents the ordinary shareholders' investment in the company: "the residual interest in the assets of an entity that remains after deducting its liabilities".

Any finance other than equity is referred to as debt, which can be divided into long-term and short-term borrowing. Borrowings with a life of less than one year appear within current liabilities and are short-term; any other borrowings are treated as long-term.

Equity shares provide a company with long-term finance. They are not normally redeemable, and have no guarantee of income, through payment of dividends, attached to them. Debt is normally borrowed for a fixed term with a fixed rate of interest. With debt, interest charges have to be paid and at some time the money borrowed will have to be repaid. With equity, there is no expectation of capital repayment and the annual dividend paid is under the control of the company. The relationship between debt and equity is crucial to an assessment of the financial structure of a company and its viability.

Gearing or leverage

Raising finance from external sources increases risk because, in the case of loans, there is a cost and the obligation to repay the loan, and, in the case of equity shares being issued to new shareholders, it can reduce the degree of control existing shareholders have over the company.

($)	A	B	C
Shareholders' funds	250	500	1,000
Long-term loans	500	500	500
Current liabilities	250	250	250
Interest charge	50	50	50

The relationship between debt and equity is referred to as gearing or leverage. Management should ensure that the balance between debt and equity finance is appropriate. Too much debt and a company is said to be highly geared; a low-geared company is financed mainly by its shareholders. The higher the level of debt in relation to equity the greater is the potential risk to shareholders of not receiving a dividend or getting back the capital they have invested. Interest on debt must be paid before any dividends, and all borrowings must be repaid before anything becomes available for equity shareholders.

Debt/equity ratio

The relationship between internal and external sources of finance, equity and the total of all non-equity liabilities, can be expressed as a percentage or a ratio: the debt to equity ratio.

$$\text{Debt/equity ratio} = (\text{current liabilities} + \text{long-term loans}) \div \text{equity}$$
$$= \text{total debt} \div \text{equity}$$

	A	B	C
%	300	150	75
times	3	1.5	0.75

The debt/equity ratio is the most commonly used measure of the relationship between internal finance (provided by equity shareholders) and external finance (provided by other sources). Company A with equity of $250 and debt of $750 has a debt/equity ratio of 3 or 300%. This can be interpreted as indicating that for every $1 of shareholder investment in the company, outside borrowing provides $3. Company C has only $0.75 of debt for every $1 of equity. Thus company A is the most highly geared company.

An alternative approach is to take long-term loans as the numerator and add it to the denominator to provide a long-term debt ratio.

Long-term debt ratio = long-term loans ÷ (long-term loans + equity)

	A	B	C
%	66.7	50.0	33.3

The time debt is scheduled for repayment is an important factor influencing the interpretation of any gearing ratio. Any borrowings not scheduled for repayment within one year are included in debt. However, a company not required to repay loans for five years may be viewed differently from one where repayment will take place in two years. The gearing ratios of the two companies may be identical, but the underlying implications are different. The notes accompanying the financial statements provide details of debt repayment terms.

Defining debt and equity

The raising of any form of finance – debt or equity – is completed by means of a "capital" or "financial" instrument. There is no standard definition of gearing, and there are considerable practical difficulties in making the distinction between equity and debt. Although a debenture or bank loan is clearly part of debt, how do you classify a convertible loan, which carries a fixed rate of interest and is capable of being repaid on an agreed future date or converted into equity?

A sound rule in financial analysis is to be conservative; when in doubt treat an item as debt.

Net debt and net tangible assets

Using the information given in the balance sheet and notes to the accounts, debt may be taken to include all non-equity shares, long-term borrowings and creditors, and borrowings appearing in current liabilities such as short-term loans, finance leases and hire purchase contracts. From this the cash and liquid balances are deducted to provide a figure for net debt.

The accounting treatment of intangibles, such as goodwill and brands, can be an important factor in deciding what figure to use to represent the assets employed in a company. Intangible assets are likely to be less certain in value than tangible assets, and therefore offer providers of finance less certain potential as security. A strict approach would be to ignore intangibles in arriving at the net asset value. This provides a figure for net tangible assets which can be used to represent equity in the ratio.

$$\text{Debt/equity ratio} = 100 \times (\text{net debt} \div \text{equity})$$

Intangibles and gearing

Despite increasing standardisation in accounting practices, the way in which companies present details of their assets and liabilities varies considerably. Charging goodwill against reserves, as used to be the case in the UK, brings about an increase in gearing compared with companies which capitalise it, as is now the practice in most countries. For example, company A acquires a subsidiary with $100 tangible assets for a payment of $150, the difference ($50) representing goodwill.

Goodwill written off against reserves ($)

Shareholders' funds (250 − 50)	200	Assets		1,000
		Subsidiary acquired	100	
Long-term borrowing	500	*Less* cash paid	150	(50)
Current liabilities	250			
	950			950

Debt/equity ratio: £750 ÷ £200 = 3.75

Goodwill capitalised ($)

Shareholders' funds	250	Assets		1,000
Long-term borrowing	500	Subsidiary acquired	150	
Current liabilities	250	*Less* cash paid	150	0
	1,000			1,000

Debt/equity ratio: $750 ÷ $250 = 3

Pressure to improve gearing ratios led some UK companies to revalue their assets or to capitalise other intangible assets, such as brand names, in order to counter the effect of the treatment of goodwill on gearing. If company A, having written goodwill off against reserves, were to insert $50 worth of brands into the balance sheet, assets and equity would rise by $50 and gearing would return to $750 ÷ $250.

Off-balance sheet items

When a company raises finance or acquires an asset and there is no identifiable change in the balance sheet, it is referred to as an off-balance sheet transaction. There is nothing new in off-balance sheet transactions; just because an event is not reflected in the balance sheet does not automatically make it suspect. Off-balance sheet items caused concern in the 1980s, when their number and variety increased as they were offered by financial experts to assist companies reduce the costs and risks of finance without all the normal disclosure being involved.

Joint ventures provide a good example of the potential for off-balance sheet financing. Two companies (X and Y) set up a joint venture, and each invests $100 in the new company (Z) for 50% of the equity. They jointly act as guarantors for a bank loan of $1,000 to purchase the assets necessary to set up Z in business. The balance sheets of X and Y show only the $100 investment in the joint venture. The loan of $1,000 does not appear; it is an off-balance sheet item. The figure of $100 will increase under the equity method of valuation as X and Y make more investment in Z or the joint venture begins to make profits, with each company taking 50% into its balance sheet.

The greater the assets and the lower the debt in a company's balance sheet, the happier everyone is. A bank lending money to a company will want to minimise the risk of loss; it may stipulate a maximum level of debt-to-equity (gearing) that it will allow the company to reach. If the company exceeds the gearing level, the bank can require the loan to be repaid immediately. Similarly, analysts, as a simple measure of credit-worthiness, may set "safe" levels of gearing that a company should not cross. In such cases, there is pressure on the company to minimise the liabilities appearing in the balance sheet. For companies X and Y, in effect their level of debt has increased by $500, but there is no evidence of this in the gearing ratios derived from their balance sheets.

Leases and debt

Leases were one of the earliest and most popular forms of off-balance sheet transactions. When a lease is agreed the asset is owned by the lessor and rented or leased to the lessee. The asset appears in the lessor's balance sheet and the lease payments in the lessee's income statement.

Until recently, it was acceptable for a company to acquire an asset under a lease and make no disclosure in the annual report apart from including the annual lease payment as part of total costs in the income statement.

Companies quickly saw the benefits of capital lease agreements, where the lease payments covered the rent element as well as the capital cost. Thus an asset became available for use in return for a series of payments. These did not have to appear as a liability in the balance sheet, and so there was no apparent increase in borrowings. In effect, all the rights and risks of ownership were retained by the lessee, but not legal ownership. Such leases, referred to as finance leases, can be compared with a mortgage or loan taken to purchase a house. It is now generally accepted that a finance lease is a means of financing the acquisition of an asset and should be treated as debt.

Sale and leaseback

Another early form of off-balance sheet transaction was sale and leaseback agreements. A company could sell an asset, such as property, and then lease it back. The asset and any associated borrowing was removed from the balance sheet, although the company still retained full use of the asset. As a result the gearing ratios came down.

With such arrangements, what matters is whether the company leasing the asset retains most of the rights and risks of owning it. If the answer is yes, the impact on the company should be made clear. Currently, any quoted company entering any major sale and leaseback agreement is under considerable pressure to disclose full details in the annual report.

Substance over form

The introduction in 1984 of an accounting standard in the UK required companies to report finance leases under the rule that "economic substance should take precedence over legal form"; in other words, they had to be capitalised and written off over their life through the income statement. It was recognised that the users of financial statements needed to know the real circumstances and actual impact of a transaction. Any asset or liability that should appear in a balance sheet to offer a true and fair view of the company should do so, irrespective of the legal form. However, even today countries in continental Europe are more flexible than the UK or the United States in requiring the capitalisation of leases.

Where a company has an unrelated activity, it can argue that it should not appear in the group balance sheet as it would distort the true picture. A decision could also be made that an activity is no longer related. A good example is retail companies offering customers a range of financial services, usually starting with a company credit card. Is the financial service operation really part of the retail business? If not, it need not appear in the group balance sheet.

Debt ratio

An easier and perhaps more practical means of interpreting a company's gearing is provided by the debt ratio.

$$\text{Debt ratio} = \text{total debt} \div \text{total assets}$$

	A	B	C
%	75	60	43
times	0.75	0.60	0.43

The debt ratio can be calculated either directly from the balance sheet or from a common size statement. The higher the ratio the higher is the gearing. A ratio of 50%, commonly viewed as the limit for accepting without question a company's level of gearing, indicates that for every $1 of assets 50¢ has been financed by long-term and short-term debt. Using this guideline, company A is highly geared with 75% of total assets financed by debt, whereas company C is low geared at 43%.

Interest cover ratio

Interest paid on debt is charged as an expense before arriving at the profit for the year attributable to shareholders. An increase in external borrowings brings higher gearing and a greater interest charge in the income statement. Once a loan is taken, the interest payments must be made in cash and the capital sum repaid on the agreed date. A company not generating enough profit to cover interest payments or having insufficient cash available to repay the loan faces serious difficulty.

An effective ratio for combining profitability with the impact of gearing is interest cover. This measures the ability of a company to generate sufficient profits to allow all interest on borrowings to be paid. It is calculated by dividing the profit before interest and tax

(PBIT) by the interest charge for the year. The figure for PBIT should exclude any exceptional or extraordinary items, and so represent the profit being generated from regular trading operations.

Interest cover = profit before interest and tax ÷ interest paid

The figure for interest used in the ratio should be that due for payment during the financial year, and care should be taken to add back to the figure appearing in the income statement any interest that has been capitalised or interest received that has been deducted.

	A	B	C
Profit before interest and tax ($)	200	100	400
Interest ($)	50	50	50
Interest cover	**4**	**2**	**8**

The higher the interest cover the lower is the risk that there will be insufficient profit available for payment of dividends to shareholders. Company C has the highest interest cover; profit could decline by eight times before it would be unable to cover the interest due on borrowings. The comparatively high interest cover of C is partly because of its profitability and partly its gearing: C has the lowest gearing.

Interest cover can be used to assess the impact of changes in profitability on the risk of shareholders not receiving a dividend. For B a 50% decline in profit would result in there being nothing available for the payment of dividends; every $1 of PBIT is required to pay interest. In the same circumstances and ignoring tax, B would have $25 and C would have $150 available for the payment of dividends.

($)	A	B	C
Profit before interest and tax	100	50	200
Interest	50	50	50
Profit before tax	50	0	150

Attractions of high gearing

Simple arithmetic supports a decision by a company to take advantage of outside sources of finance. Shareholders will clearly benefit if a loan bearing a 10% interest charge is invested in the business where it is expected to generate a 20% rate of return. For no increase in their investment shareholders' return improves, through either increased dividends or capital growth, or a combination of the two.

The situation where there is a 50% decrease in profits has been considered, but what happens when profits double? Profit, subject to tax, becoming available to the shareholders of B increases by 300% and interest cover moves from 2 to 8 times ($400 ÷ $50).

($)	A	B	C
Profit before interest and tax	400	200	800
Interest	50	50	50
Profit before tax	350	150	750

When a company is confident that the costs of external borrowings can be covered through the increased profit flowing from the investment made in the business, it makes sense to increase gearing. An added incentive for debt is that interest is normally tax deductible but dividends are not. High gearing increases the risk associated with the investment, but it can provide shareholders with high returns.

Gearing and rate of return

Alternative measures of rate of return were considered in Chapter 7, including that of return on equity (ROE) or return on shareholders' funds (ROSF). The return on shareholders' investment in a company is a result partly of its efficiency in running the business and partly of the way it is financed. Borrowed funds are employed alongside those provided by shareholders to supply the investment needed to run the business.

Using the after-tax profit figure, the ROE for the three companies is as follows.

($)	A	B	C
Profit before interest and tax	200	100	400
Interest	50	50	50
Pre-tax profit	150	50	350
Tax	75	25	175
After-tax profit	75	25	175
Total assets	1,000	1,250	1,750
Equity	250	500	1,000
ROE (%)	30.0	5.0	17.5
After tax on total assets (%)	7.5	2.0	10.0

Asset gearing ratio and return on equity

The way in which a company's assets are financed can be reviewed with the asset gearing ratio. This is directly linked to the debt ratio and identifies what proportion of the total assets or total capital employed is provided by shareholders. The impact of gearing is clearly shown; the higher the gearing the higher is the ratio.

$$\text{Asset gearing} = \text{total assets} \div \text{equity}$$

Company A's shareholders are supporting only one-quarter ($1,000 $\div$ $250) of the total assets employed in the business. For every $1 of shareholders' investment in company A there is $3 ($750 $\div$ $250) of debt and creditors finance, whereas for company C there is only $0.75 ($750 $\div$ $1,000).

$$\text{Return on equity} = (\text{profit} \div \text{assets}) \times (\text{assets} \div \text{equity})$$

Financing a business with debt can help increase returns to shareholders. For every $1 of equity in company A there are $4 of assets. This acts as the multiplier of profits becoming available to shareholders. If the after-tax profit margin (7.5%) is multiplied by the asset gearing ratio (4), the result is the return on shareholders' funds of 30%. Company C has a higher profit margin (10%) but lower asset gearing, with a multiplier of only 1.75 producing the lower rate of return to shareholders of 17.5%.

	A	B	C
Assets/equity	4.00	2.50	1.75
After tax on total assets (%)	7.50	2.00	10.00
ROE (%)	**30.00**	**5.00**	**17.50**

Dangers of high gearing

The more a company relies on debt the less control it has over its finances and the more it is at risk, because banks are less likely to accept changes in the terms of a loan agreement than shareholders are to accept a lower or even no dividend if the company is short of cash or needs money to invest in assets.

High gearing can bring high volatility in the level of profit available to equity shareholders. For a highly geared company, a small movement in profit can have a dramatic influence on equity earnings. A small drop would eat up in debt service all the profit that would otherwise be available to distribute as dividends.

When business is booming, a company may regard an increase in gearing as not only attractive but also essential. It can be seen as a sign of poor management not to borrow more to achieve returns in excess of the cost of borrowing. During inflationary times, when the real cost of debt decreases, the pressures can be irresistible. However, if the boom slows and/or ends and there is a recession, the highly geared company faces difficulties as profits decline, interest rates rise and the loans fall due for repayment.

A further danger inherent in high gearing is that as the providers of debt see gearing rise they may, to reduce their own exposure, insist that certain restrictions are built into loan agreements – for example, an upper limit for gearing or tougher levels for interest cover or liquidity. The company may lose some degree of control and flexibility of approach in its financial management. If it breaks the loan restrictions, it may be held in default and forced to make immediate repayment.

Share price and value

In general, share prices reflect views of the future rather than the clear view of the past presented by the accounts.

In the UK, shares are normally issued at a par value. The par value of a share is the nominal value at which it is issued and appears in the balance sheet. A company may issue 25p or £1 shares and this, rather than market price, is the value consistently used in the balance sheet. When shares are issued at a price higher than par value the difference is referred to as share premium. The par value of shares is of no relevance to financial analysis. In the United States, it is more common for companies issue shares of no par value.

For the majority of shareholders, it is the price quoted on the stock exchange that determines the value of their investment. Share prices and price movements of the previous day are given in the press together with the high and low points for the year.

Many factors can influence a company's share price. Some are clear and quantifiable; others are more esoteric and ephemeral. A company issuing a profit warning can expect a drop in share price. Rumours of a takeover, a technological breakthrough, changes on the board, a big order or a lost one can all influence share price. Share price will partly reflect the general mood of the market, which is in turn linked to the national and global, economic, political and social environment. General optimism produces a bull market (one in which share prices are rising) and pessimism a bear market (one in which share prices are falling).

There can be only one indisputable answer to the question: Why did the shares go up by 5% yesterday? That, as any market trader knows, is: Because there were more buyers than sellers.

The prime trigger for a movement in share price is a change in investors' confidence in the ability of a company to produce profits in the future. Shares may have been purchased on the basis of the past performance of a company, but they are held in expectation of future returns: income and capital gain.

The sector in which a company operates can also influence share price. If it is one that is seen as being static, this will hold back the share price, whereas the reverse is true for a dynamic or glamorous sector.

Each stock exchange has its own share price indicator. In the UK, the FTSE 100, commonly referred to as the Footsie, includes the share prices of the largest 100 quoted companies. This is a good real-time indicator of the market; a rise in the FTSE can be taken to indicate a general upward movement in share prices.

Betas

For any given period, movements in both a company's share price and a selected stock exchange index can be plotted to give an indication of the sensitivity of the company's share price to general movements of the stockmarket. If it was found that for every 1% move in the stockmarket the company's shares moved by 1.5%, applying the 1.5 factor to the stockmarket index should provide an indicator of the likely price of that company's shares. This is called the beta rating or beta factor.

A beta of 1.5 suggests that the company's share price will on average move 1.5% with every 1% move in the market. A beta of 1 suggests the company's share price moves precisely in tune with the market. If the buoyancy of the share market is linked to expectations of the economy, companies with high beta values are likely to be directly affected by boom or doom. With a sound economy high-beta companies can be expected to generate extremely good returns, but in a recession they will probably be poor performers. A company with a low beta is likely to be little affected by changes in the economic environment. Government stocks or gilts have a beta of 0; the interest received is not affected by stockmarket fluctuations.

A company's beta can be taken as a measure of market or systematic risk of the share. The higher the beta the more volatile the share will be in relation to changes in the market. There are also betas available for sectors of business against which to compare individual companies.

The statistical analysis behind the development of betas is complex. Both income and capital gains from each share are compared with the return from the selected market index over a number of years. Betas are incorporated in the capital asset pricing model (CAPM), which is used to quantify the cost of equity capital (see pages 231-2).

Net asset per share ratio

If a company is wound up and the assets are sold for their balance sheet values, after all external liabilities are settled what remains – net worth or net assets – is all that is available to repay equity shareholders. It is therefore worth calculating the net asset per share ratio to get an idea of the value of the assets supporting the share price. The higher the assets per share the lower is the shareholders' risk.

Asset backing = net assets ÷ number of shares in issue

($)	A	B	C
Sale of total assets	1,000	1,250	1,750
Less			
Debt	500	500	500
Current liabilities	250	250	250
Net assets	250	500	1,000
Number of shares	250	500	1,500
Net assets per share	1.00	1.00	0.67
Share price	3.00	1.00	1.50

For most companies, net asset backing per share is lower than the current share price for the simple reason that there should be more to a company than just the book value of its assets. The company's "market to book" ratio is greater than 1. Company B has net assets per share matching the current share price ($1). A share can be purchased for $1, and if the company were wound up then $1 would be returned from the sale of assets. However, there does not appear to be any value placed on the business beyond net assets employed. The share price indicates no expectation of growth or improved performance.

Where share price is found to be lower than net asset backing, this can be interpreted in a number of ways. It may be that the company has not been performing as well as others in the same sector and there is general agreement that this is likely to continue, with the result that there is little demand for the shares. If net assets per share are much higher than share price a company may be seen as beyond redemption, but it may also become a target for takeover by someone who has spotted an opportunity to acquire assets cheaply.

Note that this ratio is not appropriate for businesses such as property companies, which have a different financial structure from that of most companies.

Earnings per share

A popular means of measuring company performance is earnings per share (EPS). This ratio is produced by dividing the after-tax profit for the year, deducting minority interests and any non-voting share dividends, by the weighted average number of equity shares in issue (see page 86).

Earnings per share = after-tax profit ÷ number of shares

	A	B	C
After-tax profit ($)	75	25	175
Number of shares	250	500	1,500
Earnings per share (¢)	30	5	11.7

Comparing earnings per share

It is a mistake to assume you can compare profitability based on earnings per share. A difference in earnings per share can be brought about simply by differences in share capital structure. Two companies could have an identical after-tax profit of $50 and share capital of $100. But if one company had issued 25¢ shares and the other 100¢ shares the earnings per share would be very different: 12.5¢ and 50¢.

Diluted earnings per share

Sometimes the earnings per share figure is referred to as being diluted. This arises where a company has issued securities which have the right to convert into equity shares at some future date. The diluted earnings per share is calculated assuming that this conversion has taken place, showing the position if all the possible options were taken up and shares were issued. Often a significant factor in arriving at the fully diluted earnings per share will be the share options of directors and other employees.

Smoothing earnings

There is an understandable tendency among directors to prefer a steady and smooth profit growth over a number of years rather than a series of volatile shifts.

Companies X and Y have over the same period of time reached the same level of profit, and for most people the decision on which company to invest in for a share in next year's profits would not be difficult. Ignoring any other available information, X showing a steady profit growth will probably be preferred to Y. Although over time the profit from both is identical, there appears to be more certainty (less risk) with an investment in X.

It is generally accepted that a smooth upward profit trend is better than a track record similar to the skyline of the Swiss Alps. Given the choice, most companies would prefer to see their profit increase gradually over a number of years. Smoothing profits is attractive. A smooth profit trend indicates that management has firm and effective control.

Creative profits

But profits can be smoothed in many creative ways, for example by changing depreciation policy or capitalising expenses such as interest charges, or product development or start-up costs. The treatment of goodwill in the UK was an example of how to reduce the apparent costs of acquisition appearing in the income statement. Taking brands to the balance sheet may result in a similar profit improvement.

The time at which a transaction or profit is brought into the accounts can be an important consideration. If a major event producing large profits is not brought into this year's accounts but moved into the following year, reported profit can be effectively smoothed – quite common practice for German companies.

It is much more difficult to produce a profit immediately than to shift profit from this year to next. There is a temptation for a very profitable company, uncertain of the future, to set aside some of its current profit for a rainy day. A reserve is created. A cash sale of $100 is not taken into the income statement but placed in the balance sheet as "deferred

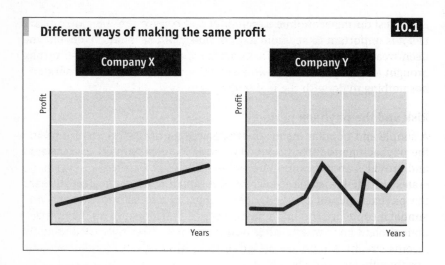

Different ways of making the same profit `10.1`

Company X

Company Y

Profit

Profit

Years

Years

revenue". Next year $100 revenue is brought into the income statement and the reserve disappears. A variation is to pre-pay expenses: pay some of next year's expenses in cash and include in the current year's cost of sales. It is to be hoped that the auditor will catch any such tricks. To date the most extreme example of manipulating reserves is World-Com, resulting in an overstatement of profit in 2000 of some $3 billion.

Pension fund accounting, off-balance sheet financing, the manipulation of provisions, year-end inventory valuations, and treatment of bad debts and exceptional and extraordinary income or expense items can all help smooth profits and influence balance sheet valuations.

A certain amount of profit smoothing is an inevitable part of business life, but a line is clearly crossed when profits are manipulated because directors' remuneration depends on them. If you think a company is employing creative accounting techniques, you should look carefully at the information in the annual report rather than rely on the ratios produced by commercial databases, which take all the figures in the financial statements at their face value.

Creative earnings per share

Because shareholders as well as financial analysts place considerable weight on earnings per share, directors are naturally keen that the figure they report is a good one, often providing an example of "what you measure is what you get". Temptation to succumb to such action, sometimes euphemistically referred to as "aggressive earnings management", is greatest during economic uncertainty and recession. When looking at EPS it is important to see how extraordinary or exceptional items have been treated. It is possible for a dramatic improvement in EPS to be brought about by the sale of an asset, thus producing a large profit that has nothing to do with the real trading activity of a company.

Risk and the payback period

A simple and popular means of taking account of risk is to be found in the payback period. Payback is used in investment project assessment and provides an indication of how long it will be before a project generates sufficient income to recover the capital investment. The shorter the payback period the better. An investment of $1,000 offering an annual income of $100 has a payback period of 10 years. An alternative option might be to invest the $1,000 in a project offering a $200 annual income stream. A payback period of 5 years is likely to be more attractive than the first option.

Price/earnings ratio

A company's earnings per share can be incorporated in an equivalent to the payback measure: the price/earnings (P/E) ratio. Share price is dependent upon investors' opinions of a company's future earning potential as much as anything else. Earnings per share (as last reported) can usefully be linked to current share price to provide some indication of expectations for future performance.

$$\text{Price/earnings} = \text{share price} \div \text{earnings per share}$$

	A	B	C
Share price (¢)	300	100	150
Earnings per share (¢)	30	5	11.7
Price/earnings	**10**	**20**	**12.9**

For company A a P/E of 10 can be interpreted as showing that when a share is purchased for 300¢ this represents the equivalent of 10 years' earnings of 30¢ a year – in other words, a payback period of 10 years.

The higher the P/E ratio the greater the confidence investors have in the future prospects and performance of the company. A high P/E ratio indicates investors have confidence that the company will maintain and probably improve its current performance in the coming year.

High or low price/earnings?

The only way of deciding whether a company has a high or a low P/E ratio is to compare it with other companies. Companies are listed in the financial media by their sector of operation. The company with the highest P/E ratio is considered, on that day, to be the sector's best future performer for investors.

As earnings per share is dependent upon share price, the P/E ratio is influenced by forecast trends, rumours or myths of the moment. It is not unusual for the company with the highest ratio one year to be the first in the sector to succumb to recession or mismanagement. By definition, a high P/E ratio indicates that it is probably too late to invest in the company since the price to be paid will be too high. It may also indicate that a company is already overvalued. Experience suggests that the only way for a high P/E to move is downwards.

It can be useful to compare a company's P/E ratio with the average for the sector or with that of a selected competitor. If the average P/E for the sector is 15, the relative position of the three example companies is indicated.

	A	B	C
Actual P/E	10	20	12
Average P/E	15	15	15
Relative position	**67**	**133**	**80**

Prospective price/earnings

If a forecast is made of a company's likely future profits, this can provide a figure for likely future earnings per share. If company A is forecast to have a profit growth of 20% in the coming year, after-tax profit will rise to $82.5 and EPS to 33¢. If current share price is divided by forecast earnings (300 ÷ 33), a prospective P/E ratio of 9.1 is produced. This prospective P/E is the product of arithmetic and is not influenced by real life.

If any item is left as unknown in the equation below, it is easy to discover its value.

$$\text{Share price} = \text{earnings per share} \times \text{price/earnings ratio}$$
$$300 = 30 \times 10.0$$
$$330 = \mathbf{33} \times 10.0$$
$$\mathbf{300} = 33 \times 9.1$$

For company A, where only one variable in the equation is adjusted, earnings per share are forecast at 33¢ and share price rises to 330. If share price were held at 300¢, with 33¢ earnings per share the P/E ratio moves to 9.1. Prospective P/E ratios can only be estimated, but once some forecast is obtained for profit and P/E these can be used to indicate likely future share price movements. If for company A earnings per share is forecast at 33¢ and it is considered that the company should command a P/E ratio of 12, the likely future share price can be calculated as follows.

Future share price = forecast earnings per share × prospective price/earnings

$$396 = 33 \times 12$$

Problems with price/earnings ratio

In most cases, the P/E ratio being used in analysis is that provided by a newspaper, not one calculated by the user. This can cause a number of problems. The profit used as the basis for a published P/E ratio is normally that shown in a company's income statement and may therefore have been arrived at creatively. Furthermore, one side of the equation is historic profit, which is not guaranteed to be a guide to future performance, and the other side is current share price, which changes from minute to minute on the stock exchange. A rumour of takeover or a major technological breakthrough in product development will not alter historic earnings, but it will certainly have an effect on share price.

Dividend per share

Dividend per share (DPS) can be calculated like earnings per share. The total dividend for the year is divided by the number of shares in issue.

Dividend per share = dividend ÷ number of equity shares in issue

	A	B	C
Dividend ($)	25	20	87
Number of shares	250	500	1,500
Dividend per share (¢)	**10**	**4**	**5.8**

Dividends

Companies normally make two dividend payments per year: an interim payment based on half-year profits and a final payment at the end of the year. In measuring shareholder returns or dividend ratios, the total dividend for the year is used.

Investors see dividends as an indicator of current performance and future profits. An increased dividend signals that a company's directors consider prospects to be good. Dividends also act as a signal to the market. Good news, indicated by an increase in dividend, usually triggers a rise in share price and bad news the reverse.

Sometimes an increased dividend is forced on a company. Shareholders may prefer to take the cash out of the business through dividends rather than leave it for management to dispose of in ways not necessarily beneficial to shareholders, such as management perks and poor acquisitions or investments.

Retained profit per share

When the profit for the year attributable to equity shareholders is known, the next step is to decide what the dividend should be and how much of the profit should be retained for use by the company. If the dividend per share is deducted from the earnings per share, what remains is the retained profit per share for the year (see page 144).

Retained profit per share = earnings per share − dividend per share

(¢ per share)	A	B	C
Earnings	30	5	11.7
Dividend	10	4	5.8
Retained earnings	20	1	5.9

Dividend cover

If after-tax profit attributable to ordinary shareholders is divided by the dividend, the result is the number of times the dividend was covered. As with interest cover, the higher the dividend cover ratio the better or safer is the position of a company. However, levels of what is considered acceptable vary across business sectors. If a company is operating in a sector that is reasonably unaffected by economic downturns, such as food manufacturing and retailing, a lower dividend cover ratio is more acceptable because the risk is lower.

Dividend cover = after-tax profit ÷ dividend
= earnings per share ÷ dividend per share

	A	B	C
After-tax profit	75	25	175
Dividend	25	20	87
Dividend cover	**3.0**	**1.25**	**2.0**

Payout ratio

Another way of looking at the safety level of dividend payments is to show what proportion of profit is being distributed to shareholders.

$$\text{Payout ratio} = 100 \div \text{dividend cover}$$

	A	B	C
Payout (%)	33	80	50

The higher the payout ratio the lower is the dividend cover; the level of profit cover for dividend is just being expressed in a different way. A company with a high payout ratio is not retaining profit to reinvest in the business. You should always try to discover why. Is management not confident about the future prospects of the business, or are they taking a short-term view of keeping shareholders happy with a dividend payment rather than providing for future long-term growth?

Gross dividend

Companies deduct tax and make a net dividend payment to shareholders. To allow comparison with other investment opportunities, tax should be added back to produce the gross dividend per share. Company A has a dividend of 10¢ per share. If the tax rate is 20% the gross dividend is 12.5¢; 2.5¢ covers the basic rate tax and 10¢ is paid to shareholders.

$$\text{Gross dividend} = \text{dividend} \div (1 - \text{tax rate})$$

Earnings yield

To obtain some indication of the return flowing from an investment, the current share price and earnings per share can be combined to give the earnings yield.

$$\text{Earnings yield} = 100 \times (\text{earnings per share} \div \text{share price})$$

	A	B	C
Earnings per share (¢)	30	5	11.7
Share price (¢)	300	100	150
Earnings yield (%)	**10**	**5**	**7.8**

Earnings yield is not an indicator of the actual return on investment. It is based on earnings per share not the dividend received by shareholders. If the P/E ratio is known, it is simple to calculate the earnings yield. Company B with a P/E ratio of 20 has an earnings yield of 5 (100 ÷ 20) and company C 7.8 (100 ÷ 12.9).

Dividend yield

Dividend yield links the current share price to the dividend received.

Dividend yield = 100 × (dividend per share ÷ share price)

	A	B	C
Dividend per share (¢)	10	4	5.8
Share price (¢)	300	100	150
Dividend yield %	**3.3**	**4.0**	**3.9**

Changes in share price bring about a change in the dividend yield. As share price changes there is an automatic adjustment in dividend yield, as illustrated below for company A, whose share price moves between 150¢ and 600¢.

Dividend (¢)	10	10	10
Share price (¢)	300	150	600
Dividend yield (%)	**3.3**	**6.7**	**1.7**

Shareholders' return

The return shareholders expect from their investment in shares is a combination of the capital gain flowing from an improvement in share price and income from dividends. A change in share price is part of the total return from their investment. If the shares in company A increase in price by 10%, the total return to shareholders, ignoring tax, in the period is 30%: the dividend yield (20%) plus the capital gain (10%). If the share price of C falls by 5% in the period, then the total return to shareholders is −1%.

To calculate the current or the likely future total return on investment, these two can be combined. If A's share price is forecast to rise to 396¢ and the dividend per share to 12¢, then the likely future return can be estimated as follows.

Capital return = 100 × (share price change ÷ opening share price)
                  = 100 × (96 ÷ 300)
                  = 32%
Dividend yield = 100 × (dividend per share ÷ share price)
                  = 100 × (12 ÷ 300)
                  = 4%
Total return   = 32 + 4
                  = **36%**

Valuing companies

There are many ways of arriving at a value for a company. The annual report can be used as a basis for valuation; the balance sheet offers comprehensive details of the assets and liabilities. However, it is not intended to offer a valuation so it is best used only as a rough guide (see page 11). The only time there can be an accurate and indisputable value for a company is when it has just been bought or sold. At other times its value is an estimate based partly on science and partly on art.

Capitalisation

If a company's shares are quoted on a stock exchange, there is a ready source of data upon which to base a valuation. Multiplying the current market price of a share by the number of shares in issue provides an indication of the company's current stock exchange value. This is its market value, or the capitalisation of the company.

	A	B	C
Share price (¢)	300	100	150
Shares (no)	250	1,000	1,500
Capitalisation ($)	**750**	**1,000**	**2,250**

Company A has a capitalisation of $750. If you wanted to acquire the company, $750 is probably a better guide to the price to be paid than, say, total assets ($1,000) or equity ($250) in the balance sheet.

The financial media publish capitalisation figures for companies daily or once a week. This provides a basis for the comparison of the size of companies according to current stock exchange values. In practice, if you decided to acquire A, as shares began to be purchased market forces would bring about a price rise. The capitalisation of $750 offers a guide to the minimum likely price for the company.

Earnings multiple

Another way of calculating a company's capitalisation is to multiply after-tax profits by the P/E ratio. Company A has a P/E ratio of 10 and after-tax profit of $75, the product of which is the $750 capitalisation.

Capitalisation can be readily produced only for quoted companies. To calculate the value of a non-quoted company, you can use the P/E ratios of stock exchange listed companies operating in an appropriate business sector. A practical source in the UK is the *Financial Times*, which has a daily list of companies by sector. The P/E ratio of three or four comparable companies or the sector average can be used as a basis for valuation.

Armed with an appropriate benchmark P/E ratio, it is possible to calculate share price. For example, a company operating in a sector with an average P/E ratio of 16.6 has earnings per share of 5¢ and no quoted share price.

Price earnings ratio	= share price ÷ earnings per share
Share price	= price/earnings ratio × earnings per share
83.3¢	= 16.66 × 5¢

Using the average P/E ratio for the appropriate sector produces a suggested share price for the company of 83.3¢. In most cases it should be possible to identify one or two quoted companies that reasonably match the activities or spread of business of the company being valued.

After-tax profit versus earnings per share

The shares in the company were valued at 83.3¢ using the sector average P/E ratio of 16.66. The basis of the valuation is the after-tax profit generated by the company and attributable to equity shareholders. This is not affected by the number of shares in issue or, ignoring tax implications, by dividend policy. It is therefore better and much simpler to use this as the basis for valuing non-quoted companies.

If the after-tax profit of $25 is multiplied by the 16.66 P/E ratio the result is $416, which when divided by the number of shares in issue (500) gives the same share price of 83¢. It is easier and more practical to use $416 as a value for the company, but the individual share price may be important if shares are being transferred between family members in a private company.

Investing in a small private company is usually considered more risky than buying shares in a quoted company. To compensate for this, the P/E ratio used in valuing a private company may be adjusted by an appropriate amount, referred to as the risk premium. If the P/E ratio selected is 16.66 and a 35% risk premium is considered applicable, the multiple to be applied to value a company is 10.8 (16.66 – 35%). If the company has after-tax profits of $25, applying the 10.8 multiple gives a value of $270 and a share price of 54¢ ($270 ÷ 500).

Further problems are encountered if only a proportion of a company's equity is being valued. In this situation the method detailed above can be used with discount factors applied to the multiple according to the quantity of shares involved. A 5% block of shares might be discounted by 60%, but if 51% of a company's shares are being acquired the discount might be only 10–20%.

The average for a sector can be used, but in most cases it should be possible to find at least one suitable company to use as a basis for direct P/E comparison. If you have access to the *Financial Times*, a simpler alternative is to use the FTSE Actuaries Share or Sector Indices. If there are no obvious sources of P/E ratios, experts suggest that a multiplier of 10 should be applied to after-tax profits to provide an indication of company value.

Dividend valuation method

If it is assumed that the value of a share is the present value of its future dividends, dividend can form the basis for valuing a company. The basic formula is:

$$\text{Value} = (\text{dividend} \times (1 + \text{dividend growth}) \div (\text{required return} - \text{dividend growth})$$

An appropriate discount factor can be applied to give the present value of the anticipated dividend stream. If the current dividend of a company is 6¢ per share, dividend growth is expected to be 5% per annum and shareholders require a 15% rate of return, a share in the company can be valued at 63¢.

$$\text{Value} = (6.0 \times 1.05) \div (0.15 - 0.05) = 6.3 \div 0.1 = 63¢$$

Government bonds and rates of return

Investors can be assumed to look for different rates of return linked to the risk of a given investment opportunity. The lower the risk the lower is the required rate of return. The rate of return investors require has a direct influence on the cost of a company's capital. The higher the risk the higher is the rate of return required, and the more it costs a company to service through dividend and interest payments the finance provided. A good starting point is to look at returns from risk-free investments.

It is generally accepted that lending money to government is risk free, as the interest rate and maturity date are fixed and certain. Thus the return from government securities can be regarded as that required from a risk-free investment. Investors in other securities, such as equities, require an additional return to compensate for the additional risk. This is called the risk premium. Using non-redeemable bonds, the interest yield can be calculated in a similar way to that of dividend and earnings yields.

Bond value ($)	100	100	100
Price paid ($)	100	50	200
Interest rate (%)	5	5	5
Interest yield (%)	**5**	**10**	**2.5**

If investors see that the returns from alternative sources are greater than 5%, they may sell their bonds to take advantage of the opportunity. The sale of bonds brings about a reduction in their price ($50) and their yield increases to 10%. When bonds are seen as a better investment, the price rises to $200 and the yield falls to 2.5%.

The base bank rate of interest, quoted daily in the media, can be used as an alternative to government securities to provide an indicator of the risk-free rate of return.

Equities risk premium

As well as the risk-free rate of return, investors can reasonably expect a premium for the risk involved in investing in equities. The equity risk premium has been 5–10% on both the UK and US stock exchanges.

An additional premium is required when considering investment in private, non-quoted companies, which are generally assumed to be a more risky investment than quoted companies. As a general rule, a minimum of an additional 25% premium should be added to compensate for the risk of unlisted company investment. Many valuation experts, however, suggest that the premium should be 30–40%

Cost of capital

The view investors take of the risk associated with buying shares in a company determines its cost of capital. The higher the risk the higher are the expected returns and the higher is the cost of raising finance. Before a company returns a profit it must cover the cost of capital. Interest on borrowed funds will have been charged before arriving at the profit for the year, but the company will not necessarily have made an appropriate allowance for the cost of equity capital provided by shareholders.

The cost of debt can be estimated from the financial statements. There will be notes providing details of the interest rates applying to loans. The after-tax cost of borrowing $500 at 10% interest with a tax rate of 50% is 5%; at a tax rate of 40% the after-tax cost of borrowing would be 6%. Inflation reduces the real cost of debt financing. With a currency decreasing in value over time, the true rate of interest adjusts and so does that repaid at the end of the loan period. Calculating the actual cost of borrowings for loan or convertible stock not issued at par is complex. For most purposes, it is adequate to take the interest rate quoted as being an approximation of the actual real cost.

There are many ways of estimating the cost of equity. One is to use dividend yield adjusted for the impact of tax. This is only an approximation as it does not take account of the fact that dividend rates may change and, of course, that share prices change from day to day. A simple adjustment to allow for some rate of growth could be applied to the dividend yield or the earnings yield could be used. The higher the P/E ratio the lower is the earnings yield. A high P/E assumes that investors have confidence in the future performance of the company so raising finance is cheaper; of course the reverse also applies.

Investing in new and untested technology can offer huge returns if it is successful, but there is also the possibility of the investment having to be written off, so a high risk is involved. If investors are to be attracted to the investment, they must have some incentive. The cost of equity is the return required by investors to provide capital to a company; the higher the perceived risk of the company the higher is the cost of capital.

The capital asset pricing model (CAPM) offers an approach to calculating the cost of equity for a company.

$$\text{Cost of equity} = \text{risk-free rate} + \text{beta (market rate} - \text{risk-free rate)}$$
$$18\% = 5\% + 1.3\,(15\% - 5\%)$$

With a risk-free rate of return of 5% and a market rate of return of 15%, the "equity risk premium" is 10%. A company with a 1.3 beta has an estimated cost of equity of 18%. If the company had a beta of 2, the cost of equity would rise to 25%.

Another way of arriving at an approximation of the cost of capital is to take a simple weighted average for equity and debt. The cost of debt is taken as the interest rate applying to each item and the cost of equity as the dividend yield.

Summary

- ◪ The debt/equity ratio is a well-tested and simple measure of the balance between the finance provided by equity shareholders and that derived from external borrowings (debt). Although the ratio may be subject to manipulation, it still provides the best starting point for an assessment of capital structure. The content of the denominator and numerator can be refined as appropriate. The lower the ratio the greater is the proportion of finance being provided by shareholders. A company with a low debt/equity ratio is said to be low geared.
- ◪ The debt ratio is helpful in interpreting the structure of a balance sheet. It shows what proportion of total assets has been funded by external sources of finance. For most businesses, when more than 50% of assets are debt financed it is advisable to complete a detailed analysis of the company and its likely future prospects before considering an investment. If only one measure of gearing were allowed, this would be the most attractive.
- ◪ Notes in the annual report will provide details of a company's

debt, showing for the next five years the amount, rate of interest and date when the borrowings mature or are to be repaid. At first glance these notes may appear overwhelming, but they are worth studying. A simple indicator of the likely demands to be made on a company's future cash flow is created by taking the total annual interest charge and adding to it any capital repayments to be made for each of the next two or three years. Based on previous experience, does it look as if the company can meet these expected cash outflows without having either to sell assets or to initiate new borrowing?

▪ For shareholders, the efficiency of a company in making debt work for them is an important consideration. Shareholders' return is a combination of profitability and gearing. Two ratios can be combined to highlight how return on equity is being achieved.

▪ The interest cover ratio is an effective way of linking the level of gearing with profitability. A company borrowing money to finance its operations must pay the agreed interest in cash each year. The greater the interest cover provided by pre-interest and tax profit the safer is the company's position. A high-geared company must guarantee to maintain a safe level of interest cover. A combination of high gearing and low interest cover is not a healthy sign.

▪ Similarly, the extent to which dividend is covered by profit is a useful indicator of the comfort or safety level for shareholders. The higher the dividend cover the greater is the proportion of retained profit being ploughed back into the company.

▪ A useful measure is to use cash flow as the basis for cash flow dividend cover. All interest, tax and non-equity dividends are deducted from operating cash flow and the result divided by the equity dividends. This ratio identifies the proportion of cash flow, after all external financing charges, that is available for equity dividends.

▪ Dividend per share should be combined with earnings per share in studying the historic record of a company. If earnings per share and dividend per share are plotted, the difference is the amount per share being retained in the business each year. Some consistency in the three figures should be evident.

▪ The financial media provide daily calculations of dividend yield and P/E ratios. When studying a listed company it is possible to make a direct comparison with the P/E ratios of similar companies, and to obtain some indication of the ranking given by investors. The higher the P/E ratio the higher are investors' expectations of that company's future performance.

◪ A company with a high P/E ratio is not necessarily a good investment. A high ratio indicates that the market has already taken into account the future prospects of the company and that it is probably already too late to buy.

◪ Published P/E ratios can be used to provide a valuation for non-listed companies. If the average ratio for the appropriate sector is found and applied as a multiplier to the after-tax profit of the company, the result is an indicator of total value.

11 Strategy, success and failure

W HEN ANALYSING A COMPANY three key areas should be examined: management, operating performance and financial position. Using annual reports and other published information to analyse the past and forecast the future in two of these three areas has been covered in earlier chapters. This chapter goes over some of that ground again, considers approaches to assessing the strength of management and discusses the unavoidable mix of the quantifiable and the qualitative necessary to make an overall assessment of a company's performance and its future prospects.

SWOT and PEST

A useful exercise is to produce a list of a company's positive and negative points. Two popular techniques (which companies use on themselves) are SWOT for Strengths, Weaknesses, Opportunities and Threats and PEST for the Political, Economic, Social and Technological influences on a company.

Sources of information

Financial analysts increasingly rely on direct communication with a company's senior executives, but the annual report remains a crucial source of financial information and acts as a basis for historic analysis and forecasting.

There are several sources from which to obtain a copy of a company's annual report. First, the company can be approached directly and asked to provide a copy. Second, services such as that offered by the *Financial Times* can be used to get a copy. The third and increasingly valuable source of company information is the internet.

The internet

Most major companies maintain a website that offers not only general information on the company and its products or services but also the latest annual report. Search for the company name and more often than not full financial information is available.

Recent moves towards the standardisation of financial reports should significantly improve the quality, value and accessibility of corporate financial information. This is to be based on the adoption of eXtensible Mark-up Language (xml) or eXtensible Business Reporting mark-up Language (xbrl), allowing through the internet instant translation of company accounts into any language using a standardised format of account presentation. The US Securities and Exchange Commission accepted xbrl filings in 2005.

Within the next few years it is probable that shareholders, unless they request otherwise, will receive only a summary financial statement replacing the annual report. Electronic reporting via the internet will increasingly act as the vehicle for financial communication between a company and its shareholders and stakeholders.

Useful sites

For UK companies, the base reference point is Companies House, and for the US, the Securities and Exchange Commission (edgar). For easy access to individual company information use Yahoo!, Google, or whichever is your favourite search engine and add "investor relations" to the company name. Good sources for company data include:

www.carolworld.com
www.companieshouse.co.uk
www.corpreports.co.uk
www.northcote.co.uk
www.prars.com
www.reportgallery.com
www.sec.gov/index.htm

The media

Newspapers, journals, magazines, tv and radio, and professional or trade publications provide further information that may help interpret the facts given in the annual report or on developments since the report was published. Media reports may provide technical analysis of the company, its current and likely future markets and operating environment, or they may give more qualitative impressions with reports of lawsuits or gossip column pieces about directors. However, bear in mind that Enron was "America's most innovative company" between 1996 and 2001 according to *Fortune*, and in 2000 was voted "energy company of the year" by the *Financial Times*.

Commercial databases

Another source of company details is commercial databases, which offer the best source of historic data. Most of them provide five years of financial statements set out in a standard and user-friendly format. They are also ideal as a readily accessible source of comparative data for both home and overseas companies.

Appearance may matter

The annual report should not be underestimated as a visual presentation of the company and its directors. A dull report may indicate a dull company; an overglamorous report may indicate a company too concerned with impressive presentation, perhaps in order to disguise poor performance – "never mind the quality, feel the width".

Photo opportunity for the board

The way in which the board is presented reflects the changing trends in corporate reporting. From the 1960s to the mid-1970s, the classic "oil painting" profile of the chairman gazing into the far distance thinking deep strategic thoughts was considered appropriate to show the company was led by a tough but fair father figure. There was little detail, beyond the statutory minimum, of the other directors.

In the late 1970s, it became important for the board to be seen to be managing the company as a team. It was recognised that a team was needed to support a dynamic leader to ensure success. The result was often a photograph of the chief executive officer (CEO) sitting in the boardroom surrounded by all the other directors (standing). Positive statements were made concerning the "diversification" policy the board was adopting.

The mid-1980s showed directors actively running the business. They were shown walking around a shop or factory and talking to employees. Typically, the director was named and looking at the camera, while the employee was anonymous and stacking a shelf or working a machine. The annual report explained the importance of "unbundling" or restructuring the group.

By the end of the 1980s, with the growth in empowerment of employees, annual reports increasingly included photographs of employees working alone or in happy groups, with no directors in sight. The board was once more relegated to a single page in the annual report.

The early 1990s saw directors back as a group at the boardroom table or a selected site, not necessarily doing anything but looking quietly confident and in control. It was often difficult to identify the leader.

In the mid-1990s, it became common to have the chairman and CEO highlighted as working well together. Other senior directors were given their own space as part of the operational review to report on their individual areas of business responsibility. Shareholder value was the aim and the in-word "focus" was linked to mention of disinvestments, spin-offs and break-ups, with common agreement that to be successful a company should be single-industry based.

This trend appears to be continuing and is allied to an increasing concern that shareholders know their company's products, services and brands. There are full-colour pages highlighting the expensive new company name and logo together with invitations to visit the website. Demergers are the vogue, with two words now perhaps somewhat tired through overexposure – "global" and "value" and "environmental issues" and "sustainable development" rapidly gaining ground.

Corporate governance

Corporate governance embraces not only the way in which a company is managed and its dealings with shareholders but also every aspect of its relationship with society. Emphasis on corporate governance was stimulated partly by apparent fraud and mismanagement in some major UK and US companies and partly by the increase in corporate failure rates during the recession years of the 1980s and early 1990s. Shareholders and others dealing with a company wanted assurance that it was being well and correctly managed. In 1992 the Cadbury Committee established a code of best practice for UK companies. It contained 19 points and required that the reasons for non-compliance with any of these should be given in the annual report. Several other committees followed, leading to the publication of the Combined Code in 1998 and its revision in 2003. "The principles on which the Code is based are those of openness, integrity and accountability"; it is now mandatory for all listed companies (see Chapter 1).

The code requires the board to present a balanced and understandable assessment of the company's position and likely prospects in the annual report. The introduction of the Combined Code for UK companies has substantially improved the quality and quantity of information on directors and their effectiveness in running a company. There has been similar experience in other countries. The OECD published *Principles of corporate governance* and in 2003 the European Commission issued *Modernising company law and enhancing corporate governance in the eu - a plan to move forward.* In the United States, following the collapse of Enron and WorldCom, the Public Accounting Reform and Investor Protection Act - normally referred to as the Sarbanes-Oxley Act (sox) - was passed to improve investor confidence and encourage full and transparant corporate reporting.

The board and its roles

The prime role of the board is to satisfy shareholders through the successful implementation of the chosen corporate strategy. Ideally, the annual report should contain an organisation chart to show the reporting lines and areas of individual authority and responsibility. At least the direct business responsibilities of each member of the board should be identified.

Who are the directors and how good are they?

The annual report should contain sufficient information on directors to enable an assessment to be made of their competence and experience. At least each director's age and length of service should be recorded. A simple aid to assessing the board is to calculate the average age of the directors. If it is the late 50s for executive directors and is over 60 for non-executive directors, the board may be getting past its sell-by date, with directors more concerned with serving their time than the shareholders' interests.

The age of directors can also indicate when succession is likely to be necessary. A board changing only as a result of death or retirement may be doing a good job, but are the directors capable of innovation or facing rapid and challenging change?

To be effective, directors must have real business experience in dealing with both hard times and good times. Investors need to be confident that the top team is capable of sure-footed management whatever the business environment.

Financial analysts assess companies in three main ways: by studying the financial statements to discover underlying strengths and expose weaknesses; through general background research into the business sector and its future; and by visiting the company and talking to the executive team. Face-to-face meetings are extremely important; if senior management fails to inspire confidence support for the company will drop, even if there was a record profit in the previous year.

One person, two jobs

It can be argued that every company needs someone, particularly in its early growth period, in firm control offering effective leadership and direction. As a company grows and becomes a more complex organisation, it becomes more difficult if not impossible for one person to manage single handed. There is eminent sense behind the separation of the roles of chairman and CEO, and this is required by the Combined Code.

Sainsbury, until the mid-1990s the UK's foremost food retailer, provides an example of the potential problems that can arise. In 1996, after profits fell for the first time in the company's history, there was immediate media comment. The Times (May 6th 1996) ran a headline "Sainsbury's decline is blamed on arrogance and complacency" and drew attention to the fact that David Sainsbury was both chairman and CEO. In 1998 the final act took place, with the Sainsbury family being separated from the management of the company. Marks & Spencer, another major UK retailer, suffered similar problems in the late 1990s, with board conflict becoming public followed by a dramatic decline in profits and share price.

The combination of an entrepreneur and a non-participating board is usually fatal in the longer term. Companies may have their powerful personalities or leaders, but to ensure continued success they must be supported by an experienced and competent team of managers.

It follows from the above that a company that seems to be overly dominated by one individual needs to be looked at carefully. The annual report may provide evidence of a personality cult, and the media often provide plenty of evidence of potentially dangerous large egos, the late Robert Maxwell being a case in point.

Non-executive directors

The role of non-executive directors is seen as increasingly important. They can provide a wealth of experience brought from other business sectors and companies, but their principal benefit should be independence of thought, view and personal income. This places them in a powerful position to reinforce the stewardship role of the board and to act on its various committees. A non-executive director who is a customer, a supplier, a friend of the family or whose only source of income is the directorship is unlikely to fulfil the independence requirement.

In much of Europe, however, there is a two-tier board structure. Large companies in Netherlands and Germany usually have a supervisory board made up of representatives of shareholders and employees. France has some two-tier companies, but the majority have a single board with two-thirds of its members being non-executive. Best practice in the UK requires at least half of the board to be made up of non-executive directors to enable them to exert an independent influence on the direction of the company.

Audit committee

To comply with best practice, a listed company must have an audit committee made up of independent and reasonably financially acute non-executive directors. Details of its membership and duties will be found in the annual report.

The Sarbanes-Oxley Act in the United States emphasised the importance of the audit committee, expanding its role to include not only responsibility for the proper treatment of employees' whistle-blowing but also all other internal and external complaints concerning financial matters. The Public Company Accounting Oversight Board (PCAOB) was set up in 2003 to work with the SEC to oversee the auditing of all US listed companies and to support the development of auditing standards.

The main purpose of the audit committee is to ensure effective external auditors are employed and to assist them wherever necessary. The audit committee should oversee accounting policies and practices and the internal control and auditing function. Its members should have direct access at any time to the CEO and chairman. A report from the audit committee should be on the agenda of the annual general meeting (AGM) or appear in the annual report. If this is not the case, the company is not fully complying with best practice.

Most companies have their own internal audit function, linked to but separate from the work of the external auditors, which should report directly to the audit committee. Internal audit is to ensure that all employees maintain and follow company procedures and systems. Best practice in corporate governance places an obligation on directors to ensure that all appropriate internal controls are applied, all assets are safeguarded and accurate accounting records are maintained, and that company risk is at an acceptable level.

Remuneration committee

Every public company should have a committee to oversee the remuneration and terms and conditions for all executive directors, including the CEO and chairman. Best practice requires that its members are non-executive directors. The fact that directors' remuneration has been set by the committee should be recorded in the annual report. It is usual for the committee also to oversee the employment terms and remuneration of all senior staff, thus ensuring that these are not solely dependent on the whim of the CEO. The intention is to ensure a completely transparent and consistent remuneration policy.

Directors' remuneration

Although money is not everything, it is clear that remuneration plays a crucial role in the motivation and retention of high-performing directors. Directors responsible for several billion pounds worth of assets and thousands of jobs rightly expect substantial rewards. It is generally accepted that reward should be directly linked to performance, and that a significant proportion of a director's remuneration package should be performance related. The aim is to provide a match between directors' and shareholders' interests.

Managing an executive remuneration policy is a considerable undertaking. It is the acid test of the quality of the non-executive directors. The remuneration committee should make sure that there is a defensible policy, and where directors' remuneration is increasing out of step with company performance there should be an explanation.

Are they worth it?

The annual report provides details of company policy on executive directors' remuneration and shows the total remuneration of the chairman and the CEO or, if they are not the highest paid, that of the highest paid director. The total remuneration and taxable benefits paid to all directors is disclosed, together with details of their service contracts with the company. In the UK, it is unacceptable for directors to have, without shareholders' agreement, service contracts of more than three years' duration.

These details can be compared with those of similar-sized companies to assess their generosity. Year-on-year changes can be set against the rate of inflation, the change in average wage rates, or growth in the company's turnover or profit to provide a benchmark to decide whether the cost of the board appears reasonable.

Changes on the board

To be effective, directors must develop a set of individual and group working relationships to support their function as the top management team. Changes in the team are inevitable through retirement, accident, illness or career opportunity. However, it is reasonable to expect that any company has a core of experienced directors continuing to run the business from year to year.

Changes on the board can be a direct signal of existing and potential problems. The annual report provides a complete listing of directors that can be compared with the previous year to see changes. Unfortunately, there is no requirement to provide the equivalent of comparative figures for directors, so it is often necessary to refer to the previous report. However, it is possible for someone to join and leave the board during the year and for this not to be noted in the annual report.

There should be a statement giving the reasons for board changes (most often these will be for retirement or career moves). A popular euphemism to disguise board conflict and disagreement is a director leaving "to pursue other interests". A continually changing board should be taken as an indicator that all is not well with the company. It can be assumed there are potentially destructive tensions at the top of the organisation that will not improve confidence in its future prospects.

A good warning sign is a continuing turnover in directors. As a general rule, where more than 20% of a board is seen to change in consecutive years, the company should be treated with additional caution. Particular significance should be attached to a group of directors all leaving at the same time; for example, all the non-executive directors resigning. Although the reasons may not be made public, history suggests it is prudent to assume the worst.

As a rough guide, the expected lifespan for the CEO of a major UK company appears to be about four years. The departure of the CEO is an important event for a company, and it should provide a quick and clear statement of the reasons for the CEO's departure. A warning signal flashed when the CEO of Enron resigned for "personal reasons" – although it was probably too late when Bernard Ebbers left WorldCom. If there is no statement, but there is adverse press comment on the CEO's departure, the apparent conflicting personal relationships of directors or the operation of the board, this should be taken as a convincing black mark against the company. If the directors cannot demonstrate that they are working as a team and are in control, you should sell.

Follow the finance director

The finance director plays a crucial role in ensuring good communication with all investor groups to keep them abreast of the business and maintain their confidence in it. A sound working partnership between the CEO and the finance director (FD) or chief financial officer (CFO) is fundamental to the successful management of any company. The CEO of Enron pledged his "unequivocal trust" in his CFO the day before the collapse. The departure of a finance director, other than for normal retirement or a non-contentious career move, is an extremely important event. What are the reasons for the departure and who is going to take over the job? The sudden departure for no apparent reason of a finance director with 3–5 years' service, to be replaced by either the chief accountant with 20 years' service or the auditor, has in the past proved to be a firm warning signal.

Relationship with the City

Successful companies in the UK may run into difficulties because they fail to establish a good relationship with the City. This is most often seen with small, rapid-growth companies in the years immediately following their listing on the stock exchange. A successful entrepreneur is not always best suited to dealing with institutional investors, who expect to be kept fully aware of what is going on.

The annual report lists a company's bankers and financial and legal advisers. Changes in the year of auditors, bankers, solicitors and advisers must be taken as negative indicators unless a clear and unambiguous explanation is given in the annual report.

Going for growth

Growth is often seen as a good measure of corporate success. A company growing at the rate of 15% per year is doubling in size every five years. Rapid-growth companies can be defined as those with annual growth rates of 20% or more, and supergrowth companies show a compound growth rate of around 40% per year.

Market share information can provide valuable support to the analysis and interpretation of changes in a company's turnover. The majority of companies display turnover growth details in their annual report, but few offer any details of market share. Where turnover is known for several firms competing in the same market, it is possible to devise a simple alternative to market share information. Four UK retail companies are used as an example.

	Morrison		Sainsbury		Somerfield		Tesco		Total	
	1999	2000	1999	2000	1999	2000	1999	2000	1999	2000
Sales (£m)	2,534	2,970	16,433	16,271	5,898	5466	17,158	18,796	42,023	43,503
Share (%)	6	7	39	37	14	13	41	43	100	100

A common view is that a rapid-growth company is a safe and sound investment. However, evidence suggests that rapid growth cannot always be sustained. There are of course exceptions, but it is probably safer to assume that rapid growth, particularly if associated with diversification, will not continue. If high compound growth rates are matched by increasing debt financing, extreme caution is called for.

For some companies, turnover growth is seen as the prime objective and measure of success, even when it is being achieved at the cost of profitability. In the late 1990s, e-business provided many extreme examples of this. Analysts decided to use a multiple of turnover as the basis for valuing internet companies. As soon as this became known, companies focused all their efforts on achieving the required numbers, and turnover growth became the only target. Inevitably, pressure to deliver turnover growth stimulated "creativity". If a big discount was offered to customers to get them to buy the product or service, the full price was taken into the income statement and the "discount" lost in marketing expenses. The provision for bad debts could be reduced. A company acting as an agent to sell holidays might take the full price of the holiday into the income statement rather than just the commission due on the sale. A single payment made by customers for the use of an internet site for a number of years might be taken into the current year's sales figure. These practices are contrary to GAAP, but they were adopted to boost apparent income growth.

Being pushed towards diversification to fuel continued growth is often the final challenge for the one-person company. Having proved itself in one business sector it moves into new areas, commonly through acquisition. More often than not its old skills prove not to be appropriate in the new business, attention is distracted from the core business, and it is viewed as having lost the golden touch. Its survival may depend on new management and financial restructuring.

When a one-person company's growth slows and criticism mounts, two scenarios may occur. In one, the individual running the company begins to take increasingly risky decisions in the hope of returning to previous levels of profit growth. In the other, recognising there is little that can be done immediately to improve operating performance, the individual steps outside the law and accepted business practice to sustain his or her personal image and lifestyle.

Creative accounting and failure

All companies can be expected to apply creative accounting techniques to some degree. For most companies, all the necessary detail and support information is set out in the annual report, but it is unrealistic to expect attention to be drawn as clearly to problems as to good news items. To some extent annual reporting is an art form, but there are clear rules that must be followed. Breaking the rules is not an act of creativity but of misrepresentation and possibly fraud. The Treadway Commission defined fraud as "intentional or reckless conduct, whether by act or omission, that results in materially misleading financial statements". A creative finance director may be justly rewarded; a fraudulent finance director should be imprisoned.

Creative accounting is not a cause of corporate failure, but it makes it more difficult for users of a company's financial statements to appreciate the underlying performance or financial position of the business. The question then is why the company thinks it necessary to adopt this approach. If the operations and finances of a company are so complex you cannot fully understand them, walk away. If the terminology is incomprehensible, take this as a firm negative point.

Enron imploded with some $3 billion liabilities described as "special purpose entities", which enabled it to remove debt from its balance sheet and shuffle assets to create fictitious profits. Profits were overstated by £1 billion in 2001. A major frustration in the United States, resulting in the Sarbanes-Oxley Act, was that although much of Enron's accounting was aggressive or creative, it was not necessarily illegal.

Any changes in accounting policy should always be examined carefully; this is particularly important when warning signals relating to the company have been picked up elsewhere. Is the change appropriate and rational, or is it made in order to give the year's profit a boost? Changes in depreciation policy, inventory valuation, use of provisions, capitalising expenses, and treatment of extraordinary and exceptional events can all indicate a desperation to improve profits rather than provide a true and fair view (see Chapter 3).

Corporate strategy

Corporate strategy encompasses a planned approach to the achievement of defined objectives: knowing where you want to go and how to get there. The objectives or goals are the "ends" or the "where" and the strategy is the "means" or the "how" of successful implementation.

Every major company must have a strategy that is recognised and embraced by the board and ideally communicated to and accepted by all employees who are actively involved and participate in its development. The annual report should provide sufficient information to identify what the strategy is and how successfully it has been implemented. Where this proves impossible it must be assumed that the company has no strategy and so is rudderless and adrift; it will either hit the rocks or someone will take the helm.

A question central to company analysis is how to recognise a sound strategy. The answer is that it must be considered realistically capable of pursuit and that proof of positive progress towards its attainment can be found in the annual report year by year.

Single solution is no solution

If a company appears to have decided that it has found a single simple solution to its strategic problems, the likelihood is that it has not. Single solutions are often attractive, but they represent companies putting "all their eggs in one basket". If the single solution does not provide the answer, there is nowhere else to go.

Examples of potentially ambitious schemes which may take up valuable management time and attention with adverse effects on other areas of the business are those that involve product development, new technology, acquisitions, diversification and high-value contracts.

Acquisition is often seen as good solution to company problems. However, when acquisitions are clearly outside a company's proven area of competence, bringing about rapid and major diversification, the problems are compounded. Managing businesses in new markets or overseas can speed decline, even though the acquisition may improve reported profitability in the year in which it takes place.

When a substantial acquisition represents a major diversification, experience in both the UK and the United States would probably support a view that the risk of the company failing has increased substantially. Diversification means new areas of activity which have to be experienced and mastered before positive returns are generated.

Mission and vision

Companies may include a mission or vision statement in the annual report which provides useful additional insight into its overall strategy and strategic management policy and practice. A mission statement normally defines a company's business, its objectives and how these will be attained. A vision statement is more concerned with defining the kind of company it wishes to be at some point in the future and the values needed to achieve its objectives and goals. However, the two terms are often combined or even used interchangeably.

Where to look for a strategy

It is reasonable to expect the annual report to provide sufficient information about a company's strategy and the success of its implementation to date. This information will not always be contained in a single section. It is usually necessary to study at least the chairman's statement, the directors' report, the review of operations and the financial review.

The information discussed below should appear, but not necessarily under the headings used here.

Chairman's statement

In their statements to shareholders, company chairmen are free to make any comments and take any view they wish. The statement is not constrained by legislation, auditing or accounting standards or even a code of best practice. It was originally developed as a personal comment on the year by the chairman to shareholders.

This section of the annual report is carefully read by typical investors. Indeed, it is often the only section they read, with perhaps a naive expectation of an objective overview of the company's performance and position. Chairmen are well aware of this, so it is not unusual to find that their statements concentrate on good news rather than less positive aspects of the business. Some are little more than public relations statements: high on presentation and low on content.

The quality of a chairman's statement is a useful guide to the quality of the individual charged with leading the company's strategic thinking and managing the workings of the board.

Directors' report

The directors' report was designed to assist in interpreting the financial statements and to provide additional non-financial information to users of the annual report. It provides an excellent basis for improving understanding of the operations of a company and its internal and external working relationships. The principal activities of the company are outlined with a broad description of the areas of business activity to be read in conjunction with the segmental notes. If you need to get a quick appreciation of the nature of the business, this is a good source.

The directors' report normally contains details of:

- principal activities;
- the review of the business and likely future developments;
- dividends;
- research and development activity;
- differences between market and balance sheet value of property;
- directors and their relationship with the company;
- employment policy;
- supplier payment policy;
- environmental issues;
- political and charitable contributions;
- purchase of own shares;
- major interests in the company's shares;
- post-balance-sheet events;
- auditors;
- compliance with the Combined Code.

The review of the business should give details of developments that are likely to affect future profitability, such as the launch of a new product, a major capital investment programme or planned acquisitions and disposals. However, sometimes the details given will be limited in order to avoid giving too much away to competitors.

A clear statement of directors' responsibilities towards the company, confirming that they have followed good accounting policies and practice and applied all appropriate accounting standards in the preparation of the financial statements, is normally provided here.

Details of anyone, excluding directors, owning more than 3% of the company's shares is listed and any transactions with a controlling shareholder described. A controlling shareholder does not have to own 50% of a company; realistically, the term is taken to refer to any investor with more than 30% of voting shares or who can control the board of directors – for example, by having the right to nominate/appoint directors or otherwise influence membership of the board. This, when combined with the details of directors' shareholdings, can provide a useful source of information on the balance of ownership of the company.

Important or significant events that have occurred after the end of the financial year should also be mentioned, as should any instance where the market value of property is substantially different from the value shown in the balance sheet.

Operating and financial review

The operating and financial review (OFR) or management discussion and analysis (MD&A) statement is where a company's strategy and its implementation should be spelled out. It should add to the amount of information available in the standard financial statements and, where things have changed, it should give the explanation (see Chapter 1).

The OFR is not meant to be another set of complex numbers, but it may contain financial ratios to support the text. These should clearly relate to the financial statements and/or be properly explained. Directors are expected to indicate their views regarding the likely future prospects of the company and any significant changes expected in its operating environment.

Typically, the OFR covers:

- significant political, economic and environmental factors;
- analysis of changing market conditions;
- turnover trends and market share;
- changes in turnover and margins;
- product development, new products;
- acquisitions, disposals and closures;
- the impact of foreign exchange, interest and inflation rates.

The Accounting Standards Board, which was responsible for the introduction of the OFR to the UK, was keen to persuade companies to use the annual report not only to report good news but also to disclose the:

> ... *principal risks and uncertainties in the main lines of business, together with a commentary on the approach to managing these risks and, in qualitative terms, the nature of the potential impact on results.*

Risk disclosure

Companies are expected to limit the impact of future changes in interest rates or currency fluctuations – they "hedge". Unfortunately, there have been several cases of apparently well-managed companies incurring significant losses owing to a failure to monitor and appreciate their exposure to risk arising from the use of financial instruments, in particular "derivatives" such as options, swaps or futures – Barings' Bank, for example.

Accounting standards (FRS 13, IAS 32 and FAS 133) were introduced to improve both control and reporting of these matters. FRS 13 defined a financial instrument as "any contract that gives rise to both a financial asset of one entity and a financial liability or equity instrument of another entity", and a derivative as "a financial instrument that derives its value from the price or rate of some underlying item". Typically, these are concerned with limiting the risks associated with foreign exchange, interest rates or commodity prices. In 2001, the German Accounting Standards Board led the field with an accounting standard (GAS 5) detailing the requirements for disclosure of risk.

Financial instruments were initially a simple and straightforward means of borrowing, but they rapidly developed in scope and complexity. Some examples are as follows:

- **Convertible debt** – carries the right to exchange for equity shares at some future date until which interest is paid.
- **Subordinated debt** – in the event of liquidation is repaid before the shareholders, but only after all other liabilities have been settled.
- **Limited recourse debt** – secured only to a particular asset.
- **Deep discount bond** – a loan with low interest issued at a substantial discount to its repayment value. A zero-coupon bond has no interest payable.

Companies must now describe their "objectives, policies and strategies" for using any financial instruments and detail their activities concerning:

- interest rate risk;
- market price risk;
- currency risk;
- financial assets and liabilities held for trading;
- hedging activities.

The objective is to ensure that where a company has "obligations ... to transfer economic benefits as a result of past transactions or events" this is fully disclosed in the annual report. It does not matter how the obligation was incurred or how it is wrapped up in a complex financial instrument. If there is an existing or potential liability, you need to know about this in order to properly assess the company.

The fair values of all instruments must be shown. FRS 13 defines fair value as:

> *The amount at which an asset or liability could be exchanged in an arm's length transaction between informed and willing parties, other than in a forced or liquidation sale.*

"New" measure of risk

An alternative approach to company risk assessment has been offered. It is suggested that if the number of times the word "new" appears in the annual report is counted this may provide a measure of risk.

Finance and investment

The OFR should give the current level of capital expenditure together with an indication of future intentions for fixed asset investment and, ideally, that allocated towards:

- marketing and advertising;
- employee training and development;
- research and new product development;
- maintenance programmes;
- technical support to customers.

This kind of detail can be helpful in assessing to what extent a company could, at least for a short time, reduce expenditure while maintaining the level of current operations. All the expenses listed might be cut for a short time without any immediate negative impact on profit.

One way of checking on the consistency of asset investment is to use the asset replacement rate and capital expenditure turnover ratios (see pages 171–2). The first provides an indication of the speed with which the company is replacing tangible assets, and the second links investment to turnover. Sudden shifts in these ratios can indicate a decision to reduce or halt investment in productive assets in an attempt to maintain liquidity or because finance has been refused.

The way in which capital investment projects are financed is worth investigation. The timescale of the planned investment should match that of the finance being applied. A company using short-term sources of finance to build a factory or make a long-term investment is more likely to run into difficulties than one using long-term finance.

You should expect finance for long-term assets to come from equity

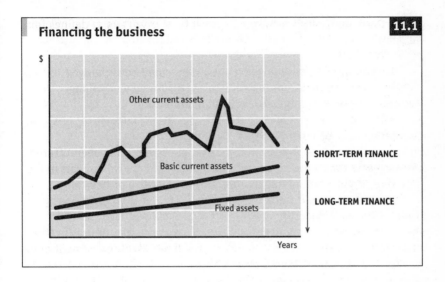

Financing the business 11.1

or long-term borrowings and for working capital to come from short-term loans or similar sources (see Figure 11.1). The financial statements and the OFR should make clear the link between borrowing requirements and capital expenditure plans.

What you generally want to see is some consistency in the debt/equity balance and when finance is raised that it is being productively employed in the business. A simple source and application analysis of the balance sheet can give an insight into where funds are coming from and where they are employed in the business. A simple rule of financial management is that a company's long-term investment in assets should be financed from long-term sources. There should be a match between the length of time funds are being tied up in investment and their repayment terms.

The OFR should explain:

> The capital structure of the business, its treasury policy and the dynamics of its financial position – its sources of liquidity and their application, including the implications of the financing requirements arising from its capital expenditure plans.

Peak borrowings

The OFR should include some discussion on cash flow linked to the cash flow statement and liquidity disclosed in the balance sheet. This can prove particularly useful where the cash flow generated from business segments is different from the profit disclosed for them in the segmental analysis report.

The OFR should define the level of a company's borrowings throughout the year, not just those applicable at the balance sheet date. That a company may have approached, or indeed exceeded, its borrowing limits during the year is an important factor in the assessment of its current financial position and future viability.

Shareholder returns

The OFR should provide some information about dividend policy and shareholder returns. It must be accepted, however, that it is difficult for companies to commit themselves to a predetermined dividend level. Next year the profit may drop, and for a variety of reasons the company may wish to move away from its previous dividend cover or payout level (see pages 144 and 225). Many factors, other than profit, can influence the dividend decision, including the requirements of major institutional shareholders, how confident directors are that profit will improve quickly, general market expectations and what other companies are doing – if they are maintaining dividends it may be difficult for one company to break the trend.

Going concern

Directors must formally state that they are of the opinion that their company is a going concern. This statement most commonly appears in either the directors' report or the OFR. It is, however, normally hedged with reminders of the uncertainties of future events and the impossibility of guaranteeing continued operations.

Share price and balance sheet values

The OFR offers an opportunity for companies to comment on the "strengths and resources of the business whose value is not reflected in the balance sheet", including such items as brands and other intangibles. This can help in calculating the value of a company. More UK companies are now discussing their shareholders' equity with reference to share price and market capitalisation; this is normally included in the OFR.

Employee training and development

The annual report should contain an explanation of a company's policy in respect of the various statutory or other guidelines for the employment of minority groups and the disabled as well as equal opportunities. However, more important are details of the way in which employees are encouraged to participate in running the business and to continue their personal development and training. Companies treating investment in employees as seriously as their investment in capital assets appear to do better in improving shareholder value and long-term profitability.

The term intrapreneurship is often used to describe a positive approach to the working relationship with employees. New ideas are welcome and employees are encouraged and rewarded for taking decisions and using their initiative within their defined areas of responsibility. Flexible working hours, teams being used throughout the organisation, a fairly flat hierarchy and employee participation in performance through profit sharing can all be taken as indicating a sound employee working relationship.

Research and development

For many companies the amount invested in research and development (R&D) is directly related to their likely future performance. A useful measure of the R&D expense is to express it as a percentage of sales revenue. The Department of Trade and Industry in the UK publishes a scoreboard of R&D expenditure based on some 300 international companies, which gives broad indicators of R&D as a percentage of sales for various business sectors. From the 1995/96 scoreboard the average R&D spend for non-UK companies was 4–5% compared with an average for UK companies of less than 2%.

Business sector	R&D as % of sales
Pharmaceuticals	14.7
Health care	12.8
Support services	12.2
Chemicals	7.0
Electronic & electrical equipment	7.0
Engineering	5.1
Telecommunications	5.0
Engineering, vehicles	3.9
Diversified industrials	3.5
Electricity	3.3
Building materials & merchants	2.7
Food manufacturers	2.5
Oil	1.3
Average for 300 companies	*4.4*

Value added

Value added is an effective means of both measuring company performance and identifying the way in which the various interest groups involved share in the resources generated. If a value-added statement is not provided in the annual report, it is quite easy to develop one based on the income statement. Retained earnings can be defined as follows.

$$\text{Retained earnings} = S - (B + Dp + W + I + Dd + T)$$

R = retained earnings
S = sales revenue
B = bought in materials and services
Dp = depreciation
W = wages
I = interest
Dd = dividends
T = tax

Value added is the difference between sales revenue and the amounts paid to external suppliers of goods and services (see page 153). This can be derived from the equation as follows.

$$S - B = W + I + Dd + T + Dp + R$$

Value added and shareholders

It can be argued that the prime objective of any company is to create value for its shareholders. Whether this should focus on maximising shareholder value or producing a balance between the interested parties (stakeholders) active in the company is open for discussion. During the 1990s companies increasingly focused on shareholder value, so much so that it almost became a mantra. Shareholder value is often mentioned in annual reports, but it is not so often or easily quantified.

Shareholders can gain value from two sources – an increase in share price or receipt of dividends. A company with high value added can decide either to reinvest funds in the business to provide continued growth or to give increased dividends to its shareholders. One simple measure of shareholder value is:

(Sale price of shares + Dividends received) – Purchase price of shares

Shareholder return can be calculated as:

(Dividend + (Current share price − Purchase share price)) ÷
Purchase share price

If the dividend for the year is 10¢, the shares cost 100¢ to buy and the current price is 105¢, if the shares were sold, the shareholder return would be 15%:

$$(10 + (105 - 100)) \div 100 = 0.15\ (15\%)$$

Such value measures can be readily understood by investors, but are not normally available from the financial figures found in the annual report.

Market value added

One way of calculating value added is to use market value added (MVA). This measures the net value of the company to shareholders – the "price to book" ratio. The total shareholders' equity (to which the market value of debt may be added) is deducted from the current market value (capitalisation) of the company (to which debt may be added). A positive figure means that value has been added to the shareholders' investment and a negative one means the investors have lost out. For example, if the capitalisation of a company is $100 and the shareholders equity in the balance sheet is $50, for every $1 of shareholders' equity the company has added $2.

Value based management

Value based management (VBM) is concerned with all aspects of a business, but particularly with the five "business drivers" from which shareholder value can be created:

- initial capital invested;
- rate of return on capital;
- rate of return required by investors;
- growth in capital invested;
- number of years involved.

Shareholder value analysis

Another means of quantifying shareholder value is through shareholder value analysis (SVA). This measure concentrates on seven value drivers such as:

- sales growth rate;
- operating profit margin;
- cash tax rate;
- fixed capital investment;
- working capital investment;
- the planning horizon;
- the cost of capital.

Free cash flow

An important factor in SVA analysis is the cash flow generating capability of a company. This is a specific measure of cash flow before taking account of the costs of shareholder or debt financing of the business. Referred to as the "free cash flow", it is normally calculated as follows:

> Operating profit
> *plus* depreciation
> *minus* cash tax paid
> = Cash profits
> *minus* investment in fixed assets and
>   investment in working capital
> = Free cash flow

Free cash flow is useful in providing an indication of the level of a company's cash flow generation. It also measures the amount of cash potentially available to cover the financing costs of the business after all necessary investment has been made.

Economic value added

A popular approach is to use economic value added (EVA), which measures after-tax profit against the estimated cost of capital – normally taken as the weighted average cost of capital (WACC). Companies should be expected to produce not only an accounting profit but also one that more than covers the cost of capital. It is argued that EVA is better than earnings per share or price/earnings ratios as these do not take account of the real cost of capital.

A simple example of the calculation of EVA is shown below. After the charge of $10 ($100 × 10%) representing the estimated cost of capital, the company shows an EVA of $30 for the period.

			$
After-tax profit	$40	After-tax profit	40
Capital employed	$100	Cost of capital	10
Cost of capital	10%	Economic value added	30

A positive EVA indicates that a company is giving investors added value. A company with a consistent EVA should have an increasing MVA; it will be generating a rate of return above the cost of capital so the share price should rise. For example, the three companies in the following example are all generating a positive return on capital employed.

($)	A	B	C
After-tax profit	50	60	50
Capital employed	200	400	600
Cost of capital (10%)	20	40	60
Return on capital employed (%)	25	15	8
Economic value added ($)	30	20	−10

Although company C produces a positive 8% return on capital employed, it is actually destroying shareholder value with a negative $10 EVA. In practice, the calculation of EVA requires several adjustments – to allow for the treatment of R&D, goodwill and brand values, leases and depreciation – to be made to the after-tax profit figure. It is claimed that EVA, as a single monetary figure, is better at concentrating management attention on the "real" results of running the business than are standard performance ratios such as return on total assets (ROTA). EVA is often used as a basis for managers' performance-related incentives.

Success or failure?

Future profit overrides current liquidity

The various ways of measuring profitability and liquidity were discussed in Chapters 7 and 10. Ideally, a company can be expected to focus on two principal objectives. The first is to provide an acceptable and continuing rate of return to investors, and the second is to maintain an adequate level of financial resources to support current and planned future operations and growth. A company can survive without profit as long as it has access to cash. A profitable company with no cash faces difficulties. No company can survive for more than a few days with neither profit nor cash.

A truism is that a profitable company is less likely to fail than an unprofitable one. The overriding factor in deciding whether to allow a company to continue in business is its profit potential, which is more important than its current liquidity. A company with low liquidity and a high profit potential will almost certainly be helped to overcome what may be regarded as a temporary problem. A highly liquid company with declining or no profit potential is unlikely to survive for long. Why should investors leave their funds to dwindle? The only decision facing such a company is whether to end operations immediately or to continue and see liquidity and profitability decline until matters are taken out of management's hands.

Financial management indicators

The interest cover ratio neatly combines profitability and gearing; a low-profit company with high debt will have a low interest cover. Gearing is an important factor in survival assessment. A highly geared low-profit company is more at risk than a low-geared high-profit company. A broad measure of the way in which the company is financed is provided by the debt/equity ratio. An alternative is the debt ratio, which expresses total debt as a percentage of total assets, allowing appreciation of the contributions by debt and equity (see page 211).

($)	A	B	C
Equity	250	500	1,000
Long-term loan	500	500	500
Current liabilities	250	250	250
	1,000	1,250	1,750
Total assets	1,000	1,250	1,750
Operating cash flow	300	200	500
Debt (%)	75	60	43
Equity (%)	25	40	57

The debt ratio measures the proportion of total assets financed by non-equity and gives an indication of short-term future viability. The higher the proportion of assets seen to be financed from outside borrowings rather than by shareholders, the higher is the gearing and the greater is the risk associated with the company. A general rule is that where the ratio is over 50% and there has been a steadily increasing trend over the last few years, this is an indication of imminent financial problems. For almost any type of business, a debt ratio of over 60% shows a potentially dangerous overreliance on external financing.

In the example, the highest geared company A with a debt/equity ratio of 200% has 75% of total assets financed by debt and 25% by equity, compared with C which has proportions of 43% and 57%. Another way of expressing this would be to use the asset gearing ratio. When equity is providing less than 50% of the total assets, the ratio moves to above 2. Company A has an asset gearing of 4 and C's is 1.75.

Cash flow indicators

Companies producing regular positive cash flow are better than those that "eat" cash flow. Operating cash flow is a crucial figure, representing the degree of success management has had in generating cash from running the business. It can be used in several illuminating measures of performance and position.

Operating cash flow ÷ interest
Operating cash flow ÷ dividend
Operating cash flow ÷ capital expenditure
Operating cash flow ÷ total debt

The first three ratios allow an appreciation of the proportion of a company's cash flow being allocated to pay for external finance, reward shareholders and reinvest in the fixed assets of the business.

For most companies, an operating cash flow ÷ interest of at least 2 or 200% is to be expected. Linking operating cash flow to dividend payments provides some assurance that sufficient cash was produced directly from the business in the year to cover the payment of dividends.

Companies cannot easily manipulate or disguise their cash flow or their financial structure. These can be combined in the cash flow/debt ratio. The higher the ratio the safer is the company. A minimum of 20% is often used as a guide level, indicating that it would take five years of operating cash flows to clear total debt. If the ratio were 10%, ten years' cash flows would be required. The cash flow from the business expressed as a percentage of the total of all non-shareholder liabilities indicates the strength of cash flow against external borrowings.

	A	B	C
Cash flow/debt (%)	40	27	67

The poor cash flow of B, the least profitable of the three companies, produces a cash flow/debt ratio of 27%. Another way of interpreting this ratio would be to say that it would take B 3.75 years ($750 ÷ $200) of current cash flow to repay its total debt. The period would be 2.5 years for A and 1.5 years for C.

To gain a better picture of the operating performance of a company, calculate the cash flow rate of return on assets (CFROA) or investment (CFROI) and treat in the manner described for ROTA analysis in Chapter 7.

100 x (Operating cash flow/total assets)

A	B	C
30%	16%	29%

Working capital and liquidity

The management of working capital is critical to company survival. Continual and careful monitoring and control of inventory levels and cash payment and collection periods is essential. Working capital, particularly in connection with inventory, is also a popular focus for fraud and misrepresentation. Inventory can be overvalued or phantom inventory devised to indicate an apparent improvement in profit.

The best way to monitor working capital and cash position is to use the liquid ratio, which is calculated directly from the balance sheet, and the cash cycle, which effectively combines operating activity with year-end position (see pages 186–7 and 195). The liquid ratio assumes that any inventory held has no immediate value. These two ratios should then be compared with those of previous years to test for consistency and identify any trends and with appropriate benchmark companies to assess conformity with the business sector.

The ability of a company to react to unexpected threats or opportunities by adjusting the timing and level of cash flows, its financial adaptability, is an important consideration. One way of assessing this from a more pessimistic viewpoint is to use the defensive interval, which indicates how long the company might survive and continue operations if all cash inflows ceased (see page 200).

Credit rating assessment

It is better to have several compatible measures than to rely on a single one in the assessment of a company. An early approach was to select a set of ratios considered to be good indicators of financial position and weight each of them to produce an index that would act as an overall credit assessment rating.

Ratio	Weight
Liquid ratio	15
ROTA	15
Interest cover	30
Cash flow/debt	20
Sales/stock	10
Equity/debt	<u>10</u>
	100

Each ratio was calculated and then multiplied by the assigned weight, the results totalled and the index for the company produced. This was then compared with an average or standard for the business sector or type of company to provide a comparative credit rating. The higher the score of the company the better was its credit rating.

This approach is still valid. It does not require substantial computer resources or a high degree of statistical competence; it can be completed on the basis of experience or personal view of a sector or type of company. It is a straightforward task to select a set of ratios that are considered to be good indicators of performance or position for companies operating in the business sector, to weight them according to their importance, to combine them and produce an overall index for each company.

It is recommended that the ratios are kept to a maximum of five or six, and that each one can be directly and independently interpreted. The simplest form of weighting is to allow a total of 100 points and allocate these to each ratio according to its perceived importance. Each ratio can be calculated as a percentage, multiplied by its assigned weight and the results totalled to give an index. It is important to remember whether a high percentage ratio represents a good or a bad position for a company. This will depend on the ratios incorporated in the analysis.

It is simplest to select ratios where a high percentage rather than a low one indicates good performance or position; for this reason the equity/debt ratio is to be preferred to the debt/equity ratio.

	Equity/debt	Weight	Index
A	0.33	10	3.3
B	0.67	10	6.7
C	1.33	10	13.3

The result is a simple composite or multivariate index that can be used to compare companies. The benchmark index level can be that of the sector leader or the average or median of the sample companies.

Predicting failure

Another truism is that it is inadvisable to lend money to a company that is about to fail. The ability to predict corporate failure before the event has been the holy grail of financial analysis for more than 50 years. There is normally a few years' warning before a company fails; a sudden and unexpected collapse is unusual.

Two major companies that were apparently healthy one day and failed the next – Rolls-Royce in the UK and the Penn Central railway company in the United States – stimulated research into whether it was possible to predict corporate failure. The first moves away from hindsight analysis were made in the late 1960s, when work in the United States broke new ground in the development of a multivariate approach to failure prediction. It was similar to that described above for producing a credit rating index, but it made use of computer power and complex statistical analysis.

A set of ratios was selected and weights assigned to produce a Z score.

$$Z = 0.012A + 0.014B + 0.033C + 0.006D + 0.010E$$

A = Net current assets ÷ total assets
B = Retained earnings ÷ total assets
C = Profit before interest and tax ÷ total assets
D = Capitalisation ÷ total debt
E = Sales ÷ total assets

A Z score below 1.8 was an indicator of probable failure, and a score of over 3 was seen as a clean bill of health. The model proved capable, for the sample companies, of predicting with an accuracy of 95% failure within one year and with an accuracy of over 70% failure within two years.

An advantage of this approach is that using a combination of several financial ratios makes it less likely that the result will be affected by manipulation of the financial statements. Each ratio attempts to provide a relevant measure of company performance or position and can be used independently as an indicator of financial viability.

The greater the proportion of net current assets (working capital) compared with total assets the healthier is the short-term position. The retained earnings used in the second ratio is the figure in the balance sheet representing the amount ploughed back from earnings to provide finance for the assets employed. The higher the figure the greater is the extent of the company's self-financing. The profit before interest and tax in the third ratio indicates the contribution of a company's profitability towards the end index score, profitable companies being less likely to fail than non-profitable ones. The fourth ratio brings market value (capitalisation) into the equation. The investors' view of the future potential of the company is set against total debt. This ratio represents the only figure, capitalisation, that is not guaranteed to appear in the annual report. The last ratio shows the ability of the company to use its assets to generate sales revenue. The higher the asset turnover the greater is the number of times cash from sales can be assumed to pass through the business. The higher the ratio the more productive are the assets and the higher is the amount of cash passing through the business.

Since the 1970s, increasingly sophisticated and arcane models have been developed to aid the prediction of failure, and those undertaking the research have not always been prepared to share their findings or index weightings. Thus the rule "keep it simple" has been neglected, and many failure prediction techniques are beyond the comprehension of the average user.

Tell-tale signs ...
There are several signs that a company may be heading for difficulties.

- It has only one product.
- It relies on a single customer or supplier.
- It is the only one in the sector showing profit improvement.
- It uses a small, unknown firm of auditors.
- The directors are selling shares.

... and fatal combinations
Identifying a number of uncomfortable factors in the annual report

should be taken as a warning sign. A company may:

- be operating a depreciation policy that is out of line with other similar companies in order to produce a profit;
- have negative operating cash flow;
- have made a series of rights issues;
- have debt that is continually rising;
- have sale and lease back agreements.

Combine these with:

- a low-quality board with little experience;
- weak non-executive directors;
- the ex-audit partner chairing the remuneration committee;
- one dominant personality as CEO and chairman;
- a newly appointed finance director.

The result will almost certainly be fatal.

Bill Mackey's list
A serious base to a light-hearted listing of possible indicators of corporate demise was provided by Bill Mackey, an experienced insolvency professional working in the UK in 1970 and 1980s.

- Rolls-Royces with personalised number plates
- Fish tank or fountain in the reception area
- Flag pole
- Queen's Award to Industry (UK only)
- Chairman honoured for services to industry
- Salesman or engineer as CEO
- Recently moved into new offices
- Unqualified or elderly accountant
- Products are market leaders
- Audit partner grew up with the company
- Chairman is a politician or well known for charitable works
- Recently announced a huge order in Afghanistan (or equivalent)
- Satisfied personnel with no strike records
- Recently announced a technical breakthrough

Yes to three or more? Call the creditors together, you're broke!

3
USEFUL BENCHMARKS

12 Practical examples of ratio analysis

The aim of this chapter is to provide useful examples of the application of ratio analysis. On pages 270–5 are a number of reasonably representative benchmarks for five sectors and six countries against which you can compare companies you are interested in. The ratios are calculated from the 1999–2000 financial statements of mature, quoted companies with a track record of consistent profitability in their sector.

On pages 276–91 more than 35 major retailers in 12 countries are used to provide a detailed comparison of performance and position. You can use the internet to access the annual report of any of these companies, or any company of interest to you, and continue the analysis to reinforce the skills developed by reading this book.

	Brewing	Construction	Food manufacture	Hotels	Pharmaceuticals
Trading profit (%)					
France	14.9	11.9	7.5	10.7	8.5
Germany	13.8	9.4	6.7	1.8	13.5
Italy	–	6.8	9.4	12.1	21.4
Netherlands	10.8	3.7	11.1	17.0	6.6
UK	8.9	5.5	6.8	26.8	29.5
US	13.7	9.0	12.5	20.6	24.5
Pre-tax profit (%)					
France	13.4	7.3	6.1	10.6	10.3
Germany	12.8	6.9	8.1	1.5	15.9
Italy	–	1.5	7.7	3.2	21.3
Netherlands	5.8	3.5	9.9	7.3	6.3
UK	8.3	4.4	5.6	15.5	27.7
US	12.4	6.2	10.9	11.1	27.5
Sales/total assets					
France	0.7	0.3	1.0	1.4	0.8
Germany	1.3	0.9	1.1	2.7	2.1
Italy	–	0.6	1.1	1.3	1.1
Netherlands	1.0	2.3	2.0	0.5	1.5
UK	1.0	1.8	1.5	0.2	0.9
US	1.2	1.0	1.0	0.5	0.9
ROTA (% trading profit)					
France	10.4	3.6	7.5	15.0	7.2
Germany	17.9	8.5	7.4	4.7	28.3
Italy	–	4.2	10.8	15.7	23.5
Netherlands	10.8	8.5	22.2	8.9	9.9
UK	8.9	9.9	10.2	5.1	26.5
US	14.7	9.2	11.4	9.6	22.3
ROTA (% pre-tax profit)					
France	9.0	2.3	6.1	14.8	8.7
Germany	16.6	6.2	8.9	4.0	33.4
Italy	–	0.9	8.7	4.2	23.4
Netherlands	5.8	8.0	19.8	3.9	9.4
UK	8.3	7.9	8.4	3.1	24.3
US	13.5	6.3	10.0	5.1	25.0

	Brewing	Construction	Food manufacture	Hotels	Pharmaceuticals
RONOA (% trading profit)					
France	11.5	4.6	8.5	20.2	10.4
Germany	20.3	4.6	8.1	7.4	34.6
Italy	–	7.2	22.6	13.5	39.4
Netherlands	11.1	13.9	16.7	9.2	12.7
UK	10.4	25.6	23.2	5.4	33.4
US	17.7	11.0	22.2	10.3	31.0
RONOA (% pre-tax profit)					
France	10.4	4.0	6.7	20.1	10.6
Germany	20.3	4.2	7.6	6.0	16.8
Italy	–	1.3	17.7	11.9	39.5
Netherlands	6.5	13.0	14.9	4.0	12.2
UK	9.5	14.6	18.8	3.1	31.5
US	16.3	7.6	19.7	5.5	34.7
ROE (% pre-tax profit)					
France	32.8	31.2	19.2	28.3	43.5
Germany	24.6	23.8	20.8	12.4	27.7
Italy	–	5.1	25.8	60.4	43.2
Netherlands	14.1	28.3	50.7	3.5	22.1
UK	12.3	15.3	20.3	4.0	77.0
US	35.5	25.0	24.3	24.5	44.4
ROE (% after-tax profit)					
France	20.4	31.1	11.2	16.5	30.8
Germany	8.0	22.5	8.6	4.4	16.9
Italy	–	2.0	15.0	24.4	22.6
Netherlands	8.3	20.7	36.0	2.1	15.6
UK	8.4	10.6	14.1	3.2	54.9
US	22.2	15.9	14.2	14.1	32.5
Liquid ratio					
France	0.7	0.9	0.5	0.8	1.3
Germany	1.8	0.8	1.1	1.2	2.3
Italy	–	0.9	1.1	0.7	1.4
Netherlands	0.4	1.0	0.7	0.5	1.0
UK	1.3	0.7	1.8	0.7	0.9
US	0.8	0.2	0.7	1.0	1.1

	Brewing	Construction	Food manufacture	Hotels	Pharmaceuticals
Cash/current assets (%)					
France	4.5	8.7	5.5	8.9	0.2
Germany	13.2	15.4	13.3	11.4	16.4
Italy	–	7.4	4.5	10.7	1.3
Netherlands	7.6	10.1	4.8	4.1	12.5
UK	16.3	10.0	3.4	8.6	6.9
US	10.3	1.1	4.0	5.6	15.7
Defensive interval (days)					
France	17	152	16	15	1
Germany	29	56	64	19	59
Italy	–	115	19	22	4
Netherlands	13	19	12	4	153
UK	133	57	23	42	26
US	50	8	9	19	78
Current liquidity ratio (days)					
France	664	411	451	136	459
Germany	−196	752	98	−319	−399
Italy	–	448	−80	82	198
Netherlands	716	3	659	106	−55
UK	−181	231	−453	215	72
US	−36	−307	−334	17	104
Sales/cash					
France	265	17	28	57	69
Germany	20	51	20	39	37
Italy	–	20	30	55	93
Netherlands	52	54	28	402	58
UK	48	57	70	459	29
US	45	97	56	49	12
Net current assets/sales (%)					
France	−36.5	−68.8	3.9	−2.9	17.4
Germany	11.5	−10.7	15.5	5.5	26.6
Italy	–	25.3	12.9	−21.6	22.1
Netherlands	−22.6	5.4	3.6	−5.3	14.0
UK	11.4	28.1	22.1	−16.2	7.4
US	1.9	67.1	2.6	5.6	12.7

	Brewing	Construction	Food manufacture	Hotels	Pharmaceuticals
Days' stock					
France	38	13	130	23	120
Germany	29	53	106	12	104
Italy	–	170	62	6	155
Netherlands	57	75	73	20	283
UK	192	53	54	10	90
US	31	121	98	20	161
Days' debtors					
France	63	112	42	28	109
Germany	55	85	37	59	86
Italy	–	116	69	73	74
Netherlands	49	49	60	28	53
UK	35	77	44	30	72
US	17	74	41	27	66
Days' creditors					
France	91	152	72	44	125
Germany	37	54	53	43	45
Italy	–	159	122	128	85
Netherlands	48	89	29	41	262
UK	179	37	80	21	35
US	51	59	61	78	85
Cash cycle (days)					
France	11	−27	99	7	104
Germany	46	84	89	28	145
Italy	–	127	10	−49	144
Netherlands	57	35	104	7	74
UK	48	93	17	18	127
US	−3	136	78	−30	142
Equity/total assets (%)					
France	27	25	53	54	18
Germany	47	20	38	33	51
Italy	–	14	33	16	47
Netherlands	39	30	23	40	38
UK	63	40	63	73	31
US	44	25	19	22	35

	Brewing	Construction	Food manufacture	Hotels	Pharmaceuticals
Debt/total assets (%)					
France	27	18	16	11	33
Germany	39	37	36	22	34
Italy	–	25	15	40	52
Netherlands	13	19	25	54	56
UK	18	15	6	17	26
US	38	58	45	71	28
Current liabilities/total assets (%)					
France	45	57	31	35	48
Germany	14	43	26	46	14
Italy	–	62	50	44	37
Netherlands	48	51	53	7	33
UK	19	45	31	9	43
US	18	16	33	7	37
Interest cover					
France	5.5	3.5	5.9	35.4	4.9
Germany	11.7	3.1	5.1	4.8	6.7
Italy	–	1.1	2.7	9.0	3.2
Netherlands	4.1	6.0	3.0	1.9	5.5
UK	7.9	5.3	10.5	2.5	13.4
US	7.2	4.0	6.8	1.8	31.4
Sales/employee ($'000)					
France	351	249	414	86	315
Germany	361	296	246	58	363
Italy	–	618	283	66	237
Netherlands	185	208	496	72	311
UK	342	315	316	71	194
US	465	437	226	64	261
Trading profit/employee ($'000)					
France	52	146	53	9	26
Germany	41	38	18	1	21
Italy	–	44	27	11	53
Netherlands	15	8	33	12	19
UK	25	22	21	18	55
US	29	39	23	13	59

	Brewing	Construction	Food manufacture	Hotels	Pharmaceuticals
Fixed asset/employee ($'000)					
France	419	858	600	41	233
Germany	167	800	386	15	95
Italy	–	256	87	148	81
Netherlands	114	33	110	126	161
UK	179	14	63	337	116
US	339	65	210	125	182
Cash flow/sales (%)					
France	24.2	10.5	15.4	15.6	12.9
Germany	20.2	14.0	11.3	5.2	17.9
Italy	–	13.9	13.7	18.5	25.5
Netherlands	16.8	5.8	14.4	25.1	10.7
UK	13.8	6.6	10.0	32.1	33.7
US	19.6	10.7	16.6	35.4	30.5

Retailers compared

			– Turnover ($m) –	
			1998	**1999**
Wal Mart	US	Jan 2000	137,634	165,013
Kroger	US	Jan 2000	43,082	45,352
Sears Roebuck	US	Jan 2000	41,575	41,071
Home Depot	US	Jan 2000	30,219	38,434
Metro	Ger	Dec 1999	39,715	37,104
K Mart	US	Jan 2000	33,674	35,925
Carrefour	Fra	Dec 1999	23,224	31,660
Safeway	US	Jan 2000	24,484	28,860
Tesco	UK	Feb 2000	24,174	26,482
Sainsbury	UK	Apr 2000	23,153	22,924
Pinault Printemps	Fra	Dec 1999	13,993	16,024
Kingfisher	UK	Jan 2000	10,507	15,336
Casino	Fra	Dec 1999	11,994	13,251
Ahold	Neth	Jan 2000	10,183	12,904
Karstadt	Ger	Dec 1999	7,963	12,572
Delhaize Frères	Belg	Dec 1999	10,939	12,123
Marks & Spencer	UK	Mar 2000	11,587	11,547
Safeway	UK	Apr 2000	10,582	10,791
Boots	UK	Mar 2000	7,107	7,308
Castorama Dubois	Fra	Jan 2000	2,613	6,225
Spar Handels-AG	Ger	Dec 1999	6,912	5,666
Galeries Lafayette	Fra	Dec 1999	4,557	4,704
GIB	Belg	Jan 2000	4,286	4,349
Rinascente	Ita	Dec 1999	3,360	3,995
Allgemeine Handles.	Ger	Dec 1999	3,804	3,810
Vendex Int	Neth	Jan 2000	2,043	3,737
Borders	US	Jan 2000	2,595	2,999
Jeronimo Martins	Port	Dec 1999	2,534	2,779
Laurus	Neth	Dec 1999	1,643	2,149
Next	UK	Jan 2000	1,746	2,008
Colruyt	Belg	Mar 2000	1,731	1,911
Amazon	US	Dec 1999	610	1,640
Valora	Swi	Dec 1999	1,423	1,577
Kesko	Fin	Dec 1999	854	871
Cortefiel	Spa	Feb 2000	432	503
Jelmoli Holding	Swi	Dec 1999	675	464
Hennes & Mauritz	Swe	Nov 1999	208	258

	Operating profit ($m)			Total assets ($m)	
	1998	1999		1998	1999
Wal Mart	6,546	8,309	Wal Mart	49,996	70,349
Home Depot	2,661	3,795	Sears	37,675	36,954
Sears	3,278	3,681	Carrefour	14,729	28,598
Safeway US	1,602	1,998	Kroger	16,641	17,966
Kroger	1,516	1,781	Printemps	10,686	17,264
Tesco	1,316	1,451	Home Depot	13,465	17,081
K Mart	1,091	1,300	Metro	16,061	16,079
Carrefour	873	1,266	K Mart	14,166	15,104
Kingfisher	891	1,070	Safeway US	11,390	14,900
Printemps	772	1,021	Sainsbury	14,160	14,867
Boots	687	777	Tesco	12,256	13,905
Sainsbury	1,241	758	M & S	10,996	11,293
Metro	707	718	Kingfisher	8,641	10,013
M & S	721	664	Casino	6,535	8,972
Delhaize	485	549	Karstadt	4,637	6,713
Ahold	391	544	Safeway UK	6,285	6,456
Castorama	160	514	Ahold	4,393	5,493
Casino	375	458	Boots	4,547	4,963
Safeway UK	594	447	Delhaize	3,847	4,852
Next	219	251	Rinascente	3,284	3,734
Vendex Int	119	203	Castorama	2,352	3,125
Borders	167	166	Gal. Lafayette	2,490	2,576
Jer. Martins	118	125	Amazon	649	2,472
Colruyt	94	117	Jer. Martins	1,901	2,293
Gal. Lafayette	96	111	Borders	1,767	1,915
Allg. Handles	43	91	Vendex Int	1,768	1,848
Rinascente	71	86	GIB	1,675	1,704
Valora	58	81	Spar	1,634	1,493
Karstadt	103	78	Next	1,202	1,334
Laurus	48	70	Allg. Handles	976	1,084
Cortefiel	48	57	Valora	1,029	952
Jelmoli	39	49	Colruyt	827	892
GIB	17	46	Jelmoli	768	798
H & M	31	42	Laurus	498	532
Kesko	19	17	Kesko	362	366
Spar	−103	−140	Cortefiel	313	360
Amazon	−109	−606	H & M	106	131

	Profit margin[a]		Asset turn[b]		% ROTA	
	1998	**1999**	**1998**	**1999**	**1998**	**1999**
H & M	14.8	16.4	2.0	2.0	29.0	32.3
Home Depot	8.8	9.9	2.2	2.3	19.8	22.2
Next	12.6	12.5	1.5	1.5	18.2	18.8
Castorama	6.1	8.3	1.1	2.0	6.8	16.4
Cortefiel	11.0	11.3	1.4	1.4	15.2	15.8
Boots	9.7	10.6	1.6	1.5	15.1	15.6
Safeway US	6.5	6.9	2.1	1.9	14.1	13.4
Laurus	2.9	3.3	3.3	4.0	9.6	13.2
Colruyt	5.5	6.1	2.1	2.1	11.4	13.1
Wal Mart	4.8	5.0	2.8	2.3	13.1	11.8
Delhaize	4.4	4.5	2.8	2.5	12.6	11.3
Vendex Int	5.8	5.4	1.2	2.0	6.7	11.0
Kingfisher	8.5	7.0	1.2	1.5	10.3	10.7
Tesco	5.4	5.5	2.0	1.9	10.7	10.4
Sears	7.9	9.0	1.1	1.1	8.7	10.0
Kroger	3.5	3.9	2.6	2.5	9.1	9.9
Ahold	3.8	4.2	2.3	2.3	8.9	9.9
Borders	6.4	5.5	1.5	1.6	9.5	8.7
K Mart	3.2	3.6	2.4	2.4	7.7	8.6
Valora	4.0	5.1	1.4	1.7	5.6	8.5
Allg. Handles	1.1	2.4	3.9	3.5	4.4	8.4
Safeway UK	5.6	4.1	1.7	1.7	9.5	6.9
Jelmoli	5.8	10.5	0.9	0.6	5.1	6.1
Printemps	5.5	6.4	1.3	0.9	7.2	5.9
M & S	6.2	5.7	1.1	1.0	6.6	5.9
Jer. Martins	4.7	4.5	1.3	1.2	6.2	5.4
Casino	3.1	3.5	1.8	1.5	5.7	5.1
Sainsbury	5.4	3.3	1.6	1.5	8.8	5.1
Kesko	2.2	1.9	2.4	2.4	5.3	4.6
Metro	1.8	1.9	2.5	2.3	4.4	4.5
Carrefour	3.8	4.0	1.6	1.1	5.9	4.4
Gal. Lafayette	2.1	2.4	1.8	1.8	3.9	4.3
GIB	0.4	1.1	2.6	2.6	1.0	2.7
Rinascente	2.1	2.1	1.0	1.1	2.2	2.3
Karstadt	1.3	0.6	1.7	1.9	2.2	1.2
Spar	−1.5	−2.5	4.2	3.8	−6.3	−9.4
Amazon	−17.9	−36.9	0.9	0.7	−16.8	−24.5

a Profit margin = operating profit/sales revenue (%)

b Asset turn = sales revenue/total assets

	Profit margin[a]		% ROTA	
	1998	**1999**	**1998**	**1999**
H & M	15.4	17.1	30.3	33.5
Home Depot	8.8	9.9	19.7	22.3
Next	13.5	13.7	19.6	20.6
Colruyt	5.6	7.6	11.8	16.4
Boots	3.4	10.8	5.3	15.9
Cortefiel	9.1	10.7	12.5	15.0
Castorama	4.7	7.3	5.2	14.5
Wal Mart	5.3	5.5	14.6	12.9
Laurus	2.7	3.0	8.9	12.3
Safeway US	5.7	5.8	12.3	11.2
Kingfisher	8.4	6.7	10.3	10.2
Vendex Int	5.6	4.9	6.5	10.0
Tesco	4.9	5.0	9.7	9.5
Delhaize	3.5	3.6	10.0	8.9
Valora	4.4	5.2	6.1	8.7
Allg. Handles	0.7	2.2	2.7	7.8
Borders	5.8	4.9	8.6	7.7
Ahold	2.9	3.1	6.8	7.3
Jelmoli	6.2	12.2	5.5	7.1
Sears	4.5	5.9	5.0	6.5
K Mart	2.2	2.7	5.3	6.4
Kroger	2.0	2.5	5.2	6.3
Printemps	5.1	5.9	6.6	5.5
M & S	6.6	5.1	7.0	5.2
Safeway UK	4.5	3.1	7.6	5.2
Sainsbury	5.4	3.1	8.8	4.8
Kesko	2.6	2.0	6.1	4.8
Casino	2.8	3.1	5.1	4.5
Carrefour	3.6	3.5	5.7	3.8
Gal. Lafayette	1.9	2.0	3.5	3.7
Metro	1.2	1.5	3.1	3.4
Jer. Martins	3.3	2.7	4.4	3.3
Karstadt	1.5	1.5	2.6	2.8
Rinascente	2.6	2.4	2.6	2.5
GIB	−1.3	0.7	−3.3	1.7
Spar	0.6	−1.4	2.6	−5.3
Amazon	−19.9	−39.2	−18.8	−26.0

a Profit margin = pre-tax profit/sales revenue (%)

	Tangible fixed assets ($m)		Stock ($m)		Trade debtors ($m)	
	1998	**1999**	**1998**	**1999**	**1998**	**1999**
Sears	6,380	6,450	4,816	5,069	–	–
H & M	223	277	299	333	32	36
Colruyt	275	296	172	193	43	48
Metro	5,108	3,320	3,828	4,152	261	500
Printemps	1,064	1,408	2,120	2,478	1,604	1,940
Laurus	229	244	125	136	49	56
Castorama	899	1,299	819	1,005	38	81
Cortefiel	86	111	118	139	46	48
Next	388	407	213	207	397	406
Safeway US	5,183	6,445	1,856	2,445	200	293
Home Depot	8,160	10,227	4,293	5,489	469	587
Casino	1,912	2,490	1,065	1,178	274	295
Boots	2,520	2,535	1,017	971	379	398
Allg. Handles	217	209	463	520	6	6
Wal Mart	25,973	35,969	17,076	19,793	1,118	1,341
Carrefour	6,051	10,263	2,071	4,177	135	828
Kroger	7,220	8,275	3,493	3,938	587	622
Delhaize	1,925	2,343	1,161	1,392	266	330
Rinascente	1	1	–	–	–	–
Kingfisher	4,065	4,836	2,162	2,488	573	571
Gal. Lafayette	706	723	602	624	201	238
Ahold	2,594	3,259	768	981	276	343
Borders	494	558	1,020	1,078	63	69
Vendex Int	970	993	508	574	58	66
Tesco	10,010	11,469	940	1,048	0	0
Valora	438	458	127	150	100	131
Jer. Martins	812	1,014	301	371	95	96
GIB	468	510	348	385	154	159
K Mart	5,914	6,410	6,536	7,101	–	–
M & S	6,182	5,977	725	668	64	63
Kesko	126	123	71	70	74	67
Safeway UK	5,312	5,351	461	555	6	14
Sainsbury	9,030	9,247	1,188	1,389	76	76
Jelmoli	447	472	93	89	52	69
Karstadt	1,835	2,338	1,380	2,083	523	1,170
Spar	300	255	514	498	122	139
Amazon	30	318	30	221	–	–

Trade creditors ($m)		Net operating assets ($m)		Operating profit ($m)		% RoNOA	
1998	1999	1998	1999	1998	1999	1998	1999
6,732	6,992	4,464	4,527	3,278	3,681	73.4	81.3
55	82	499	563	307	423	61.6	75.1
227	248	263	289	94	117	36.0	40.5
5,365	6,014	3,832	1,958	707	718	18.4	36.7
2,363	2,864	2,425	2,962	772	1,021	31.8	34.5
194	224	209	211	48	70	22.8	33.1
706	812	1,050	1,574	160	514	15.2	32.6
85	106	165	191	48	57	28.9	29.7
94	102	904	918	219	251	24.2	27.4
1,596	1,878	5,643	7,304	1,602	1,998	28.4	27.4
1,586	1,993	11,336	14,310	2,661	3,795	23.5	26.5
1,643	2,100	1,608	1,862	375	458	23.3	24.6
507	501	3,408	3,403	687	777	20.2	22.8
226	286	459	449	43	91	9.3	20.2
10,257	13,105	33,910	43,998	6,546	8,309	19.3	18.9
4,144	8,535	4,112	6,733	873	1,266	21.2	18.8
2,926	2,867	8,374	9,968	1,516	1,781	18.1	17.9
818	970	2,535	3,095	485	549	19.1	17.7
1	1	–	–	–	–	16.2	17.2
1,359	1,512	5,441	6,383	891	1,070	16.4	16.8
855	889	654	696	96	111	14.7	16.0
857	1,100	2,781	3,483	391	544	14.1	15.6
607	580	969	1,124	167	166	17.3	14.8
115	141	1,420	1,491	119	203	8.4	13.6
1,550	1,758	9,400	10,758	1,316	1,451	14.0	13.5
98	118	567	620	58	81	10.2	13.0
461	514	748	967	118	125	15.8	12.9
586	656	383	398	17	46	4.3	11.5
2,047	2,204	10,403	11,307	1,091	1,300	10.5	11.5
302	309	6,668	6,399	721	664	10.8	10.4
71	78	199	183	19	17	9.6	9.2
941	987	4,838	4,932	594	447	12.3	9.1
1,527	1,616	8,766	9,096	1,241	758	14.2	8.3
30	36	562	594	39	49	7.0	8.2
463	753	3,275	4,838	103	78	3.1	1.6
432	393	505	499	−103	−140	−20.3	−28.1
133	463	−74	75	−109	−606	147.4	−805.6

	Operating profit/ equity (%)			After-tax profit/ equity (%)	
	1998	1999		1998	1999
Ahold	65.5	66.6	Ahold	37.0	45.4
Kroger	79.1	66.4	Laurus	26.1	32.3
Delhaize	62.9	59.7	H & M	27.2	29.9
Sears	54.0	53.8	Delhaize	32.2	29.6
Laurus	42.7	52.4	Colruyt	22.5	29.0
Safeway US	52.0	48.9	Vendex Int	25.8	27.3
Vendex Int	35.1	45.0	Valora	12.2	26.4
H & M	39.6	44.5	Kroger	25.8	23.8
Castorama	17.6	37.9	Safeway US	26.2	23.8
Jer. Martins	35.7	37.8	Next	22.8	23.1
Printemps	29.5	32.4	Printemps	19.1	22.8
Colruyt	33.6	32.4	Wal Mart	21.7	22.2
Wal Mart	31.0	32.2	Sears	18.4	22.2
Valora	13.7	31.0	Boots	1.3	21.6
Home Depot	30.4	30.8	Castorama	7.8	21.4
Boots	27.4	29.8	Kingfisher	19.8	19.9
Next	28.7	29.4	Cortefiel	16.5	19.5
Kingfisher	28.1	28.9	Home Depot	18.5	18.8
Cortefiel	26.5	26.9	Jer. Martins	21.5	18.7
Allg. Handles	13.5	26.3	Jelmoli	13.6	17.3
Carrefour	26.4	23.6	Allg. Handles	4.2	14.2
Metro	23.0	23.4	Tesco	13.8	14.1
Casino	22.2	21.8	Karstadt	7.5	13.2
Tesco	21.3	21.6	Carrefour	16.1	12.8
Gal. Lafayette	21.2	21.3	Casino	11.9	11.6
Borders	23.4	20.7	Borders	12.9	11.3
K Mart	18.2	20.6	Gal. Lafayette	12.1	10.3
Jelmoli	14.5	17.7	Metro	10.3	10.1
GIB	5.7	15.5	K Mart	8.7	10.0
Safeway UK	19.9	15.5	Safeway UK	11.0	7.8
Sainsbury	19.0	11.3	Sainsbury	12.8	7.3
M & S	10.5	9.6	GIB	−23.9	7.1
Rinascente	10.5	8.6	Kesko	8.1	5.9
Kesko	9.5	8.3	M & S	7.6	5.3
Karstadt	9.0	5.5	Rinascente	7.2	5.0
Spar	−35.2	−84.8	Spar	7.1	−53.4
Amazon	−78.7	−227.5	Amazon	−87.7	−241.5

	Interest cover[a]			Dividend cover[b]	
	1998	**1999**		**1998**	**1999**
H & M	238.6	306.3	Gal. Lafayette	25.0	16.1
Next	312.2	298.2	Home Depot	9.6	9.1
Home Depot	72.9	136.5	Wal Mart	6.6	6.5
Castorama	20.3	59.5	Delhaize	5.0	5.0
Cortefiel	18.8	46.4	Colruyt	3.2	4.4
Colruyt	13.5	21.2	Sears	3.1	4.3
Boots	16.2	19.6	Rinascente	2.5	4.0
Laurus	10.8	11.7	Printemps	3.5	4.0
Kingfisher	15.0	11.2	Valora	3.2	3.7
Allg. Handles	3.3	10.9	Castorama	2.7	3.6
Kesko	6.5	10.6	Vendex Int	3.6	3.4
Borders	11.3	10.3	Cortefiel	2.8	3.3
Gal. Lafayette	7.7	9.8	Ahold	2.4	3.1
Wal Mart	9.2	9.1	Jelmoli	2.7	3.0
Tesco	10.0	8.0	Karstadt	2.2	3.0
Safeway US	7.8	6.5	Laurus	2.3	2.9
Valora	4.5	6.4	Casino	2.5	2.8
Vendex Int	6.5	6.0	H & M	2.8	2.8
Sainsbury	9.8	6.0	Kingfisher	2.5	2.6
Delhaize	5.9	6.0	Allg. Handles	1.4	2.6
Printemps	5.9	5.5	Carrefour	3.3	2.6
M & S	7.7	5.4	Jer. Martins	3.0	2.5
Safeway UK	7.0	5.1	Tesco	2.2	2.2
K Mart	4.2	4.9	Kesko	1.9	1.9
Casino	5.2	4.7	Next	1.8	1.8
GIB	2.1	4.6	Boots	0.1	1.8
Ahold	4.2	4.4	Safeway UK	1.5	1.8
Jelmoli	3.5	4.2	Sainsbury	2.0	1.3
Sears	3.3	3.9	Metro	1.2	1.2
Carrefour	5.4	3.9	M & S	0.9	1.0
Kroger	3.4	3.7	GIB	−2.2	0.6
Metro	3.1	3.6	Amazon	na	na
Rinascente	2.7	3.3	Borders	na	na
Jer. Martins	3.4	3.0	K Mart	na	na
Karstadt	2.1	1.6	Kroger	na	na
Spar	−1.5	−3.3	Safeway US	na	na
Amazon	−3.1	−6.2	Spar	na	na

a Operating profit + interest paid/interest paid
b After-tax profit/dividends

	Equity[a]/ total assets (%)		Debt[b]/ total assets (%)		Current liabilities/ total assets (%)	
	1998	1999	1998	1999	1998	1999
Amazon	21	11	54	59	25	30
Borders	40	42	4	4	56	54
Home Depot	65	72	14	6	21	21
K Mart	42	42	32	31	26	27
Kroger	12	15	56	53	33	32
Safeway US	27	27	48	49	25	24
Sears	20	22	42	41	37	37
Wal Mart	46	39	21	25	34	37
Boots	55	53	8	15	37	33
Kingfisher	43	43	13	9	44	48
M & S	63	61	11	12	26	27
Next	64	64	2	2	34	34
Safeway UK	47	45	19	22	34	33
Sainsbury	47	45	8	10	45	45
Tesco	50	49	14	16	35	35
H & M	73	73	6	5	21	23
Kesko	56	56	8	6	36	38
Cortefiel	58	59	7	4	35	37
Jer. Martins	22	19	32	26	46	55
Rinascente	21	27	27	22	52	51
Colruyt	34	42	12	9	54	49
Delhaize	38	35	23	23	38	43
GIB	21	20	26	21	53	59
Ahold	16	17	44	40	40	43
Laurus	22	25	25	18	52	57
Vendex Int	22	25	51	45	27	31
Jelmoli	36	35	47	44	17	22
Valora	42	28	39	49	19	23
Allg. Handles	33	32	22	22	46	46
Karstadt	25	22	47	45	28	34
Metro	22	20	31	29	47	50
Spar	19	11	43	40	38	49
Carrefour	27	22	17	24	57	54
Casino	32	29	24	28	45	43
Castorama	39	44	13	8	48	48
Gal. Lafayette	25	27	17	16	58	57
Printemps	29	31	20	23	51	46

a Equity = Shareholders' funds + minority interests
b Debt = Long-term borrowings and creditors + provisions

	Total debt/ equity (%)		Total assets/ equity (%)	
	1998	1999	1998	1999
Amazon	367	828	468	928
Borders	147	139	247	239
Home Depot	54	38	154	138
K Mart	137	140	237	240
Kroger	768	570	868	670
Safeway US	270	265	370	365
Sears	396	351	496	451
Wal Mart	118	159	218	259
Boots	81	90	181	190
Kingfisher	134	130	234	230
M & S	59	63	159	163
Next	57	56	157	156
Safeway UK	111	125	211	225
Sainsbury	114	120	214	220
Tesco	99	106	199	206
H & M	36	38	136	138
Kesko	77	77	177	177
Cortefiel	72	69	172	169
Jer. Martins	357	427	457	527
Rinascente	383	273	483	373
Colruyt	194	140	294	240
Delhaize	161	188	261	288
GIB	373	398	473	498
Ahold	536	480	636	580
Laurus	347	299	447	399
Vendex Int	347	308	447	408
Jelmoli	179	189	279	288
Valora	138	260	238	360
Allg. Handles	207	212	307	312
Karstadt	306	364	406	464
Metro	355	396	455	496
Spar	437	780	537	880
Carrefour	276	348	376	448
Casino	213	244	313	344
Castorama	159	127	259	227
Gal. Lafayette	297	265	397	365
Printemps	240	221	340	321

	Liquid ratio[a]				Cash[b]/current assets (%)	
	1998	**1999**			**1998**	**1999**
H & M	2.4	2.3		Amazon	88	70
Sears	1.7	1.7		H & M	58	62
M & S	1.4	1.5		Printemps	13	38
Next	1.3	1.4		Colruyt	48	37
Valora	2.3	1.4		GIB	39	36
Amazon	2.4	1.1		Rinascente	19	33
Kesko	1.0	1.0		Valora	51	29
Jelmoli	1.1	0.9		Boots	10	28
Printemps	0.6	0.9		Casino	19	27
Colruyt	0.8	0.9		Tesco	29	26
Karstadt	0.8	0.8		Safeway UK	25	21
Boots	0.5	0.7		Next	12	21
GIB	0.9	0.7		Carrefour	11	20
Spar	0.9	0.7		Kesko	17	19
Rinascente	0.6	0.7		Ahold	13	17
Metro	0.4	0.6		Gal. Lafayette	18	17
Sainsbury	0.6	0.5		Kingfisher	19	16
Cortefiel	0.6	0.5		Jelmoli	14	15
Gal. Lafayette	0.5	0.5		Sainsbury	21	15
Casino	0.4	0.4		Delhaize	13	14
Ahold	0.4	0.4		M & S	14	13
Kingfisher	0.5	0.4		Metro	21	12
Carrefour	0.3	0.4		Jer. Martins	9	12
Allg. Handles	0.3	0.4		Spar	32	10
Vendex Int	0.5	0.4		Castorama	12	9
Delhaize	0.4	0.4		Wal Mart	9	8
Laurus	0.4	0.4		Allg. Handles	2	6
Castorama	0.5	0.4		Kroger	6	5
Kroger	0.3	0.3		Karstadt	10	5
K Mart	0.4	0.3		K Mart	9	4
Home Depot	0.2	0.2		Cortefiel	5	4
Jer. Martins	0.3	0.2		Vendex Int	3	4
Wal Mart	0.2	0.2		Safeway US	2	3
Tesco	0.2	0.2		Borders	4	3
Safeway US	0.2	0.2		Laurus	6	3
Safeway UK	0.2	0.2		Home Depot	1	3
Borders	0.1	0.1		Sears	2	3

a (Current assets – stock)/current liabilities
b Cash includes cash equivalents

	Defensive interval (days)			Current liquidity ratio (days)	
	1998	**1999**		**1998**	**1999**
Amazon	286	191	Spar	2,586	−1,614
H & M	170	190	Sears	−919	−798
Printemps	27	128	M & S	−396	−538
Rinascente	39	65	H & M	−329	−305
Boots	17	55	Valora	−986	−290
Valora	127	54	Next	−190	−242
Jelmoli	26	52	Kesko	−52	21
Colruyt	67	52	Amazon	1,280	49
Next	28	47	Jelmoli	−63	53
GIB	51	45	Colruyt	243	121
M & S	33	33	Boots	376	168
Carrefour	10	31	Home Depot	267	236
Casino	17	29	Printemps	807	237
Kingfisher	41	26	Cortefiel	243	310
Gal. Lafayette	28	25	Safeway US	415	403
Kesko	17	19	Vendex Int	441	410
Metro	17	13	Karstadt	300	426
Sainsbury	18	13	K Mart	497	532
Castorama	34	13	Kroger	576	550
Ahold	10	13	Ahold	557	559
Delhaize	9	12	Castorama	1,073	562
Jer. Martins	9	12	Delhaize	458	581
Cortefiel	16	12	Allg. Handles	844	652
Karstadt	20	10	Laurus	771	674
Sears	7	10	Wal Mart	551	694
Safeway UK	9	8	Tesco	710	723
Spar	23	8	GIB	406	745
Tesco	8	7	Metro	925	747
Borders	8	7	Kingfisher	635	754
Allg. Handles	1	5	Sainsbury	515	810
Wal Mart	6	5	Safeway UK	758	902
K Mart	10	4	Rinascente	1,153	962
Vendex Int	6	4	Casino	1,046	1,098
Kroger	3	3	Gal. Lafayette	1,473	1,332
Home Depot	1	2	Carrefour	1,441	1,494
Safeway US	1	2	Jer. Martins	1,119	1,519
Laurus	3	2	Borders	1,877	1,952

	Stock[a] (days)		Debtors[b] (days)		Creditors[c] (days)		Cash cycle (days)	
	1998	1999	1998	1999	1998	1999	1998	1999
Rinascente	55	52	7	5	150	147	−88	−90
Amazon	23	60	0	0	102	125	−80	−66
Carrefour	41	62	2	10	83	126	−39	−55
Sears	64	68	0	0	90	94	−25	−26
Casino	43	43	8	8	66	77	−15	−26
Metro	45	52	2	5	64	76	−16	−18
GIB	41	45	13	13	69	76	−15	−18
Safeway UK	20	24	0	0	41	42	−21	−18
Gal. Lafayette	73	73	16	18	104	105	−15	−13
Tesco	15	16	0	0	25	26	−10	−11
Jer. Martins	53	60	14	13	81	83	−14	−10
Laurus	33	27	11	9	50	45	−7	−8
Colruyt	46	47	9	9	61	61	−6	−4
Sainsbury	20	24	1	1	26	28	−5	−3
Ahold	36	37	10	10	40	41	6	5
Safeway US	39	44	3	4	34	34	8	14
Kroger	40	43	5	5	33	31	11	17
Spar	34	39	6	9	29	30	12	17
M & S	34	32	2	2	14	15	22	19
Wal Mart	57	56	3	3	34	37	26	22
Castorama	172	94	5	5	148	76	29	23
Kesko	35	35	32	28	35	38	31	24
Delhaize	51	55	9	10	36	39	24	27
Printemps	84	88	42	44	94	102	32	30
Allg. Handles	60	69	1	1	29	38	31	31
Valora	55	61	26	30	43	48	38	43
Kingfisher	113	89	20	14	71	54	62	48
Home Depot	72	74	6	6	27	27	51	53
Boots	98	90	19	20	49	46	68	64
K Mart	91	92	0	0	28	29	62	64
Vendex Int	151	89	10	6	34	22	127	74
H & M	107	100	6	5	20	25	93	80
Cortefiel	204	201	39	35	147	154	96	82
Borders	200	183	9	8	119	99	90	93
Next	65	55	83	74	29	27	119	102
Karstadt	116	113	24	34	39	41	101	106
Jelmoli	76	120	28	54	25	49	79	126

a Stock/average daily cost
b Debtors/average daily sales
c Creditors/average daily cost

	Sales/cash[a]			Net current assets/sales (%)	
	1998	1999		1998	1999
Laurus	124	279	Sears	36	36
Safeway US	536	272	H & M	29	28
Home Depot	487	226	Next	20	20
Kroger	144	161	M & S	16	19
Vendex Int	104	131	Jelmoli	15	17
K Mart	47	104	Amazon	43	17
Allg. Handles	396	96	Valora	27	16
Wal Mart	73	89	Cortefiel	17	15
Borders	61	72	Karstadt	14	13
Karstadt	34	67	K Mart	12	11
Cortefiel	47	60	Printemps	0	10
Spar	20	57	Kesko	9	8
Sears	84	56	Colruyt	5	7
Safeway UK	49	55	Home Depot	7	7
Tesco	52	54	Boots	1	7
Castorama	16	44	Allg. Handles	4	6
Delhaize	51	39	Borders	6	6
Ahold	50	38	Vendex Int	14	6
Jer. Martins	52	36	Spar	7	5
Metro	27	35	GIB	5	2
Sainsbury	22	30	Metro	−1	2
Kesko	24	23	Delhaize	2	1
Gal. Lafayette	19	22	Castorama	8	1
Kingfisher	19	21	Kroger	−1	0
M & S	17	17	Wal Mart	3	−1
Casino	28	17	Kingfisher	3	−2
Carrefour	48	15	Safeway US	−2	−2
Boots	39	12	Laurus	−2	−3
Jelmoli	21	12	Ahold	−2	−3
Valora	5	12	Gal. Lafayette	−4	−3
Next	19	11	Rinascente	−6	−4
GIB	10	11	Sainsbury	−6	−7
Colruyt	7	9	Casino	−5	−7
Rinascente	12	7	Safeway UK	−12	−11
Printemps	20	4	Tesco	−11	−11
H & M	4	4	Carrefour	−17	−16
Amazon	2	2	Jer. Martins	−14	−22

a Cash includes cash equivalents

$'000s	Sales/ employees		Fixed assets/ employees		Operating profit/ employees	
	1998	1999	1998	1999	1998	1999
H & M	148	146	16	16	22	24
Jelmoli	245	209	163	212	14	22
Home Depot	193	191	52	51	17	19
Colruyt	217	217	34	34	12	13
Castorama	79	160	27	33	5	13
Printemps	198	202	15	18	11	13
Sears	128	126	20	20	10	11
Safeway US	144	150	30	33	9	10
Cortefiel	82	85	16	19	9	10
Boots	81	86	29	30	8	9
Kingfisher	120	130	46	41	10	9
Next	86	71	19	14	11	9
M & S	153	153	82	79	10	9
Wal Mart	151	145	29	32	7	7
Valora	140	142	43	41	6	7
Tesco	127	129	53	56	7	7
Carrefour	175	163	46	53	7	7
Sainsbury	212	196	83	79	11	6
Kroger	202	149	34	27	7	6
Safeway UK	139	134	70	66	8	6
Borders	166	100	32	19	11	6
Casino	169	159	27	30	5	6
K Mart	121	133	21	24	4	5
Delhaize	92	97	16	19	4	4
Jer. Martins	97	87	31	32	5	4
Vendex Int	65	72	31	19	4	4
Gal. Lafayette	137	141	21	22	3	4
Rinascente	183	171	59	54	4	4
Allg. Handles	146	143	8	8	2	3
Metro	159	165	20	15	3	3
Ahold	63	62	16	16	2	3
Laurus	45	54	6	6	1	2
Kesko	76	79	11	11	2	2
GIB	139	133	15	16	1	1
Karstadt	89	111	21	21	1	1
Spar	212	157	9	7	−3	−4
Amazon	290	216	14	42	−52	−80

	Tangible fixed assets/ depreciation[a]			Cash flow[b]/ sales (%)	
	1998	1999		1998	1999
Amazon	1	1	H & M	16.3	18.1
Allg. Handles	2	3	Jelmoli	9.0	15.1
Spar	3	3	Next	14.6	15.0
Metro	5	3	Cortefiel	14.8	15.0
GIB	5	5	Boots	12.5	13.5
Colruyt	6	6	Home Depot	10.0	11.1
Cortefiel	5	6	Sears	9.9	11.0
Printemps	6	6	Castorama	8.1	10.1
H & M	7	7	Safeway US	8.7	9.3
Borders	7	7	M & S	9.1	8.9
Laurus	9	7	Colruyt	8.1	8.8
Gal. Lafayette	8	7	Kingfisher	10.4	8.7
Karstadt	7	7	Vendex Int	8.8	8.6
Sears	8	8	Jer. Martins	8.3	8.5
Kesko	9	8	Borders	9.0	8.4
Next	11	8	Printemps	6.8	7.8
Vendex Int	16	8	Tesco	7.8	7.8
K Mart	9	8	Valora	6.5	7.7
Rinascente	9	8	Carrefour	6.5	7.1
Delhaize	8	8	Delhaize	6.7	6.8
Kroger	8	9	Ahold	6.4	6.8
Jer. Martins	9	9	Safeway UK	7.9	6.6
Safeway US	10	9	Wal Mart	6.1	6.5
Ahold	10	10	Kroger	5.7	6.0
Casino	9	10	Rinascente	5.8	6.0
Carrefour	9	10	Sainsbury	7.7	5.9
Castorama	17	11	K Mart	5.2	5.8
Valora	12	11	Casino	5.0	5.4
Boots	12	12	Laurus	4.5	4.9
Wal Mart	14	15	Metro	4.4	4.6
Sainsbury	17	16	Gal. Lafayette	4.2	4.5
M & S	19	16	Allg. Handles	3.6	4.4
Kingfisher	20	18	Kesko	3.9	3.7
Tesco	18	19	GIB	2.7	3.4
Safeway UK	22	20	Karstadt	4.5	3.1
Jelmoli	21	22	Spar	0.1	−0.9
Home Depot	22	22	Amazon	−9.0	−19.7

a Depreciation includes amortisation

b Cash flow = operating profit + depreciation

Glossary

English	French	German	Italian
assets	actif	Aktiva	attivitá
balance sheet	bilan	Bilanz	bilancio
cash and bank balances	trésorerie, disponibilités, caisse	Kassenbestand und Bankguthaben	cassa e banche
cost of sales	cout des ventes	Kosten der verkauften Erzeugnisse	costo del venduto
current assets	actif circulant	Umlaufvermögen	attivitá correnti
current liabilities	dettes à court terme	Kurzfristige Verbinlichkeiten	passivitá correnti
depreciation	amortissement	Abschreibung	ammortamenti
earnings per share	bénéfice par action	Gewinn je Anteil	utile per azione
fixed assets	immobilisations	Anlagevermogen	immobilizzazioni
going concern	continuité	Unternehmens-fortführung	continuitá operativa aziendale
goodwill	écart d'acquisition, survaleur	Geschäftswert	valore di avviamento
income statement	compte de résultat	Gewinn- und Verlustrechnung	conto economico, conto profitti e perdite
intangible assets	actif incorporels	immaterielles	attivitá immateriali
inventory	stocks	Vorräte	inventario
liabilities	passif, dettes	Passiva	passivitá
profit	bénéfice	Gewinn, Jahresüberschuss	utile
public company	Société Anonyme (SA)	Aktiengesellschaft (AG)	societa per azioni (SpA)
sales revenue	ventes, produits, chiffre d'affaires	Umsatzerlöse	vendite
shareholders' funds	capitaux propres	Eigenkapital	patrimonio netto
trade creditors	dettes fournisseurs	Verbindlichkeiten	altri debiti, fornitori
trade debtors	créances	Forderungen	crediti

Index

net current assets 33–60, 64, 90–1, 139–40, 178–204, 264–5, 272
types 59–60, 179–84
current cost accounting (CCA) 11
current liabilities
see also liabilities; working capital and cash flow 99
balance sheet 32–60, 90–1, 139, 179–204, 205–6
concepts 34, 40–1, 90–1, 99–100, 179–204, 271–2, 286
definition 34, 179, 205–6
liquidity 105, 107, 184–204, 271–2, 286–7
types 179–80, 205–6
current purchasing power accounting (CPP) 11, 46
current ratio 185–6, 189–90
current liabilities/total assets ratio, benchmark comparisons 274, 284
current liquidity (days) ratio, concepts 187–90, 272, 287
customers, profit perspectives 130

D
daily sales and costs 192–7
Daimler-Benz 21
DaimlerChrysler 57
databases
commercial databases 119–20, 237
Datastream 128
financial analysis 127–8
days' cash cycle 193–7
days' creditors ratio 195–8, 273, 288
days' debtors ratio 194–8, 273, 288
days'/inventory (stock) ratio 193–8, 273, 288
debentures, concepts 42, 207
debits, double entry book-keeping 3, 30–1
debt
see also creditors; long-term...
balance sheets 41–2, 205–34, 251–4
cash flow/debt ratio 261–4
concepts 7, 41–2, 100–10, 122, 130, 205–34, 251–4, 260–2, 266, 274, 284
convertible shares 39, 42, 143, 207, 231, 251
cost of debt 231–2
definitions 106, 205, 207, 284
equity 7, 122, 205–34, 253, 260–1, 263–4, 285
financial instruments 251
gearing 7, 30, 33, 49, 122, 206–34, 260–1, 285
inflation 231
leases 209–10
limited recourse 251
net debt 106, 208–34
notes to the accounts 42, 231–3
repayment dates 42
subordinated 251
debt ratio, concepts 211, 260–1

debt/equity ratio 7, 122, 206–34, 253, 260–1, 263–4, 285
see also gearing
debt/total assets ratio 274, 284
debt factoring 53
debtors 41, 59–60, 63–4, 90–110, 178–204, 273, 280–1, 288
see also trade...
bad debts 14, 60, 181–2, 220
concepts 41, 59–60, 63–4, 90–110, 178–9, 191–2, 273, 280–1, 288
factoring 60
liquidity 180–4
overtrading dangers 41, 63–4, 178–9
debtors (days) ratio 194–8, 273, 288
debtors to creditors ratio 191–2
decision-making 8, 103–4, 221
declining assets, efficiency measures 170–2
deep discount bonds 251
defensive interval (days) ratio
benchmark comparisons 272, 287
concepts 200–4, 272, 287
retail sector comparisons 287
"deferred" debtors 60
deferred revenue, reserves 219–20
deferred taxation 81–2
Deloitte Touche-Tohmatsu 23
demergers 238
Denmark 10
Department of Trade and Industry 255–6
depreciation 11, 16, 19–20, 44–8, 70, 77–88, 94–5, 97–8, 102, 131, 219, 246, 266, 291
see also fixed assets
balance sheet 44–8, 78–80, 94–5, 131
cash flow 94–5, 97–8, 102
concepts 44–8, 77–82, 94–5, 97–8, 102, 131, 219, 246, 266, 291
funds flow statement 94–5, 97–8
income statement 44, 70, 77–82, 102, 131
methods 79–80, 219, 246, 266
profit affected by 77–80
tangible fixed assets/depreciation ratio 291
taxation 79, 81–2
derivatives 106, 250–2
Diageo 49
dilution factors, EPS 143–4, 218–19
direct costs 70–3
directors 3, 4–5, 10, 12–13, 17, 25–6, 43, 73–5, 145–6, 158–9, 164–6, 219, 237–66
see also boards; management
accountability 25
ages 239
annual reports 25–8, 164–6, 237–42, 247–62
"big bath" provisions 43
compensation payments 74
corporate governance 12–13, 25, 164–6, 238–46